Peter Chaadaev

Ex Oriente Lux

New Perspectives on Russian
Religious Philosophers

SERIES

VOL. 2

Edited by Artur Mrówczyński-Van Allen,
Teresa Obolevitch, and Paweł Rojek

We believe that the Russian religious philosophy of the nineteenth and twentieth centuries has a great importance for Christian theology and philosophy. Russian thinkers, rooted in the tradition of the Church Fathers, avoided the theological dualism that so deeply penetrates Western thought. Such philosophers and theologians as Peter Chaadaev, Alexei Khomiakov, Vladimir Soloviev, Evgeni Trubetskoy, Pavel Florensky, Sergey Bulgakov, Nikolai Berdyaev, Georges Florovsky, and Aleksei Losev developed unique views on the relationships between religion and culture, science, philosophy, and social life, which, unfortunately, are missing from contemporary Western debates. The pressing task is to include their legacy to the contemporary philosophical and theological discussions.

The series *Ex Oriente Lux* aims to meet this need. It serves as a way to bring Eastern Christian intuitions into the current post-secular philosophical and theological context. Each volume focuses on one Russian thinker and includes a selection of essays on his main ideas in historical and contemporary perspectives. The books are prepared by both Western and Russian scholars, thus creating a space for intellectual dialogue.

The series come out of research connected with the annual conferences on Russian religious philosophy held in Krakow, Poland. The "Krakow Meetings" are organized jointly by the Pontifical University of John Paul II in Krakow, the Institute of Philosophy Edith Stein and the International Center for the Study of the Christian Orient, both in Granada, Spain.

Previous Volume

Beyond Modernity: Russian Religious Philosophy and Post-Secularism

Next Volumes

Alexei Khomiakov: We Are Sobornost'

Evgeni Trubetskoy: Icon and Philosophy

Peter Chaadaev

Between the Love of Fatherland and the Love of Truth

EDITED BY

Artur Mrówczyński-Van Allen,
Teresa Obolevitch,
and Paweł Rojek

PICKWICK *Publications* • Eugene, Oregon

PETER CHAADAEV
Between the Love of Fatherland and the Love of Truth

Ex Oriente Lux Series 2

Pickwick Publications
An Imprint of Wipf and Stock Publishers
199 W. 8th Ave., Suite 3
Eugene, OR 97401

www.wipfandstock.com

PAPERBACK ISBN: 978-1-5326-4359-0
HARDCOVER ISBN: 978-1-5326-4360-6
EBOOK ISBN: 978-1-5326-4361-3

Cataloguing-in-Publication data:

Names: Mrówczyński-Van Allen, Artur, editor. | Obolevitch, Teresa, editor. | Rojek, Paweł, editor.

Title: Peter Chaadaev : between the love of fatherland and the love of truth / edited by Artur Mrówczyński-Van Allen, Teresa Obolevitch, and Paweł Rojek

Description: Eugene, OR : Pickwick Publications, 2018 | Ex Oriente Lux Series 2 | Includes bibliographical references and index.

Identifiers: ISBN 978-1-5326-4359-0 (paperback) | ISBN 978-1-5326-4360-6 (hardcover) | ISBN 978-1-5326-4361-3 (ebook)

Subjects: LCSH: Chaadaev, P. I͡A.—(Petr I͡Akovlevich),—1794–1856. | History—Philosophy.

Classification: B4238.C47 A5 2018 (print) | B4238.C47 A5 (ebook)

11/28/18

Contents

Part II: Contexts

Part III: Influences

Contributors

Konstantin Antonov, Professor at St. Tikhon's Orthodox University, Moscow, Russia.

Janusz Dobieszewski, Professor at University of Warsaw, Warsaw, Poland.

Yuriy Ivonin, Professor at the Siberian Institute of Management, Novosibirsk, Russia.

Olga Ivonina, Professor at the Novosibirsk State Pedagogical University, Novosibirsk, Russia.

Fr. Pavel Khondzinskiy, Professor at St. Tikhon's Orthodox University, Moscow, Russia.

Bernard Marchadier, Chairman of the Société Vladimir Soloviev in Paris, Paris, France.

Artur Mrówczyński-Van Allen, Professor at the International Center for the Study of the Christian Orient and the Institute of Philosophy "Edith Stein"—International Academy of Philosophy, Granada, Spain.

Teresa Obolevitch, Professor at the Pontifical University of John Paul II in Krakow, Poland.

Grigory Olekh, Professor at the Siberian State University of Water Transport, Novosibirsk, Russia.

Paweł Rojek, Assistant Professor at the Jagiellonian University in Krakow, Poland.

Atsushi Sakaniwa, Professor at the Waseda University, Tokyo, Japan.

Andrew Schumann, Assistant Professor at the University of Information Technology and Management, Rzeszow, Poland.

Daniela Steila, Professor at the University of Turin, Turin, Italy.

Olga Tabatadze, Assistant Lecturer at the International Center for the Study of the Christian Orient, Granada, Spain.

Boris Tarasov, Professor at the Maxim Gorky Literature Institute, Moscow, Russia.

Andrzej Walicki, Professor emeritus of the University of Notre Dame, Indiana, USA.

INTRODUCTION

The Critique of Adamic Reason

Peter Chaadaev and the Beginning of the Russian Religious Philosophy[1]

Artur Mrówczyński-Van Allen
Teresa Obolevitch
Paweł Rojek

Peter Chaadaev (1794–1856) is rightfully considered one of the forerunners of modern Russian philosophy. In order to approach this impressive figure and contextualize him in reference to the subsequent tradition of Russian religious philosophy which he played such a crucial role in generating, it is well to approach him from a concrete scene in his life. Chaadaev spent three years in Western Europe visiting a few countries and meeting various people. In 1825 he became personally acquainted with Friedrich Wilhelm Joseph von Schelling, with whom he continued to correspond. When he returned to Russia in 1826, he continued with his studies. Chaadaev was one of the first in Russia to read Hegel. At that time, he also carefully studied Kant's *Critique of Pure Reason* and it is significant that, upon finishing it, Chaadaev crossed out the title on the cover and wrote beneath it: *Apologete adamitischer Vernunft—An Apology for Adamic Reason.*[2]

1. This publication was generously supported by a grant from the National Science Center, Poland, No. 2014/15/B/HS1/01620.

2. Lossky, *History of Russian Philosophy*, 49. For Chaadaev's complicated relationships with Kant, see Zeldin, "Chaadayev's Quarrel with Kant" and "Influence of Kant on Chaadayev."

Three Features of Russian Thought

This gesture made by Chaadaev may helps us to understand the extent to which he continues to affect Russian religious philosophy to this day, as well as to point out three fundamental features of Russian thought in the nineteenth, twentieth, and twenty-first century.[3]

First, as it is easy to see, the "*Vernunft*" (reason) accompanies the figure of "Adam." Chaadaev seems to suggest that theology form a characteristic unity with philosophy and, ultimately, with all spheres of life, culture, politics, economy, etc.[4] This unity is revealed in the strong correspondence between metaphysics, anthropology, and the philosophy of history on the one hand and trinitology, christology, and ecclesiology on the other. Moreover, philosophy in this view is not just a theoretical issue, but rather a real and rational way of thinking and living that can be defined as eschatological pragmatism.

Second, Chaadaev's gesture reveals the most profound experience of the formation of Russian identity. We can find it behind the answer to the question of what this "*adamitischer Vernunft*" means for Chaadaev. Put in the simplest way, it refers to a form of reasoning that has been tampered with and distorted by Adam's sin, by the *ego*, which took place at the center of our reality. This decisive and categorical assessment can only be made from a perspective deeply rooted in the event of the Incarnation of God, in the principle defined at the Council of Chalcedon, the Godmanhood of Christ. This theological aspect is fundamental for the identity of the political, cultural, and religious community that we know today as Russia. It is so important that ignoring it would make it impossible for us to understand the country's past, present, and future. This theological aspect of Russian identity does not need to explicitly appear in political statements or strategic analyses, since it is present in the very way in which Russian understand themselves and interpret the world around them: a way in which ontology and anthropology take shape together in the divine-human space, acquiring a dynamic of theosis, and historiosophy is expressed with a specific apocalyptic tension.[5]

3. See Mrówczyński-Van Allen, *Between the Icon and the Idol*, 52–80.

4. For more on the integrality of Russian thought see Mrówczyński-Van Allen, Obolevitch, and Rojek, "Apology of Culture," 2–3. For our analysis of the relationship between theology and philosophy in Georges Florovsky, see Obolevitch, "Faith and Knowledge," and Rojek, "Post-Secular Metaphysics."

5. For a brief discussion of the theological aspects of Russian identity, see Rojek, *Przekleństwo imperium*, 35–54.

Third, the act of crossing out the title was definitely unilateral. Kant did not responded to it, and not only because he was already dead at the time. The third feature of Russian religious philosophy, revealed by Chaadaev's gesture, might be termed a "strange dialogue." It was strange, because although two parties were involved in the conversation, only one ever replied to the other. Russian thinkers always followed the development of Western philosophical movements, studying them in depth and offering up responses with enduring value, but only in a very few cases did the rest of Europe started to answer back.

Therefore, we can summarize the three fundamental features of Russian religious thought, which can be found in Chaadaev's starting point, as: (1) the unity of theology and philosophy, (2) the central importance of theology in revealing the experience of the life of the community and the way it generates and regenerates the identity of that community, and finally (3) the kerygmatic or apologetic function of philosophy.

Beyond the Slavophiles and the Westerners

Beginning with Chaadaev's works, two great currents in Russian thought were born, the Slavophiles and the Westerners, and they began a specific debate that grew out of the strong dichotomy in Russian culture. As expressed by Chaadaev himself:

> Since time immemorial the world has been divided into two spheres, into East and West. That is not simply a geographical division, it is an order of things resulting from the very nature of intelligent being. There are two principles which respond to the two dynamic forces of nature, these are two ideas which embrace the whole economy of mankind. It is through self-concentration, meditation, and withdrawal that the human spirit discovered its powers in the East; it is through expansion to the outside, spreading out in every direction through the fight with all the obstacles, that the human spirit developed in the West.[6]

This dichotomy specifically marks the Russian idiosyncrasy and seems to be present in it to this day.[7] But this division led to a simplified interpretation of what these two groups actually had in common, relegating the debate to a reductionist, and therefore misleading, contest between the European

6. Chaadaev, "Apologia of Madman," 106.

7. It might be seen, for instance, in Patriarch Kirill's thought; see Mrówczyński-Van Allen, "From Chaadaev to Patriarch Kirill."

and the Slavic, the Western and the Eastern, which only permitted the two groups to offer simplistic sketches of the complex, underlying controversy. For, at its heart, this was a debate about three intimately related issues: (1) the definition of the human person, or anthropology, (2) the kind of society that people create or should create, or historiosophy, and, finally, (3) the account of universality, whether ecclesiological or national, that framed both anthropology and historiosophy. The debate about the Russian Idea was a debate about the idea of Europe, and even more universally, about the idea of humanity, because it was also a debate about the human person and what it meant for human persons to relate to the reality that surrounds them and to the history in which they participated.

In this debate, God and the church clearly acquired a leading role. Any attempt to interpret the discussion initiated by Chaadaev that ignores this background reveals either an unjustifiable tendentiousness or a disturbing ignorance of the profound unity between Christian tradition and experience in the social and historical context of nineteenth-century Russian philosophy. Such an attempt would therefore only arrive at conclusions of very little value because they are basically false. Nikolai Berdyaev, in his *Russian Idea*, puts it this way: "The question of socialism, the Russian question of the organization of mankind in terms of new personnel, is a religious question; it is a question of God and immortality. In Russia the social theme remains a religious theme, even given atheistic thought."[8] In Berdyaev's words, we once again perceive the three intimately related issues we noted above in the birth and the development of the Russian Idea: a vertical ontological unity always articulates and grounds the tripartition of anthropology, historiography, and ecclesiology.

First, the anthropological aspect consists in the way in which any philosophical reflection is at the same time intrinsically and primarily ontological self-definition, and therefore, an anthropological self-definition. As Berdyaev writes,

> The ethical ideas of the Russians are very different from the ethical ideas of Western peoples, and they are more Christian ideas. Russia's moral values are defined by an attitude towards man, and not towards abstract principles of property or of the state, nor towards good in the abstract.[9]

Isaiah Berlin confirmed Berdyaev's claim: "The central issue of Russian society was not political but social and moral. The intelligent and awakened

8. Berdyaev, *Russian Idea*, 123.

9. Ibid., 267.

Russian wanted above all to be told what to do, how to live as an individual, as a private person."[10]

Second, the aspect of the philosophy of history consists not only in the reference points that appeared over the course of the debate about the history of Europe in general and Russian history in particular, but especially in the very purpose of the debate itself, which centered upon Russia's fate in its own history and in the history of humankind. As Berdyaev wrote, "There are two prevailing myths which are capable of becoming dynamic in the chorus of the peoples—the myth of the beginning and the myth of the end. Among Russians, it was the second myth, the eschatological myth, which prevailed."[11] He continued:

> Russian nineteenth-century thought was mainly preoccupied with problems of the philosophy of history which, indeed, laid the foundations of our national consciousness. It is no accident that our spiritual interests were centered upon the disputes of the Slavophiles and Westerners about Russia and Europe, the East and West. Chaadaev and the Slavophiles had helped to turn Russian speculation towards these problems, for, to them, the enigma of Russia and her historical destiny was synonymous with that of the philosophy of history. Thus the elaboration of a religious philosophy of history would appear to be the specific mission of Russian philosophical thought, which has always had a predilection for the eschatological problem and apocalypticism. This is what distinguishes it from Western thought and also gives it a religious character.[12]

Third, we can identify, as specific for Chaadaev and for posterior Russian thought, the development of anthropological and historiosophical aspects into an ecclesiological narrative (which is the case, for example, both for Marxists and Slavophiles). This ecclesiological aspect of Russian thought reveals its existential roots and vocation, because "we are called upon to resolve most of the problems in the social order, to accomplish most of the ideas which arose in the old societies, to make a pronouncement about those very grave questions which preoccupy humanity."[13] As Vasilii Zenkovsky highlights:

> Eighteenth- and nineteenth-century Russian humanism—in its moral or aestheticizing form—grew from this *theurgical* root,

10. Berlin, *Russian Thinkers*, 174.
11. Berdyaev, *Russian Idea*, 32.
12. Berdyaev, *Meaning of History*, xxv.
13. Ibid., 109.

> from the religious need to serve the ideal of justice. This same theurgical motif found expression in the occult searchings of the Russian freemasons, and in the mystical flurry of various spiritual movements during the reign of Alexander I; it was also expressed with exceptional force in Chaadaev.[14]

His understanding of Russia's future as a space open to the intervention of God's will was deeply rooted, as Zenkovsky emphasizes, in a "Christocentric conception of history,"[15] a "conception of history," for example later ingrown by Alexei Khomiakov in an ecclesiological principle of *sobornost'*.

This distinction of the three fundamental aspects of Russian thought, it seems, continues to be valid today. But valid not only as an academic theory applied to Russian thought, but as an instrument that supports the identification of the contemporary evolution of the *adamitischer Vernunft*, modern secular faith with its attendant worship of the state. As such, what Peter Chaadaev wrote in his *Apologia of a Madman* also remains valid for us today:

> Love of the fatherland is certainly a very beautiful thing, but there is one thing better than that; it is the love of truth. Love of fatherland makes heroes, love of truth makes wise men, the benefactors of humanity; it is love of fatherland which divides peoples, which feeds national hatreds, which sometimes covers the earth with mourning; it is love of truth which spreads light, which creates the joys of the spirit, which brings men close to the divinity. It is not by way of the fatherland, it is by way of the truth that one mounts to heaven.[16]

These words, in fact, take on a particular importance today, and not only in Russia, but in countries around the world. Therefore through the essays presented here we hope to provoke a fresh study of Chaadaev's personality and works, and his thinking on the relation between love of fatherland and love of truth, analyzing the links between philosophy, theology and nationality, and tracing these tensions between the universal and the particular in the Russian thought he generated. In this way we propose a new encounter with Chaadayev's thought and his "love of truth."

14. Zenkovsky, *History of Russian Philosophy*, 155–56.

15. Ibid., 157.

16. Chaadaev, "Apologia of a Madman," 102.

Bibliography

Berdyaev, Nikolai. *The Meaning of History*. Translated by Boris Jakim. San Rafael, CA: Semantron, 2009.

———. *The Russian Idea*. Translated by Reginald Michael French. Hudson, NY: Lindisfarne, 1992.

Berlin, Isaiah. *Russian Thinkers*. New York: Penguin, 1994.

Chaadayev, Peter. "Apologia of a Madman." In *Philosophical Works of Peter Chaadaev*, edited by Raymond T. McNally and Richard Tempest, 102–11. Dordrecht: Springer, 1991.

Lossky, Nikolai O. *History of Russian Philosophy*. New York: International University Press, 1951.

Mrówczyński-Van Allen, Artur. *Between the Icon and the Idol: The Human Person and the Modern State in Russian Thought and Literature*. Translated by Matthew Philipp Whelan. Eugene, OR: Cascade, 2013.

———. "From Chaadaev to Patriarch Kirill: The Russian Orthodox Counterdiscourse." in *Peter Chaadaev: Between the Love of Fatherland and the Love of Truth*, edited by Artur Mrówczyński-Van Allen, Teresa Obolevitch, and Paweł Rojek, 46–54. Eugene, OR: Pickwick, 2018.

Mrówczyński-Van Allen, Teresa Obolevitch Artur, and Paweł Rojek. "Apology of Culture and Culture of Apology: Russian Religious Thought against Secular Reason." In *Apology of Culture: Religion and Culture in Russian Thought*, edited by Artur Mrówczyński-Van Allen, Teresa Obolevitch, and Paweł Rojek, 1–12. Eugene, OR: Pickwick, 2015.

Obolevitch, Teresa. "Faith and Knowledge in the Thought of Georges Florovsky." In *Faith and Reason in Russian Thought*, edited by Teresa Obolevitch and Paweł Rojek, 197–218. Krakow: Copernicus Center Press, 2015.

Rojek, Paweł. "Post-Secular Metaphysics: Georges Florovsky's Project of Theological Philosophy." In *Beyond Modernity: Russian Religious Philosophy and Post-Secularism*, edited by Artur Mrówczyński-Van Allen, Teresa Obolevitch, and Paweł Rojek, 97–135. Eugene, OR: Pickwick 2016.

———. *Przekleństwo imperium: Źródła rosyjskiego zachowania*. Krakow: Wydawnictwo M, 2014.

Zeldin, Mary-Barbara. "Chaadayev's Quarrel with Kant: An Attempt at a Cease-Fire." *Revue des études slaves* 55 (1983) 277–85.

———. "The Influence of Immanuel Kant on Peter Yakovlevich Chaadayev." *Studies in Soviet Thought* 18 (1978) 111–19.

Zenkovsky, Vasilii V. *A History of Russian Philosophy*. Translated by George L. Kline. 2 vols. New York: Columbia University Press, 1953.

PART I

Ideas

1

Peter Chaadaev

Prolegomena to the Philosophy of Russia as a Peripheral Empire[1]

Andrzej Walicki

It may sound strange, but my interest in Chaadaev began as early as the fifties and thus it is already sixty years old. I wrote about Chaadaev in my first book *Personality and History*, published in the late fifties,[2] then in the large monograph on the great debate of the Slavophiles and Westernizers[3] (the title of its English version is *The Slavophile Controversy*), then in *A History of Russian Thought: From the Enlightenment to Marxism* (for many years an academic textbook in the USA), recently published in Russian,[4] and finally in the book *Russia, Catholicism and the Polish Question* (2002).[5]

I had a happy opportunity to discuss the Chaadaev legacy with people such as Isaiah Berlin and Leonard Schapiro—in England; Zakhar Kamenskij—in the USSR; Martin Malia, Raymond McNally and Richard Tempest—in the USA; Francois Rouleau—in France; Tsuguo Togawa and Haruki Vada—in Japan, as well as, which is really important, with the outstanding representatives of the "first wave" of Russian emigration such as Fr. George Florovsky, Roman Jakobson, the well-known historian of the Russian religious Renaissance Nikolai Zernov, and the Harvard economist

1. First published in Russian as "Petr Chaadayev—Prolegomena k filosofii Rossii kak periferiynoy imperii," *Logos i Ethos* 43 (2016) 9–26.

2. Walicki, *Osobowość a historia.*

3. Walicki, *W kręgu konserwatywnej utopii*; Walicki, *Slavophile Controversy.*

4. Valitskiy, *Istoriya russkoy mysli.*

5. Walicki, *Rosja, katolicyzm i sprawa polska.*

of the Russian origin Alexander Gerschenkron, an author of the influential book *Economic Backwardness in Historical Perspective*.[6]

My interpretation of Chaadaev's thought mainly focused on the problem which I defined as "Chaadaev's paradox." I saw a paradox in Chaadaev's ideas when the author of *Philosophical Letters* found it impossible to apply his social philosophy to his own country; in the European context, he was a convinced conservative, a disciple of the French traditionalists—Joseph de Maistre and Louis de Bonald, whereas he defined his native country as "a blank sheet of paper," *tabula rasa*,[7] on which a rationalistic reformer was free to write anything. In other words, he saw Russia as a country without history, without traditional foundations and inner, spontaneous development; as a country rejected by Providence, devoid of its own "moral idea," unable of being conservative since it had no heritage which was worth maintaining. Thus, as a European, Chaadaev was a staunch conservative in the spirit of French "theocrats," whereas as a Russian patriot, he could only be a radical reformer "from above" whose desire for Russia was a new Peter the Great.

This is how it is; however, in the light of the twentieth-century historical experience various combinations of the conservative worship of traditions, on the one side, with the approval of autocratic reforms "from above," on the other side, do not appear as something exceptional, solely characteristic of countries devoid of the so-called "organic development."

In the present chapter, I will discuss Chaadaev's "philosophy of Russia" in terms of general problems related to peripheral development as they are described in works of Immanuel Wallerstein. In the context of these problems, Chaadaev's philosophy of Russian history stands out as an important attempt at understanding the fate of Russia as a *peripheral empire*[8] which seeks its place and tasks in the world history. Chaadaev's ideas pertinent to this theme may be grouped in three interrelated parts:

1. Peripheral status as a misfortune,
2. Peripheral status as a privilege,
3. Overcoming peripheral status as a task.

My own work on the place of economics in the intellectual history of pre-revolutionary Russia, which I wrote in connection with the project on the inheritance of the so-called Warsaw school of the history of ideas,[9]

6. Gerschenkron, *Economic Backwardness*.
7. Chaadaev, "Apologia of a Madman," 104.
8. See Kagarlitskiy, *Periferiynaya imperiya*.
9. Walicki, "Miejsce ekonomii."

helped me in selecting and formulating these problems. The problems which I focused on unwittingly revived in my memory talks with the above-mentioned Alexander Gerschenkron, in Harvard in 1960, on two stages of the debate on the economic modernization of Russia, namely: the dispute of the Slavophiles with the Westernizers in the first half of the nineteenth century and the later dispute of the populists with the Marxists. Already then did I succeed in drawing the attention of my conversationalist to the fact that the priority in recognizing a specific *privilege of accelerated development* typical of *tarde venientibus*, that is, of countries which were late in joining social development, belonged to Chaadaev. Gerschenkron defined this as *the privilege of backwardness*, and he agreed with me that Alexander Herzen (to whom he used to ascribe the authorship of this thought) was indebted to Chaadaev in this respect. Soon I developed these ideas in the comprehensive introductory article to the two-volume anthology on Russian populists and further in the book on this subject published in English in 1969[10] (translated into Spanish, Italian, and Japanese).

In this chapter, I will not limit myself to solely economic issues. My task is to identify those issues as part of the general, integral history of ideas.

Peripheral Status as a Misfortune

In spite of our wide-spread opinion, the Russian Empire created by Peter the Great was not born under the conviction of the orthodox Russia's central position in the Christian world, which found its expression in the idea of Moscow as the Third Rome. By contrast, the tsar-reformer despised orthodoxy and saw a much greater value in Lutheranism (to which he sympathized) or Catholicism. Similar to this was his attitude to the national identity of the country's population which was eloquently manifest in the tsar's attitude to the project of introducing in Russia the Dutch language as an official language of educated social classes.

As known, Peter's reforms in Russia resulted in a deep chasm between the educated "society" (i.e., Europeanized aristocracy) and the Orthodox "people." This chasm did not decrease under the influence of the social character of the victory over Napoleonic France. In spite of the Christian religiosity renaissance, declared from above by the emperor Alexander, the chief ideologue of the Holly Alliance, this act did not entail

10. Walicki, *Controversy over Capitalism*. In 1986 Immanuel Wallerstein suggested me to write about it in a collection of articles under the title "The Forerunners of the Development Debate" which he was planning to compile. Sadly enough, this plan has not been realized.

a return to the *orthodox* Christianity. The religious renaissance of that time had a distinctly aristocratic character; it disregarded the orthodoxy of common people as being unable to satisfy spiritual needs of the elites. Far more attractive was, as a rule, the mystical "universal Christianity"; at the same time, the growing interest in educational values of intellectually disciplined Catholicism became noticeable, and a remarkable number of formally forbidden conversions to Catholicism among aristocratic circles testified to this. Moreover, at that time the Russian Orthodox Church itself was under the process of latinization, and the tsar Alexander seriously regarded his own conversion to Catholicism with the aim of leading the Russian Church toward the union with Rome.

This is the atmosphere in which Chaadaev's world view, with its critical universalism and longing to introduce Russia to the world history as well as his pro-Catholic sympathies, took its form.

A starting point in Chaadaev's reflections about Russia was his acknowledgement of contrasts between the state's grandeur and the absence of inward meaning in its existence, insignificance of its contribution to the world history. In the eyes of the thinker, this was equal to the absence of a "historical idea," in reality—to the absence of history as such. In his opinion, Russia never kept pace with other nations, belonging to neither West, nor East, having thus no traditions of either of them. It was a country devoid of history, i.e., it had neither historical mission nor moral personality, aiming to give the world a certain important lesson; it was organically unable of genuine progress. In spite of its vast territory, it was, in fact, a sort of God's forgotten bastard, lonely in the world. The conclusions of these reflections sounded gloomy:

> We grow but we do not mature; we advance but in an oblique line, i.e., in a line which does not lead to any goal . . . Alone in the world, we have given nothing to the world, taken nothing from the world, bestowed not even a single idea upon the fund of human ideas . . . nothing from the first moment of our social existence has emanated from us for man's common good.[11]

Chaadaev saw the main reason behind this state of affairs in Russia's isolation and "detachment" from the all-European unity caused by the religious schism. Russia, subordinating Christianity to its national prejudice, departed from the Universal Church and thus excluded itself from the human history, dooming itself to the isolated, barren existence outside history. To be exalted in the spiritual life, Russians had only one way: "we

11. Chaadaev, "Philosophical Letters," 22, 25.

must, in a certain sense, repeat the whole education of mankind,"[12] i.e., all past European development.

Transferring these thoughts into terms of the theory of relations between the center and the periphery, one can say that the author of the *Philosophical Letters* created a gloomy picture of the peripheral status of the Russian empire, seeing the only way out of this situation in an incredibly complicated and hardly imaginable reverse to the spiritual center of the Western world, with a total subordination to its supreme authority. Within this perspective (common in the undeservedly forgotten movement which I termed as "religious westernism"),[13] Russia's return to the world history was only possible through the restoration of the Christian unity, i.e., its subordination to the authority of the Catholic Rome.

In this interpretation, however, peripheral position as such would not represent any positive aspects. It would remain a great misfortune, a curse of fate.

Peripheral Position as a Privilege

Nonetheless, this was not the only possible interpretation. Chaadaev himself mitigated it after the scandal caused by the publication of the first of *Philosophical Letters* in 1836. In his work under the eloquent title *Apologia of a Madman* (1837), he admitted the excessive severity of his recent judgments about Russia; however, he emphasized loyalty to his main thesis, i.e., the concept of Russia as a country without history and independent internal development.

Peter's reforms proved the correctness of this concept. Those reforms would have been impossible had Russia been a historical nation with strong, deeply rooted traditions. Meanwhile, Russia was just "a blank sheet of paper"; the autocratic monarch could write anything on it, facing no public confrontation. Love for such a country would not go with respect of its great past; on the contrary, freedom from the "burden of history" would make its ruler focus exclusively on a rational arrangement of its future. This is exactly how the great tsar understood his mission, and Chaadaev agreed with him: "I love my country in the way that Peter the Great taught me to love it."[14]

Hence, the absence of history could be a specific privilege. European nations, bound and pressed down by the legacy of their past, had to create their future in a heavy struggle against conservative forces, whereas in

12. Chaadaev, "Philosophical Letters," 22.

13. See Walicki, *Flow of Ideas*, 147–66.

14. Chaadaev, "Apologia of a Madman," 108.

Russia (in Chaadaev's words) "it is enough for a sovereign will to be pronounced among us, in order to have all our opinions disappear, to have all our beliefs waver, to have all our minds open up to the new thought offered to them."[15] Thereby Russia could create its future by applying the experience of European nations, avoiding their mistakes and "by obeying only the voice of enlightened reason with a deliberate will."[16] The conclusion provided by this analysis sounded optimistic: "History is no longer ours, it is true, but science is ours; we could not begin the whole work of humanity again, but we can participate in its latest works. This past is no longer within our power, but the future belongs to us."[17]

Moreover, based on the "freedom from the past" concept, the thinker grounded a hope that Russian was destined to perform the majestic task of mankind's earthly salvation: "We are called upon to resolve most of the problems in the social order, to accomplish most of the ideas which arose in the old societies, to make a pronouncement about those very grave questions which preoccupy humanity."[18]

In this argument, the tragic paradox of Chaadaev's ideas reveals itself with particular force. In his social philosophy, Chaadaev was a convinced conservative; he emphasized the importance of traditions and, in particular, "the inheritance of human thought,"[19] sharply criticizing the atomistic conception of society which disables people to confront the ruler's will. At the same time, justifying his view of Russia's specific privilege as a country without history, Chaadaev indirectly admitted that all his ideas about man, society and history had no direct relevance to his own fatherland. It was obvious that the idea of "scientific" construction of the future, recommended for Russia, contradicted all tenets of the conservative system of values, professed by Chaadaev as an European traditionalist.

In Europe, the view of Russia as a virgin country was first formulated by proponents of the enlightened absolutism. This was already stated by Leibniz in connection with Peter's reforms and Diderot in connection with the legislative activity of Catherine II. However, these thinkers never meant to ascribe to Russia a special historical mission of performing the great tasks of social progress. They just meant that in Russia *the rational will of the enlightened legislator would meet less resistance* than in the case of countries with autonomous social forces and a rich historical heritage. The

15. Chaadaev, "Apologia of a Madman," 109.

16. Ibid., 110.

17. Ibid., 109.

18. Ibid.

19. Chaadaev, "Philosophical Letters," 46.

very thought that the absence of the "burden of history" could be a great privilege, enabling a peripheral country to become a leader of mankind on its way to universal progress, was born in Russia much later—under the direct influence of Chaadaev's *Apologia of a Madman.*

The history of this important and fateful idea for Russia begins with Alexander Herzen. His conversations with Alexei Khomyakov and readings of Adam Mickiewicz's Parisian lectures made him think that the future would belong to the Slavic world as it remained faithful to the values of community, which to a large extent attuned with the ideas of European Socialists.[20] However, Chaadaev's influence was decisive in convincing Herzen that only Russians, a people-proletariat, could perform the great task of the world renewal as they would only win in the revolution since they had nothing to lose, as we know, but their chains. Poles, being so proud over their history as a Catholic nation, did not have this advantage. Even though Herzen himself proclaimed the "Polish-Russian revolutionary alliance," he used to predict that at the decisive hour Poland would take the side of the "old world." From this perspective, the task of building a really new world was feasible only for Russians as they alone were totally free from the burden of history and had the audacity of denial required for such a feat.

Thus, Chaadaev's concept of history absence as a specific privilege laid basis for Herzen's "Russian socialism." His motto was: "Preserve the community while liberating the individual."[21] The first postulate reflects the influence on Herzen of the Slavophilic concept of *sobornost'*, the second emphasized his loyalty to the Western idea of a free autonomous personality. The very possibility of this ideological synthesis was associated with Chaadaev's concept of Russia's rather sad privilege, the privilege of the isolated and lonely country which was free from historical devotions and had nothing in the world besides a hope for the future.

In exile, Herzen developed these ideas in anticipation of revolutionary events in Europe and later—in a state of bitter disappointment—with their results. Therefore he overlooked the possibility of applying Chaadaev's ideas to support the idea of a privilege of *accelerated internal development.* This privilege is inherent in a country lagging behind in its economic development and thereby able to consciously use the experience of more developed countries, avoiding their mistakes and applying their achievements. Gerschenkron termed it as *the privilege of backwardness* and fairly noted that in

20. See Walicki, "Alexander Herzen's 'Russian Socialism.'"

21. Gertsen, "Staryy mir i Rossiya," 189–90. In original: *obshchina*, i.e., "village community."

Russia the thought about such privilege was born during the preparation of the "great reforms" of Alexander II.

The author of this idea was Nikolai Chernyshevsky who in his *Critique of Philosophical Prejudices Against Communal Ownership* (1858) developed a thought about the possibility of "skipping" through middle stages of development as a kind of specific privilege—*tarde venientibus*—of peoples which were late in joining the mainstream of human history. In 1861, the revolutionary version of this idea was formulated by Nikolai Shelgunov and Mikhail Mikhailov in their proclamation *To the Younger Generation*, particularly in the words: "We are a belated nation, and in this is our salvation."[22] The rationale for this thought directly echoed Herzen's interpretation of Chaadaev's ideas: "Nobody goes so far in denial as we Russians. And why is that? For we have no political past, we are not bound by traditions, we stand for the new things . . . That is why we do not fear for the future as Western Europe does."[23] Chaadaev and Herzen could have subscribed to these words, but they would have been horrified by their further development: "There is no salvation without faith, and our faith in our strength is great. If to achieve our aspirations . . . we had to cut out one hundred thousand landlords, we would not be afraid of this."[24]

The best representatives of the Europeanized gentry elite from the generation of so-called "superfluous men" could not accept such a coarse radicalism of revolutionary commoners. Chaadaev was looking forward a new Peter the Great for Russia, while Herzen pinned his hopes on the enlightened part of the educated nobility. It should be added that Chernyshevsky also defended the constitutional ideas of liberal nobility in his *Letters without Addressee*, although he considered them "a betrayal of the people," inevitable in view of the people's ignorance.[25]

The influential book under the title *The Fate of Capitalism in Russia* (1882),[26] by Vasily Vorontsov, the chief theorist of non-revolutionary populism, was a most comprehensive and scientifically convincing analysis of the "privilege-of-backwardness" concept. There the author expanded an idea that owing to various reasons, mainly due to the lack of external markets (since they had been already divided between the developed countries of the world) as well as due to the lack of domestic market demand, capitalism

22. Mikhaylov, "K molodomu pokoleniyu," 69.

23. Ibid., 69–70.

24. Ibid., 70.

25. Chernyshevsky's article "Apologia of a Madman," which quoted almost the whole of Chaadaev's "Apologia of a Madman," was written for the January issue of *Contemporary* in 1861, but was subjected to censorship and banned.

26. Vorontsov, *Sud'by kapitalizma v Rossii.*

in Russia could not develop spontaneously as it did in Western Europe. However, this circumstance, characteristic of all "late newcomers to the arena of world history" was, at the same time, a privilege which could enable a conscious use of the experience of developed countries and a rational control of natural processes. Through this Russia could skip or maintain the capitalist stage of development, substantially avoiding the horrors of its primitive accumulation as well as the ruthless proletarization of small producers, described in Marx's *Capital*.

Interestingly, Marx himself was under the influence of this idea—a key idea in all versions of Russian populism. Here I am referring to his letter to Vera Zasulich from March 8, 1881, in particular, to the wealth of argumentation in the drafts to this letter. By studying Russian economic literature and, especially, by getting familiar with ideas of Chernyshevsky, Marx became convinced that Russia—owing to its acquaintance with the historical experience of more developed countries and using their technology—could make a direct transition to socialism, relying for this purpose on the archaic communalism of the Russian population.

In contrast to Vorontsov, Marx thought that this possibility was solely dependent on the revolutionary overthrow of the Russian autocracy and unrelated to the socialist revolution in Europe.[27] Besides, the Russian Marxists of the Georgi Plekhanov school, who considered the idea of capitalist development of Russia a historical dogma and the foundation of the socialist westernism, had to carefully conceal these arguments of their master. This is, of course, a theme for a separate paper that would focus on complexities of Russia's special path. My only wish in the context of the present paper is to draw attention to the fact that there was a link between the ideas of Chaadaev and Marx's ideas of the later period. I mean Chernyshevsky, who knew Chaadaev's concept of "privilege of backwardness" and who had an impact on a significant change in Marx's views on specific possibilities of the future development of Russia and other "belated newcomers to the arena of history."

Overcoming Peripheral Status as a Task

The question of the possibility of using the privileges of backwardness in order to accelerate economic development and to solve social problems was,

27. See Walicki, *Controversy over Capitalism*, 179–94. The Japanese version of this book was published in 1975 and aroused a great deal of interest in Japan which resulted in my visit to this country, at the invitation of the Japan Society for the Promotion of Science, in June 1977.

however, only one side of Chaadaev's interpretation of Russia as a "country without history." The key problem of this concept was the peripheral status of a great country, being alone in the world, belonging neither to the West nor to the East, and devoid of a great moral idea which gives meaning to its existence. From this perspective, the peripheral empire was facing the problem of the *inner meaning* of its existence, and, thereby, overcoming of its peripheral status by entering the world history.

According to Chaadaev, Russia was excluded from world history as a result of the Orthodox schism which tore the country away from the Universal Church, headed by the successor of St. Peter. This view, common to all representatives of "Russian religious westernism (*zapadnichestvo*)," substantiated the idea of reconciliation of Orthodoxy with Roman Catholicism and the dream of ecumenical mission of the Russian monarchy.

No doubt, this contradicted the widespread thought about the alleged survivability of the Russian idea of Moscow as the Third and the last Rome. In reality, this idea was almost completely forgotten in the post-Petrine Russia, only vegetating in church circles and remaining completely alien to "Russian Europeans" of Chaadaev type. If Russia had thought of itself as the center of the Christian world, the emergence of Chaadaev would have been impossible.

Chaadaev's idea about the possibility of overcoming Russia's peripheral position and simultaneously legitimizing its imperial status by associating the Russian Orthodox Church with the universal Roman Catholic Church found its enthusiastic supporter in the person of Prince Ivan Gagarin, a publisher of Chaadaev's writings, who under his influence became a Jesuit and devoted his whole life to the idea of unification of the churches.[28] His work *La Russie sera-t-elle catholique?* (1856), published in Russian under a less provocative title, namely *Russia and the Universal Church*,[29] developed the idea of practical benefits which could be gained in case the Russian Church would recognize the authority of the Pope: Russia would make a truly universal European empire, defending Christian civilization against internal and external enemies, which would be of great help in its expansion into Asia and which would contribute, within the country, to the possibility of a compromise with Catholic Poles. Thereby the Orthodoxy would be Westernized, and there would be an end to the painful chasm between the "people" and the "educated society."

28. See Walicki, "Religious Westernism of Ivan Gagarin." The revised version: Walicki, *Rosja, katolicyzm i sprawa polska*, 285–360.

29. Gagarin, *La Russie sera-t-elle catholique?*

Less well-known and underrated is the fact that Chaadaev's idea of overcoming Russia's "loneliness" by bestowing on it the great mission of the unification of churches was further developed in the theocratic utopia of the greatest Russian religious philosopher Vladimir Soloviev, and that Gagarin was definitely a link between Chaadaev and Soloviev. Soloviev wrote his book *La Russie et l'Eglise Universelle* (1889) in France in the Jesuit center created by Gagarin and in working contact with the Jesuit Ivan Martynov who presented Soloviev with the portrait of Chaadaev. Chaadaev's closeness to Soloviev was deeper than his relationship with Gagarin: it was reflected in their mutual understanding of Russia's possible mission in christianizing political relations and thus paving the way for the kingdom of God on earth. Doubts of some researchers[30] as regards Soloviev's acquaintance with the ideas of Chaadaev are for me a mere manifestation of excessive pedantry in the search of "solid evidence." If Soloviev had no interest in his predecessors, he would not have called Chaadaev the main representative of the "theocratic westernism" in Russia, and he would not have written the article on this matter for the popular Brockhaus and Efron encyclopedia.

Thus, Chaadaev's idea about overcoming Russia's peripheral position and its inclusion in world history—in his own opinion—should take the form of a dream of a spiritual union with St. Peter's capital as the center of Christian history. The very existence of this dream contradicted the understanding of Russia as the Third Rome, i.e., the opinionated, final center of the world history. The average nineteenth-century Russian did not identify itself as such a center; on the contrary, this was the reason why it intensely sought for its own ideological justification.

As it is well-known, many Russian thinkers, beginning with Herzen, tended to identify the meaning of Russia's existence with the realization of the "last word" in the European intellectual history, understood, one way or another, as socialism. Herzen was fully aware of the close relationship of this choice of the historical path with Chaadaev's concept of Russia; other supporters of the "socialist choice of Russia" could only know about Chaadaev by hearsay, but for them to grant Russia a socialist mission which provides a peripheral country with a prestigious place in world history was an alternative to the passive consent to a historical oblivion and solitude. In this sense, the complex and tragic history of Russian searches of a shortened path to the "universal harmony" of socialist future begins with Chaadaev. The fact that Chaadaev's concept of Russia quite eloquently showed the main dangers of the Russian *Sonderweg*[31] is also important. I will try to delineate points of these dangers.

30. See Trubetskoy, *Mirosozertsanie Solov'eva*, 1:71.

31. A special route, exclusiveness (German).

First, the view of Russia as a "white paper," i.e., a country without rooted traditions and independent social forces, is presented in *Apologia of a Madman* as an argument for the thesis on unprecedented opportunities for reforms from above since nobody in Russia dared to oppose the ruler's "powerful will." Thus, Russia happened to be a *promised land of enlightened authoritarianism*.

Second, the "privilege of backwardness," implying that an independent country with the educated elite can employ the experiences gained by the mankind and freely choose its path of development, was sure to create a *danger of rationalist constructivism and social experimentation*, aggravated, in the context of Russian conditions, by the lack of organized interests and independent public opinion.

Third, the program of overcoming Russia's peripheral status by submitting the Russian Empire to a selfless service of the great universal all-human idea harbored the danger of the total ideologization of politics, which has become particularly evident in our times in the light of the experience of twentieth-century ideological authoritarianisms; especially, since Chaadaev used to preach that religious universalism was paving the way to salvation in the world.

Chaadaev's dependence on the ideas of the French Catholic traditionalist theocrats was evident when he strongly emphasized that man by his nature is seeking not for individual liberty but for the hierarchical subordination to the super-individual whole. From this perspective, it appeared that the Russian disaster was not a lack of personal freedom, but on the contrary, an *excess* of freedom from a certain range of responsibilities and obligations due to its social atomization and spiritual anarchism. This explains why the ideological leaders of the liberal and democratic Russian westernism, for whom a free, autonomous person was the goal of historical development could not recognize in Chaadaev their advocate. In turn, the leaders of the Slavophilism, accused Chaadaev of his preaching the Catholic "unity without freedom," the truly Russian, in their opinion, idea of "free unity," defined as the idea of *sobornost'* was their contraposition.

All this testifies to the complexity of the ideological position of the author of *Philosophical Letters* and, at the same time, to his central place in the intellectual history of Russia as a peripheral empire.

May 2016
Translated by Larisa Gustafsson

Selected Bibliography

Chaadaev, Peter. "Apologia of a Madman." In *Philosophical Works of Peter Chaadaev*, edited by Raymond T. McNally and Richard Tempest, 102–11. Dordrecht: Springer, 1991.

———. "The Philosophical Letters Addressed to a Lady." In *Philosophical Works of Peter Chaadaev*, edited by Raymond T. McNally and Richard Tempest, 18–101. Dordrecht: Springer, 1991.

Gagarin, Ivan. *La Russie sera-t-elle catholique?* Paris: Douniol, 1856.

Gerschenkron, Alexander. *Economic Backwardness in Historical Perspective: A Book of Essays*. Cambridge: Belknap Press of Harvard University Press, 1962.

Gertsen, Aleksandr I. "Staryy mir i Rossiya." In *Sobranie sochineniy*, 12:167–200. Moscow: Akademiya Nauk SSSR, 1957.

Kagarlitskiy, Boris. *Periferiynaya imperiya: tsikly russkoy istorii*. Moscow: Algoritm, Eksmo, 2009.

Mikhaylov, Mikhail I. "K molodomu pokoleniyu." In *Politicheskie protsessy M. I. Mikhaylova, D. I. Pisareva i N. G. Chernyshevskogo*, edited by Mikhail K. Lemke, 62–80. Moscow: Gosudarstvennoe Izdatel'stvo, 1923.

Trubetskoy, Evgeniy. *Mirosozertsanie Vl. S. Solov'eva*. 2 vols. Moscow: Put', 1913.

Valitskiy, Andzhey. *Istoriya russkoy mysli ot Prosveshcheniya do marksizma*. Translated by Vitalij Makhlin. Moscow: Kanon+, 2013.

Vorontsov, Vasiliy P. *Sud'by kapitalizma v Rossii*. Saint Petersburg: Tipografiya M. M. Stasyulevicha, 1882.

Walicki, Andrzej. "Alexander Herzen's 'Russian Socialism' as a Response to Polish Revolutionary Slavophilism." In *Russia, Poland, and Universal Regeneration: Studies in Russian and Polish Thought of the Romantic Epoch*, 1–72. Notre Dame: University of Notre Dame Press, 1991.

———. *The Controversy over Capitalism: Studies in the Social Philosophy of the Russian Populists*. Oxford: Clarendon, 1969.

———. *The Flow of Ideas: Russian Thought from the Enlightenment to the Religious-Philosophical Renaissance*. Translated by Hilda Andrews-Rusiecka and Jolanta Kozak. Frankfurt am Main: Peter Lang, 2015.

———. "Miejsce ekonomii w moim ujęciu intelektualnej historii Rosji. Próba zwięzłego podsumowania." *Przegląd Humanistyczny* 3 (2014) 5–45.

———. *Osobowość a historia. Studia z dziejów literatury i myśli rosyjskiej*. Warsaw: PIW, 1959.

———. "The Religious Westernism of Ivan Gagarin." In *The Cultural Gradient: The Transmission of Ideas in Europe 1789–1991*, edited by Catherine Evtuhov and Stephen Kotkin, 33–54. Lanham, MD: Rowman and Littlefield, 2003.

———. *Rosja, katolicyzm i sprawa polska*. Warsaw: Prószyński i S-ka, 2002.

———. *The Slavophile Controversy: History of the Conservative Utopia in Nineteenth-Century Russian Thought*. Translated by Hilda Andrews-Rusiecka. Oxford: Clarendon, 1975. 2nd ed, Notre Dame: Notre Dame University Press, 1989.

———. *W kręgu konserwatywnej utopii*. Warsaw: PWN, 1964.

2

The Lessons of History in Chaadaev's Reflections

Boris Tarasov

World History Represented in Chaadaev's Thoughts and Aspirations

Chaadaev's ideological longing for an impeccable social system on earth clearly demonstrates the extraordinary yearning which the people of his time had for social justice and ideals. According to his point of view, such ideals are impossible to be reasonably grounded and carried out outside of the Christian creed which—being subject to spiritual and moral principles rather than materialistic ones—is the real source of truly universal, constant and infinite progress. He constructed a speculative "extract" from the practical biblical mysteries, deeming Christianity a global force, active and moralistic, which on one hand is assisting the development of the historical process and, on the other hand, sanctions its graceful completion by reaching the state of "heaven on the earth."

To understand the specific nuances of Chaadaev's ethical and social ideas it is necessary to examine the particular specifics of the spiritual changes that took place in his personality under the influence of the Christian beliefs, affecting the evolution of his philosophical system. "There are two very distinct things in Christianity," he writes: "one is its action upon the individual, the other is the action upon universal intelligence."[1]

Chaadaev remarks as he describes the position of the people who like himself in an earlier period are not captured by absolute ideals, eternal values and invariable traditions—"It is in man's nature to lose himself when

1. Chaadaev, "Philosophical Letters," 27.

he doesn't find the means of referring his condition to what preceded and what follows him; then all consistency, all certitude escapes him; without the feeling of continuity to guide him, he discovers that he has wandered aimlessly in the world."[2]

Such individualistic self-perception of the "lost" ones and of the "aimless wanderers" inevitably separates them from the whole and invariably leads them to indulge in their uniqueness and self-admiration. So the development of this isolating individualistic principle shows that a free will which is not grounded is chained, after all, to the "earthly amusement" and leads to the "foolish satisfaction in oneself" and a "more foolish indifference towards all that surrounds us."[3]

Thus the deeds and actions of a seemingly "free" man turn out to be based on a natural egocentrism of which we are often unaware as it stays undetectable for us. "The principle is nothing but the instinct for self-preservation," he concludes,

> The sole genuine principle of our own activity is the idea of our interest circumscribed within the limits of a given time-period which we call life . . . No matter how much we ardently desire to act with a general good in sight, this abstract good which we think up is simply the one which we ourselves want. We are never able to abnegate ourselves completely; we always include ourselves in what we desire for others.[4]

Such a "rebellious" substitution is entwined with the evil spreading in the world since the idea of absolute individualistic liberty is entwined with another

> awesome idea, its terrible, merciless consequence which is the misuse of my liberty and *evil* which results from it. Assume that one single molecule of matter would make an arbitrary movement once, for example, instead of tending towards the centre of its system it would deviate a little from the radius in which it's located. What would happen? Would not the whole order of the world disturbed at once? Would not each atom be moved out of place into infinite space? As if that were not enough, would not all bodies collide together at the opening and destroy one another? Very well, do you realize that each of us does this very thing each moment in the day? And it is not only our exterior

2. Ibid., 23.
3. Chaadaev, "Fragments," 132.
4. Chaadaev, "Philosophical Letters," 37.

> movements that cause this awesome devastation within creation but each pulsation of our soul, each of our most intimate thoughts.[5]

According to Chaadaev's logic, the greatest treasure of a man (that is his free will) *is* the biggest stumbling rock of his growth if it is disconnected from the whole, being centrifugal and egotistic. So he believed that it was the matter of utmost importance in reaching the spiritual perfection to diminish the demands of the "fatal Self," to leave the limits of the self-efficient outlook, to break out from the isolation within the system of one's own passions, to transmutate the force of the false liberty which denies life unto the force of the true liberty which establishes life and is projected centripetally.

Chaadaev himself had a distinct need to overcome the addiction to the quaint movement of irregular waves and to submit himself to the "universal order" which inclines the "wandering" atom to move along its radius to the center of the system of isness. Each soul, he notes, has "a confused instinct for moral good"[6] without which people would have been confused at facing their own liberty and which manifests itself variously. A man, apart from sensing his own personality, senses his connection with his family, his friends, his native land. Compassion, love and sympathy help him understand other people's worries and induce him to participate in solving these. "If we so choose," he stresses,

> we can mingle with the moral world so well that, provided we know about it, we may experience everything that happens in Nature as if it were happening to us; more than that, it is not even necessary that events in the world preoccupy us extraordinarily; just the general but profound idea of the affairs of men, just the intimate consciousness of our real link with humanity is enough to make our heart start to beat for the destinies of all mankind and to make each of our thoughts each of our actions harmonize with the thoughts and actions of all men in one harmonious whole.[7]

Expanding "a confused instinct for moral good" and converting it into "the deep realization" of oneness, solidarity, co-creativity on the path to the ultimate goal a man, as Chaadaev asserts, approaches such a height that he can see himself as a moral being, originally connected by a multitude of invisible strings and by some obvious traditions with the "universal

5. Ibid., 56.
6. Ibid., 34.
7. Ibid., 48.

intelligence," "the supreme idea," "God"; never as "the individual and personal being circumscribed by the present moment, an ephemeral insect which is born and dies on the same day, and which is linked with the totality of things merely by the law of birth and corruption."[8] Then, surrendering completely to "the divine will" a man would not be exercising the separated personal mind but would be able to turn to the universal consciousness and feel himself an integrated part of "the great spiritual whole," moving steadily toward "the absolute synthesis" as every movement of his will would be triggered by the totally graceful principle.

Generally speaking, Chaadaev imagined this "absolute synthesis"—that is, the perfect social system on earth—as "the complete renovation of our nature within the given conditions"[9]—by which he meant the final retreat of all personal features as well as the end of a man's separation from the creation in its allness (destruction of one's individual existence and its substitution for another existence which would be quite social). As he says: "The definitive point of our progress can only be a complete fusion of our nature with the nature of the whole world."[10]

The development of Chaadaev's traditionalistic views in regard to a given person corresponds with his understanding of history, which is supposed to examine various ages "not with cold, scientific interest, but with the deep sense of moral truth."[11]

The ideas related to the enigmatic meaning of the historical process and to the role which particular countries play in the fate of all mankind are central to Chaadaev's mental examinations.

Poking the past and aspiring to solve the prophecies of the days of yore did not give him the answers to the questions of, as he calls it, "mundane history" which intrigued him so. Chaadaev's "mundane history" is that the empirical, descriptive approach to various social events lacks both the moral vector and the proper conceptual outcome of man's activity. He believes that such "dynamic, psychological"[12] history whose hero is "a man and nothing else" who exercises his boundless free will can only see in its endlessly piling facts and events mere repetitions of "the world's miserable comedy"[13] and "the human play." This fact-gathering, which "trivial" history is so fond of, leads only to futile, empty conclusions, he claims; either to the idea of the

8. Ibid., 97.
9. Ibid., 47.
10. Ibid., 48.
11. Ibid., 86.
12. Ibid.
13. Ibid., 69.

mysterious "mechanical improvement" or to the idea of its meaningless and groundless meandering motion. "The human spirit nothing more than a snowball which grows by rolling, that is all."[14]

Yet the accumulation of any number of facts does not lead to a totally probable account which is achieved by their grouping and distribution and by understanding them in the light of knowing the moral background of various historical ages. True history, as Chaadaev tells us, should be comprehended philosophically and must acknowledge the plan, intention and intelligence in the way the things are going, as well as assimilate the idea of a man as of a moral being originally connected by many strings with those basic traditions which appear to be the moving force of "the great law of the constant and direct influence of a supreme principle."[15] Only then will the art of history be able to achieve the wholeness and the sheer instructiveness which springs inevitably from the clear understanding of the global law which conducts the change of historical ages. Hence history must become a part of theosophy and acquire the truthfulness not through a chronicle but through the work of the moral intelligence which can detect manifestations and the impact of "a perfectly wise intellect."[16]

According to Chaadaev, it is by the reinforcement of the spirit of self-sacrifice and of revolting from separation—the spirit which had been brought to us by Christianity—in every aspect of our being is how "the idea revealed from above is preserved, in this way the grand operation of the fusion of souls and of the world's different moral forces into one soul, into a single force is completed through this idea"[17] as to solve "the universal drama" and to introduce to life "the accomplished moral law."[18]

"The Christian truth" and the idea of the moral law being applied serve him as a curious imperative which brings order to the system of understanding different historical ages. Not every nation and not every age, he writes, could enforce "the divine thought" equally fully and actively; hence there are the chosen minds existing in different ages who are able to sacrifice their egocentric liberty and to submit themselves to the "supreme intelligence." Such, within Chaadaev's frame of history, are the biblical prophets, those "heroes of thought" whom "God had committed the preservation of his first words"[19] which transmit the fact of the moral

14. Ibid., 70.
15. Ibid., 63.
16. Ibid., 67.
17. Ibid., 101.
18. Ibid.
19. Ibid., 73.

existence being the primary one. Due to misconceptions of independent self-awareness, Chaadaev writes, these "colossal figures" are now lost in the crowd of historical characters as a man's mind is reluctant to enter "a region where the mind does not like to travel, a region of importunate forces commanding inflexible submission, where men exist perpetually in the presence of implacable law, and where the only thing to do is to kneel down and adore."[20] Yet belonging to the realm of direct perception of the "implacable law" is exactly what allows the prophets to preserve the idea of the singular God for the whole world and for all oncoming generations and to prepare the human souls to perceive the more vital influence of Christ's personality. Incarnation, which separates the old world from the new one, lies at the heart of Chaadaev's thoughts; it expands and fortifies the religious wholeness of history and spreads "the truths of Revelation" among the masses of people of different nations. The adequate understanding of Incarnation is prevented, as the author insists, nor by the lack of required facts and neither by the want for the sources devoured by Time; but by the imperfection of our moralistic historical logic. However, "all times and ages come together" and the past of the mankind merges with its future at the beginning of the Christian era. The age of "mankind's regeneration,"[21] as Chaadaev writes, is reflected in the pure and martyr-like life of the first Christians; it then continues in the early Middle Ages when there were "luminaries bright" hiding in the deep darkness and numerous forces were preserved among the apparent stillness of mind, left undetected by the later researchers due to the "philosophic prejudice."[22] These forces and luminaries kept and developed the "mysterious unity which contains the whole divine idea of Christianity and all its power."[23]

The author says that in order to prevent this oneness from becoming an imaginary one and disappearing altogether, the original Christianity had to fight with the numberless manifestations of human imperfection and the baleful remnants of paganism; changing itself accordingly, depending on the particular features of the given historical period and the specific needs of various nations. Hence Christianity, as understood by Chaadaev, faced the necessity to "pass through all the phases of corruption and to bear all the characteristics which the freedom of human reason had to imprint upon it"[24]—in order to preserve itself and to find itself victorious.

20. Ibid., 90–91.

21. Ibid., 71.

22. Ibid.

23. Ibid., 82.

24. Ibid.

Chaadaev seems to believe that an example of such reasonable strategy which reflects "the divine action" can be found in the papacy which, in spite of its mistakes, of all the misfortunes that befell it and the accusations of unbelievers, remains for Chaadaev "a visible sign of unity"[25] or "the symbol of unity."[26] It "*centralizes* Christian thoughts today, attracts them to one another, reminds even those who have disavowed the unity of the supreme principle in their faith, and always majestically towers above the world of material interests by means of this characteristic divine vocation imprinted on it."[27]

Nothing other than papacy, he notes, made it possible to unite the European nations into a single social body and one spiritual family which was vital for the global progress.

> This is what makes the history of the Middle Ages so profoundly philosophical; it is literally the history of the human spirit. The moral movement, the movement of thought accomplished everything; purely political events always occupied only a secondary place in the whole picture.[28]

According to Chaadaev, the dominance of spiritual interests (which by the way were bringing the material goods as well) over "one nation" of Europe appears to be the bonding element of stability and progress of the modern civilization which absorbs those achievements of the past ages which will be needed for solving the social question in the future. "The Christian society alone is genuinely animated by interests in thought and in the soul. And that is precisely what constitutes the perfectibility of modern people and that is where the mystery of civilization is to be found,"[29] as opposed to the enlightenment of the ancient nations where the fleeting material principle was celebrated. Therefore, he assumes, "it is certain that a Chinese immobility, a Greek decadence or even less likely any total annihilation of civilization will never become a part of our experience."[30]

Chaadaev believes that a great obstruction to the adequate understanding of Christianity as of the "mysterious unity" and the chief source of the cultural and scientific progress was caused by Protestantism which erased "the fertile, sublime idea of universality and unity from the

25. Ibid., 83.
26. Chaadaev, "Apologia of a Madman," 102.
27. Chaadaev, "Philosophical Letters," 84.
28. Ibid., 75.
29. Ibid., 80.
30. Ibid., 82.

consciousness of intelligent being"[31] and damaged the links connecting the European nations.

In Protestantism Chaadaev found a crucial diversion from the original indoctrination, too deep an imprint of the independent mind's liberty and a far-gone phase of degradation; but Islam gives him the vision of the providential sideways which assist "the realization of the plan conceived of by divine wisdom for the salvation of mankind."[32] The threat of the Muslim nations made the Europeans forget their personal interests and fuse together in the global search for security; which strengthened the consolidation of the Christian society (which itself was not averse to using the achievements of the Arabic civilization for its own prospect of infinite progress). Yet apart from that, he continues, Islam—as one of the numerous forces that follow blindly "the truths of Revelation"—directly assisted the spread of "the idea of one God and one universal faith" across the vast territories of the globe by eradicating paganism and thus preparing an immense number of people for "definitive destiny of mankind."[33]

Revising certain historical reputations as he elaborates his providential logic of oneness, Chaadaev mentions the bad reputation wrongly attributed to Epicurus which remained unnoticed by him for a very long time. Yet this Greek philosopher attracted him by his common sense, by a lack of false pride, by heartiness and modesty, in other words, by "contained something of the principle in Christian morality";[34] as opposed to the arrogant instructions of the Stoics and the vague, nebulous moral principles of the Platonists. Epicurus's greatest advantage, he reckons, rests in having the essential detail in his teaching—the detail which is absent from the practical doctrines of antiquity—namely, "an element of unity, solidarity and good will among men."[35]

History, as we can see, should, according to Chaadaev, not be limited by the calculation of the "universal law" of the change of the historical ages or by the ability to discover in these the traditions of obedient continuation of "the primitive fact of moral order";[36] but it should revise diligently "every glory"[37] from this perspective and to hold a merciless court over the pride and beauty of all ages and to provide the nations that had left the world's

31. Ibid., 72.
32. Ibid.
33. Ibid., 93.
34. Ibid., 92.
35. Ibid.
36. Ibid., 67.
37. Ibid., 74.

stage with convenient seats in accordance with the role they had played in upbringing the humanity. He believed it was necessary to annihilate all of the false examples and unrighteous authorities so that man's intelligence could penetrate, upon seeing the past in its true light, the moral universality of history and turn its vision to the graceful prospects. Then people will learn the chief lesson extracted from history of the known ages and especially noticeable at the beginning of the Christian era "when the time of a great catastrophe in the intellectual world arrived, and all man's vainly-created powers disappeared at once and amid the general conflagration only the sole tabernacle of eternal truth remained standing."[38]

We can also learn from this lesson that a man left to himself, rebelling against "the truths of Revelation" and abusing his own liberty will always turn to the path of endless degradation. Despite the high aspirations of the soul and temporal periods of success, nothing in the life of a man not engaged in Christianity can grant him perpetual and continuous evolution. So, India, the bearer of the enlightenment of the highest antiquity, the land which planted the first seeds of all human knowledge finds itself devastated by the colonialists. China won't give us a merrier picture. And how come that such powerful empires of the old world as Egypt, Greece, and Rome ceased to make discoveries and inventions upon achieving a particular stage of evolution?

Chaadaev thinks that the explanation of instability and the brevity of the ancient civilizations is contained in this idea that a man left to himself inevitably finds the material principle becoming the central one and as he satisfies this principle he evolves no more. Thus the "typically human" evolution which is not linked to the highest realms where "the genuine principle of social life is to be found"[39] and defines the dominance of the spiritual interests and consequently the prospect of the infinite perfectibility will unfailingly end up in the state of immobility.

Chaadaev names Greece as one of the most amusing examples of the invalidity of conventional historical reputations resulting from the scholastic habits of thinking and from the spiritual sweet deception, delusions, and illusions.

Ancient arts represent in his system of thought the idealization and heightening of the bodily aspect of man's existence, the "apotheosis of matter"[40] the result of which was that "our physical being grew while our

38. Ibid., 68.

39. Ibid., 75.

40. Ibid., 87.

moral being was shrunk"[41] although "some wise men such as Pythagoras and Plato fought against this fatal tendency";[42] but they themselves were influenced by this spirit. The Grecians employed their mighty imagination not to meditate upon the imperceptible or to take pains to light up the horizontal of life with the invisible vertical but to render "the sensuous even more sensuous, the earthly even more earthly."[43]

Chaadaev sought for the hardest words to revise and condemn Homer's poetry which, as he believed, was the prototype of ancient sculpture. There will come a day, our philosopher declares, when the name of this "delinquent seducer" and "debaucher of people" who was singing about "the deadly heroism based on passion, impetuous ideal of beauty and unbridled taste for the earth"[44] will be recalled with "a cry of shame." In Homer's deeply material, "harmful poetry"[45] which patronizes sins, Chaadaev discovers a wondrous glamour which lulls the mind and "leads astray the stream of thought which linked men with the great days of Creation"[46] and consequently diverts it from meditating upon the future fates of mankind.

The same patronizing tendency toward sin with all the consequences of such an attitude are found, he believes, in Socrates's life as well; this sage left nothing but "the incertitude of thought to posterity."[47] Chaadaev insists on the appropriate revision of the reputation of Marcus Aurelius (who "is basically simply a curious example of artificial greatness and pompous virtue"[48]) and of Aristotle ("intellectual mechanic,"[49] "angel of darkness" who "repressed all the forces for good in mankind during a number of centuries"[50]).

Chaadaev perceives the whole spiritual and geographical region of ancient culture as the land of "deceptive and illusory earth from which the genius of deceit disseminated seduction and falsehood upon the rest of the world for such a long time me."[51] Yet he is known to admit the existence

41. Ibid.
42. Ibid.
43. Ibid.
44. Ibid., 94.
45. Ibid.
46. Ibid., 95.
47. Ibid., 91.
48. Ibid., 71.
49. Ibid., 92.
50. Ibid., 72.
51. Ibid., 73.

of various characters coming from that land and worthy of "the truths of Revelation" and more or less following their command.

Yet he deemed the overall negative influence of the ancient culture which through science, philosophy, and literature of Renaissance became an integral active and essential element of our intelligence to be so grand that he doubted even his own favorite idea of the perpetual and consistent motion of humanity toward "the ultimate synthesis":

> In order to regenerate ourselves completely in accordance with revealed reason we still need *some immense penance, some dreadful expiation* decidedly felt by the Christian community and generally suffered like a great physical catastrophe on the whole surface of our world; without it I cannot conceive how we could rid ourselves of the mire which still stains our recollections.[52]

However, his optimistic inclination was nurtured by the hope of creating the true philosophy of history which would be able to distinguish in the course of the latter the actions of the "divine," "inferior," "human," and "free" principles.

Each nation, he remarks, has to revise various ages of its past in accordance with this plan of the Creator, to make clear for itself the peculiarity of its present existence in order to feel the oncoming future and to some extent foresee the course it is destined to take in future. During such a revision, he writes, all nations would practice the real national self-awareness which contains a number of obvious truths, deep beliefs, and positive ideas which can free people from local passions and delusions and lead them to the single universal aim. Only such self-awareness, he points out, and not any general success of broad education (as the Decabrists believed) can grant "the harmonious universal outcome" when the nations can join their hands in "the right understanding of the common interest of mankind" which corresponds with "the correctly perceived interest of every given nation" since the activity of both individual people and great human families results from the intimate sensation of being separated from the rest of the kind, as well as from the awareness of one's independent existence and mission.

Thus, he concludes as he elaborates his analogy between the individual existence and the collective one,

> the cosmopolitan future of philosophy is only an idle dream. First, men must concentrate upon drawing up a set of domestic morals different from their political morality; people have to learn how to know themselves first and how to evaluate

52. Ibid., 95.

> themselves just as individuals, so that they may recognize their own vices and virtues; so that they may learn to admit the faults and the crimes which they have committed, and repair the evil which they have done, or else to persevere upon the good path which they are following. Those are the inevitable moral conditions leading to genuine perfectibility for the masses, just as for individuals; in order to fulfill their destinies in the world, both have to look back upon their past lives and discover their future in the past.[53]

Russia and Europe

The universal moralistic and traditionalistic logic which frames Chaadaev's view on the course of world's history implies the discovery, within each given nation, of its "moral element," specific ways of life, manner and culture in light of "the Christian truth" in the matter of the universal progress. He unfolds a new round of ethical and historical musings upon the fates of Russia and Europe from these positions. He believes that Western countries achieved a more notable success on the path to the sought-for earthly prosperity than Russia due to their particular historical traditions.

He gives the leading role in the formation of the European cultural ethnographical region to Catholicism which attracted him first of all by the fusion of religion and politics, science and cultural changes, in other words, by its integration in the historical process. "The principle of Catholicism," he informs Alexander Turgenev, "is first and foremost a principle of action, a social principle."[54] Chaadaev characterized Catholicism as "the religion of things" and not as the religion of scholars and nations. Chaadaev believed that it "understood the reign of God not only as idea, but as a fact,"[55] so everything in it works toward the establishment of the ultimate social system on earth.

This was supported, he says, by the theocratical powers of the Catholic Church allowing it to contest with the government and to force the application of "the sublime teaching of the Bible"[56] in social life in order to achieve the desired unity and the well-being of the Christian community. He isn't taken aback by the fact that it used exactly the opposite means such as the

53. Ibid., 73.

54. Chaadaev to Alexander Turgenev, 1835, Chaadaev, "Fragments," 163.

55. Ibid.

56. Chaadaev to Count Adolphe de Circourt, 15 June 1846, Chaadaev, "Fragments," 208.

Inquisition's bonfires and religious wars as it pursued the goal—"we can only envy the fate of people who, in the clash of convictions, in these bloody conflicts for the cause of truth have created for themselves a world of ideas which we cannot even imagine."[57]

The formation of this world of ideas, the realm in which the Europeans dwell to this day and which includes the spiritual and material achievements of Europe became possible, as Chaadaev asserts, only due to the existence of a continuous string of an active successive evolution of the social and political aspects of the Western Christianity where the principles of "development, progress and future"[58] became reinforced. The historical mission of the Catholic Church, as he writes to princess Sofiya Meshcherskaya, is "to civilize the world in a Christian way." "It had to be constituted with force and with power for that," he continues, since "if the church had taken refuge in an exaggerated spiritualism or in a narrow asceticism, if it had never left the sanctuary, it would have been struck down with sterility."[59]

Chaadaev thought that the European achievements in the fields of culture, science, law and material prosperity come as the direct as well as an indirect result of Catholicism as of a "political religion" and estimated them to be the height of a man's spirit and a peculiar guarantee of the future ultimate social system on earth, being, so to speak, a transitional stage. Chaadaev in spite of admitting the imperfect state of the Western world, tends to believe that "in European society as it stands today, yet it is nonetheless true that God's reign has been realized there in some way, because it contains the principle of indefinite progress and possesses basically and essentially all that is needed for God's reign to become established definitively upon earth one day."[60]

First, an "intelligent," as Chaadaev calls it, life in empirical reality, that is, mundane facilities and comfort, decent manners and rules etc. Second, a high level of education and of culture of the Western nations which "always created, invented, and discovered."[61] The dominance of ideas, powerful beliefs, and great religious faiths were typical for their creativity and inventions and were used by sages and thinkers for leading the masses to a better life; at the same time, logical progression and the spirit of method were equally typical for them. The treasury of European

57. Chaadaev, "Philosophical Letters," 28.

58. Chaadaev to Circourt, 203.

59. Chaadaev to Princess Sofiya Meshcherskaya, December 1841, Chaadaev, "Fragments," 181.

60. Chaadaev, "Philosophical Letters," 29.

61. Chaadaev to Turgenev, 1835, 161.

nations contains many exemplary discoveries. Third, the presence of well-organized legal relations and a developed legal consciousness. Thus the spirit of the West or "the physiology of the European"[62] consists of "the ideas of duty, justice, law, and order."[63]

Chaadaev's interpretation of Christianity as a historical progressive social evolution that includes attributing an absolute importance to culture and education, his identification of "Christ's business" with the final establishment of "the earthly kingdom" and the logic of his musings unfolding upon these grounds became his foundation for a severe criticism of the modern position of Russia and its history which led it to such a state. He could find neither the "elements" nor the "premises" of European progress in Russia of his time. He explained it in accordance with the ideas of oneness and the perpetual and gradual successive religious and social evolution postulated by him; he says that in separating ourselves from the Catholic West during the religious schism we made a mistake in our approach to the true spirit of religion, did not embrace the purely historical aspect and the social transformative principle as an innate aspect of Christianity and consequently did not collect all its fruits although we did submit ourselves to its command, meaning here the "fruits" of science, culture, civilization, and comfortable life. "We have something or other in our blood which alienates any real progress"[64] for "has placed us outside the universal movement in which the social idea of Christianity was developed and formulated."[65] When the "sanctuary of the modern civilization" was being formed under the energetic influence of this idea, the Russian people obtained the moral codex from Orthodox Christianity of Byzantium which became the foundation of the moral education of the Russian nation and was embraced in all its dogmatic purity and completion. "A good-natured and simple-souled people," Chaadaev remarks in his letter to Count Adolphe de Circourt,

> whose first steps on the social scene were marked by this famous abdication in favor of a foreign people so naively related by our annalists—this people, I say, embraced the sublime teachings of the Bible in their original form, i.e. before the movement of Christian society had on them imparted social character, now the germ of social character was there but it would and could only manifest itself at a given epoch.[66]

62. Chaadaev, "Philosophical Letters," 23.
63. Ibid.
64. Ibid., 25.
65. Ibid., 28.
66. Chaadaev to Circourt, 15, 208.

According to Chaadaev's thoughts, the original purity of "the sublime teaching of the Bible" combined with undeveloped rudiments of social nature had amplified extraordinarily the ascetic element of the Russian nation and left this nation in the shadow of the social and cultural principles of the Western type of construction: "there was really no social development in it, this was an intimate fact, a factor of the inner moral consciousness, a family affair."[67] The social and historical "exclusion" of the Orthodox Church from the construction of the "earthly kingdom" agrees with the weakness of its theocratical power and with the lack of its dominance in the profane governmental realm: "spiritual power [in Russia] was far from enjoying the fullness of its natural rights in society."[68]

"Domesticity" and "kinship unity" of Orthodox Christianity of Russia, he believed, discourages—unlike the expansive religious system of the West—the active progressive evolution of society and correspondingly the foundation of the perfect life on earth in the end of all things. Hence the Russians lack the traditional continuity of social progressive ideas which forms the "premises" and the "elements" of the "earthly kingdom" in Europe.

Chaadaev deemed it essential in order to reach the achievements of the European society and to participate in the global evolution that Russia must not merely assimilate, blindly and superficially, Western forms. Upon absorbing the social idea of Catholicism unto its flesh and blood it must repeat all the successive traditions and stages of European history.

Such is the course of his musings which led him to the conclusions expressed in the "First Philosophical Letter" stating the secondary role and insignificance of the historical fate of Russia and declaring the "negative patriotism" which involves an organic reshaping of the authentic ways of life after the fashion of European Catholic traditions and achievements.

There is no doubt that Chaadaev's thoughts and conclusions tend to be one-sided, and are not always just and correct. But at their core we discover a great life-affirming impulse, a sincere concern about the mission of Russia. "I love my country in my way, that's all," he admitted in his letter to Yuriy Samarin. "More than I could tell you, it cost me to pass for an unfaithful Russian."[69] The very acuteness and authenticity of the presentation of the question concerning the specifics of the historical ways of Russia and Europe were appealing for a creative dialogue and turned out to be extremely fruitful for Russian culture, the best members of which were ready to raise serious objections against a number of essential points in Chaadaev's reflections

67. Ibid., 206.

68. Ibid., 201.

69. Chaadaev to Yuriy Samarin, 29 January 1847, Chaadaev, "Fragments," 211.

while admitting the genuineness of his patriotic feelings and an element of truth of his statements. Peter Vyazemsky, Vasily Zhukovsky, Yevgeny Baratynsky, Alexei Khomiakov, Vladimir Odoyevsky were going to write a rebuttal essay against his article published in *Teleskop* magazine but had to delay it due to strict governmental measures.

The Slavophiles, whose activity was in many aspects stimulated by his ethical strain of philosophical and publicist ideas, also entered into the dialogue with Chaadaev. In the article "On the Old and New" which set in motion the Slavophilic ideas in social movement, Khomyakov wrote that even though the past of Russia abounds with instances of internal wars and upheavals, there is an equal number of opposite examples. At the heart of our history, he continues, there are no stains of blood and conquests; our traditions and legends bear no lessons of injustice and violence, hate or vengeance. "These very instincts, the best instincts of a Russian soul educated and dignified by Christianity, these very memories which belong to unknown antiquity but which live secretly in us produced all our goodness of which we can be proud."[70] Another Slavophile, Peter Kireevsky, used a collection of folk songs to argue, in his way, against Chaadaev's conclusions about Russian past by showing the elegant effigies in the recollections of the nation and powerful teachings in its legends, finding the noble sources in folklore recreating all heroism and magnificence of the national historical events.

The intricate peculiarity of Russian history marked by the Slavophiles found another supporter in Nikolai Karamzin's works which Chaadaev kept re-reading more and more closely. In his letter to Alexander Turgenev he confesses that he learns to treasure the memory of the famous historian more and more each day.

> How sensibly, how intelligently he loved his country! . . . And yet how he knew the worth of everything foreign and gave it its just due! . . . The vividness of his pen is extraordinary; and in the history of Russia this is the most important thing; reason would have destroyed our history; only an artist's brush can re-create it.[71]

(This last idea can be traced back to Tyutchev's lines—"Russia is a thing of which / The intellect cannot conceive"[72] etc.).

Chaadaev, longing so desperately to discover the truth, could not ignore the extensive complexity of the historical picture unfolding before his

70. Khomyakov, "O starom i novom."

71. Chaadaev to Turgenev, 1837, Chaadaev, "Fragments," 173.

72. Translation by Frank Jude.

eyes and noticeably adjusting the straightforward selectiveness of his religious and progressive logic. Besides, the deeply controversial development of contemporary Europe was in itself affecting in many ways his ethical and social beliefs regarding the Western civilization as a transitional stage on the path to the perfect social system on earth.

In his *Apologia of a Madman* Chaadaev calls the reader to look at the things going in those countries which appear to be the most complete models of civilization in all its aspects and which he, to use his own words, has praised too much: "There when a new idea occurs, all the egoisms, vanities and partialities on the surface of society throw themselves upon it, seize hold of it, disfigure it, make a travesty of it, and a moment later, pulverized by these diverse agents, there it lies, transported into the abstract regions in which all the sterile dusts of the human mind are accumulated."[73]

The social evolution of these countries shows more and more clearly that neither a life of comfort nor the discoveries of science and formally developed legislation can bring the bourgeois society the desired "ultimate synthesis"—that is, overcoming any egocentricity in social and metaphysical state of harmony—but serve only "the insolence of capital"[74] and germinate, on the contrary, "this mass of artificial needs, violent interests, and agonizing preoccupations which invade our lives."[75] Now Chaadaev calls the premises of "the earthly kingdom" "the futzing of the West" as they are "ignoble"—that is, they lack the most essential element: the true and absolute love for man. More than that, any social progress that is not inspired by such love would conceal great obstacles to the moral growth of an individual and of society as the state of concentration on the development of the external aspects and comforts of life leads only to the cultivation of a complexity of sensual perception and to an infinite multiplication of purely materialistic needs. Moral apathy, a lack of beliefs, universalistic egotism and life by a plan—such is the other side of the violent development of bourgeois well-being.

In the midst of the bourgeois revolutions of the middle of the nineteenth century, when "poor humanity fall again into barbarity, sink into anarchy, swim in its blood,"[76] "the lamentable golden mean"[77] as Chaadaev calls it, becomes more visible. He anticipates some of Herzen's ideas in his criticism of the unspoken glamour of the golden mediocrity. "The

73. Chaadaev, "Apologia of a Madman," 109.

74. Chaadaev, "Fragments," 234.

75. Chaadaev, "Philosophical Letters," 97.

76. Chaadaev to Sergei Poltoratskii, 30 May 1848, Chaadaev, "Fragments," 223.

77. Chaadaev to Turgenev, 1835, 159.

autocratical crowd of conglomerated mediocrity," "*bourgeoisie*, the last word of civilizations,"[78] Herzen will repeat after Chaadaev.

This "last word of civilizations" and the obvious imperfection of the "premises" and "elements" of the desired earthly prosperity in general led Chaadaev to another revision of the direct and unbreakable link between the external social achievements and the "Christian truth" and made him change somewhat his view at the historical "inclusion" and social transformative activity, the theocratic power of Catholicism which, as we know from his system of thought, initiates the fruits of enlightenment and culture by means of the successive development of social and political aspects of the Western Christianity. Now, not without some influence of the Slavophiles, Chaadaev was ready to discover "human passions" and "earthly interests" in the social idea of Catholicism which corrupt the purity of "the Christian truth" and thus lead to such imperfection. And as if that was not enough, he began to doubt the very possibility of the fusion of the religious principle and of the social progressive one into "a single thought," began to doubt the possibility of establishing "God's kingdom" on earth and so consequently he started revising the "religion of things," "political Christianity" which perceived the Holy Spirit as "the Spirit-of-the-century."[79] This "single thought" divides itself, in a way, into components which touch each other through a principal and deeply indirect connection. "Christianity," Chaadaev remarks in his letter to Alexander Turgenev,

> first of all postulates that truth resides not on earth but in heaven . . . Political Christianity has outlived its usefulness . . . political Christianity was replaced by a purely spiritual Christianity . . . which must act upon the civil world only indirectly, through the power of ideas rather than matter. More than ever before it must dwell in the realm of the *spirit* and illuminate the world from there, and seek its final expression there.[80]

He discovers such "spiritual Christianity" in Russia in those aspects of the Orthodox faith (its historical "exclusion" from the construction of the "earthly kingdom," the weakness of its theocratical principle, asceticism and so on) which did not affect the traditional succession of the social progressive ideas and thus previously had been perceived by him negatively but now obtained a completely different perspective. "Christianity [in Russia—B. T.] had remained pure from contact with human passions and earthly interests, because it had, like its divine founder, done nothing but pray and

78. Herzen, *My Past and Thoughts*, 4:1688, 1692.

79. Chaadaev to Turgenev, 1835, 165.

80. Chaadaev to Turgenev, 1837, 171.

humiliate itself, because it was probably due to that very fact alone that it would be favored with the last and most powerful inspirations."[81]

He deemed these particular traditions of the "spiritual Christianity" to lie at the core of the Russian religious and mental ways of life, being a fertile principle of the specific evolution of Russia. He tells Vyazemsky in 1847:

> We have always been quiet of mind and humble of character; this is how we were raised by our church, our only teacher. Woe to us if we prove ourselves unfaithful to her wise teachings! We owe this teaching our best national traits, our grandeur and everything that distinguishes us from other peoples and is shaping our destiny.[82]

Unlike Catholicism, which brought science and a life of comfort to the Western community, Orthodox Christianity had gifted Russia with a special modality of a man's soul and spirit—namely, an unselfish heart and a humble mind, patience and hope, conscience and self-sacrifice. Chaadaev could now discover these aspects where he could only perceive "the dumbness of faces" and "a careless life," a lack of "beauty" and "elegance" before. They, these very qualities—and not only the external achievements and advances of the Western cultural construction—can assist to override individualism and to promote the reunion of people of all mankind in harmony with the true moral ("noble") principles and are the premises of Russia's special mission. Even before publishing the letter in *Teleskop* magazine he notes in one of his letters to Alexander Turgenev that "if Russia understands her mission she should take the initiative in all noble ideas because she doesn't have European affectations, passions, ideas or interests."[83]

The "First Philosophical Letter" demonstrates already some vague digression from the thrust of the "negative patriotism" and begins to germinate the seeds of a completely different course of thinking—of "the positive patriotism." Despite placing a number of grim descriptions of Russian history in this essay, Chaadaev still had a vague awareness of Russia having to "give some important lesson to the world"—even though in order to accomplish this mission it might find itself destined to experience many a calamity and numerous woes. Afterward this sensation kept growing stronger, becoming more and more persistent. Chaadaev writes, in many aspects foreseeing Dostoevsky's idea of the Russian panhumanism, that the mission of Russia was to "provide the solution to all the questions which are being debated in Europe

81. Chaadaev to Mikhail Orlov, 1837, Chaadaev, "Fragments," 170.

82. Chaadaev to Peter Vyazemsky, 29 April 1847, Chaadaev, "Fragments," 215.

83. Chaadaev to Turgenev, 1835, 160.

one day"[84] that "Providence . . . has charged us with the interests of humanity . . . there's our future, there is our progress."[85]

An important premise for such a supreme calling now rested in the very thing which was regarded in Chaadaev's "First Philosophical Letter" as the most fundamental negative aspect of Russian history—that is, the aloofness of Russia from the past and the present of Europe, its independence and "otherworldliness." "Placed . . . outside of the times," "we have never advanced along with other people," "we are not related to any of the great human families."[86] Later in his studies he began to evaluate this aloofness in a different light and—deemed no more that it was essential for Russia to repeat every stage of the historical evolution of Europe from the very beginning.

Chaadaev gradually came to believe that the historical isolation of Russia did not merely account for "the most profound feature of our social physiognomy"[87] but also provided the foundation for "our future prosperity."[88] The spiritual distance which parts stationary Russia from the unquiet ever-busy West, he says, allows the former to assess European events calmly and with a sense of detachment: "We are the public, over there are the actors, it's up to us to judge the play."[89] This Russian disengagement from the ambiguity of "the lofty past" of Europe and from "the rapid movement which carries along the spirits there"[90] in the present position of Russia enables it to examine soberly and objectively "great play which is being acted out by the European people"[91] without repeating "the long series of follies and calamities,"[92] to extract the lessons for future in order to avoid those fallacies which had led the Western community to "the last word of civilizations." "I find that our situation is a fortunate one," he tells us, "provided that we know how to evaluate it, and that the ability to contemplate and to judge the world from the heights of a thought freed from unbridled passions, from miserable interests which encroach upon it, is a lovely privilege."[93] A deeper, more thorough penetration unto the essence of the national peculiarity and

84. Chaadaev to Turgenev, 1 May 1835, Chaadaev, "Fragments," 158.

85. Chaadaev to Turgenev, 1835, 160.

86. Chaadaev, "Philosophical Letters," 20.

87. Chaadaev, "Apologia of a Madman," 105.

88. Chaadaev to Ekaterina Sverbeeva, 10 July 1842, Chaadaev, "Fragments," 185.

89. Chaadaev to Turgenev, 1835, 159.

90. Chaadaev to Turgenev, 1 May 1835, 158.

91. Chaadaev to Turgenev, 1835, 159.

92. Chaadaev, "Apologia of a Madman," 109.

93. Ibid.

of our own history, combined with a critical assimilation of the Western experience, would grant, he believed, the supreme role of Russia. After all, he came to a conclusion which was diametrically opposite to the one presented in the end of the "First Philosophical Letter": "It's Europe, on the contrary, which we are destined to teach about an infinity of things which Europe could not understand alone . . . This will be the logical result of our long solitude: great things have always come out of the desert."[94]

As we can see, Chaadaev's reflections had undergone remarkable transformations in the course of their development (and at that, all the positive signs changed to the opposite ones and his whole logical construction from premises to conclusions adopted the reverse characteristics). However, Chaadaev's studies kept returning quite perpetually to the intonations of the "First Letter." Thus, for instance, in his letter to Mikhail Orlov he calls his own opinion about the providential role of Russia in the matter of bringing the Christian promises to life "chimerical";[95] in his letter to Peter Vyazemsky he criticizes the Slavophiles for attributing the role of "a teacher of other nations" to "our modest, pious Russia"[96] albeit it were his own words heard from him repeatedly; in his message to Circout he mentions that "any progress here would be impossible without a reference to the European court."[97]

Such logical contradictions are scattered across the pages of Chaadaev's correspondence and his other works. They can be found not only throughout some particular time-period of his life and work but even within the same piece of writing. The philosopher's thought did not evolve but rather pulsated, unfolding in a forward-backward motion. Herzen writes on the warfare between the Slavophiles and the Westernizers—which aimed for the well-being of Russia, understood differently by the parties—such lines: "And like Janus, or the two-headed eagle, they and we looked in different directions, while one heart throbbed within us."[98] The complexity and strangeness of Chaadaev's character lies in him being inwardly such a "double-headed eagle" and consequently absorbing in his writings all the motley questions that disturbed both the Slavophiles and the Westernizers. One of the eagle's heads was looking at the Western peoples, expecting a graceful transformation of their inner world by the total and directed external activity of people; another head was looking at the East in hope that the profound spiritual concentration and the convenient mood of a man's

94. Chaadaev to Turgenev, 1835, 162.

95. Cf. Chaadaev to Orlov, 170.

96. Chaadaev to Vyazemsky, 214.

97. Chaadaev to Circout, 16 June 1846, Chaadayev, "Pis'ma," 186.

98. Herzen, *My Past and Thoughts*, 2:549.

soul would harmonize the whole system of his relations with everything that surrounds him. The more acute the contradictive visions were getting, the more tension there was in his heart. The very coexistence of the ethical problems related to the mystery of "the Sphinx of the Russian life"[99] (to use Herzen's expression) in his mind was getting a dramatic turn of an intimate dispute which could and would never come to an end.

I believe that it is hard to overrate the lessons which we can get from the very sways and contradictions of Chaadaev's philosophical beliefs in the field of the realistic understanding of the results of various historical experience and moral values. An enlightener's confidence of the philosopher in the time-proved achievements of an external education in the matter of the moral transformation of personality and of the reunion of the brotherhood of man faced some unexpected paradoxes. There is a little doubt that he couldn't ignore how in the process of the centuries-long motion of history the external appearance of humanity kept changing due to the improvement of the material aspect of its existence which in its turn was caused by the interconnectedness of intellectual breakthroughs in manufacturing, science and technology. However, in the spiritual and mental core of man there still resided ineradicably things like vanity, cravings for power, envy and other egotistic principles which disharmonized any social relations. Thus the social achievements and theories of the progressive social development were in quite a violent contrast with the spiritual image of a person and its actual relationship with other people.

Apart from that, the utopian chiliastic understanding of evolution of the global social process gives, to some extent, the ethical and historical conceptions of Chaadaev too abstract a tone, distracts him from the more actual and particular contradictions in the moral content of the given ages and induces him to exclude the eschatological teachings of Christianity from his field of attention. The Bible does not tell us about a harmonious end of profane history; on the contrary, it stresses its apocalyptic termination.

The peculiarity of the providential scale chosen by the author of the *Philosophical Letters* and his selectively limited review of various traditions made him "sift out" the facts, leaving and correspondingly interpreting, out of the historical existence of all the different ages and nations, only such evens and occurrences which would not damage the general logic of his construction of a social church without the paradoxes of the New Testament and the "madness" of Calvary. He places the question of balance between goals and means of the social progress in an emotional manner and in a blazingly artificial way, justifying the religious wars and the

99. Ibid., 525.

bonfires of the inquisition in the Middle Ages as well as "the gory battles in the name of Truth" in Europe. So if we examine his speculations upon, for example, Moses who preserves "his sublime monotheism"[100] and at the same time destroys tens of thousands of people, or upon Muhammad's teaching which discovers, in the name of the extermination of any idolatry, the ability "to know how to become linked, when necessary, even with error, in order to achieve its total result"[101] in Christianity, we'll see that the same enduring capital contradiction is equally typical for them since the fusion of good and evil reflected in the whole course of history replicates perpetually the imperfection of social relations and seems to be the biggest stumbling stone for the graceful conclusion of "the definitive destiny of mankind"[102] which was so desired by Chaadaev.

The urge for the "external" establishment of universal harmony of all mankind does not take into account the contradictive complexity of human liberty, the imperfect fluctuations of which have originally been designed to expand its rights, individuality, will-power and to make them more sublime and which cannot be corrected by jurisdictional statutes, social institutions or scientific knowledge. Neither the utopian theories, nor civilization nor education can augment the regions of goodness in a man's soul and neither they propel it to brotherly affection. Quite the opposite, evil and selfishness appear to guise themselves in the course of history, adapting to the new circumstances, becoming more subtle, more dangerous. And only the unprompted willingness for goodness which lies much deeper in the soul than the sphere of influence of an external enlightenment can lead to the truly human relations. Here one cannot but refer to Dostoevsky who writes that brotherhood is impossible lest there be brothers in whose nature the principle of love to other people would naturally develop. The metamorphosis of the self-interested modality of a soul into a loving one is only possible when there is either a heartfelt experience or a clear understanding of abilities and paradoxes of the human nature and of the history of mankind. Revitalization of the roots of desires only happens when a soul is captured, directly and essentially close to life, by the absolute ideal of Christ which is all opposite to the egotistic nature and which erases from it all other "ideals" and idols and dictates the evolution of an inner enlightenment, spiritual harmony and the moral prosperity of a given individual. Piety, love of truth, deep thought, sublimity, nobility, justice, honesty, proper pride, commitment, the sense of duty and responsibility, the wholeness and seamlessness of mentality, noble

100. Chaadaev, "Philosophical Letters," 89.

101. Ibid., 93.

102. Ibid.

appearance and chastity—such are the qualities, bred by the true enlightenment, that is by brightening the whole structure of life forces, of the spirit and the soul of people who could overcome their original imperfection and find the ability to be brother-like to others. Such very qualities will prevent the confusion between good and evil and the endless reproduction of more and more new social conflicts; they help reaching the balance between goals and means and finding an "internal" path to the universal harmony. Hence it becomes clear why Chaadaev gradually begins to pay more attention to the specific moral qualities and centuries-long traditions of the true enlightenment which cures the egotistic principles of the unrighteous human relations with the help of the "Calvarish" principles and which creates the spiritual identity of particular individuals as well as of whole nations.

Any nation has a special identity, the moral foundation of which rests in the values that had been collected over centuries by the way of national traditions. The philosophical heritage left by Chaadaev helps us work out a sober and unbiased perception of cultural traditions of each nation, seeing their controversial aspects, separating the wheat from the chaff and revealing their spiritual and moral essence.

Bibliography

Chaadaev, Peter. "Apologia of a Madman." In *Philosophical Works of Peter Chaadaev*, edited by Raymond T. McNally and Richard Tempest, 102–11. Dordrecht: Springer, 1991.

———. "Fragments and Various Thoughts." In *Philosophical Works of Peter Chaadaev*, edited by Raymond T. McNally and Richard Tempest, 112–255. Dordrecht: Springer, 1991.

———. "The Philosophical Letters Addressed to a Lady." In *Philosophical Works of Peter Chaadaev*, edited by Raymond T. McNally and Richard Tempest, 18–101. Dordrecht: Springer, 1991.

Chaadayev, Petr. "Pis'ma." In *Polnoe sobranie sochineniy i izbrannye pis'ma*, 2:6–409. Moscow: Nauka, 1991.

Herzen, Alexander. *My Past and Thoughts*. Translated by Constance Garnett. 4 vols. London: Chatto and Windus, 1968.

3

From Chaadaev to Patriarch Kirill

The Russian Orthodox Counterdiscourse[1]

Artur Mrówczyński-Van Allen

When we look into Peter Chaadaev's works, we find the fundamental elements of contemporary Russian thought, especially apparent in the Russian Orthodox Church's complex, often dramatic, and always inspirational relationship with the modern world. The core of this relationship is the understanding of culture put forth by Father Pavel Florensky in the *Philosophy of Cult*. In order to explore this relationship in this work (which owes much to prior investigations), we propose to more succinctly (and, therefore, I hope, more clearly), present the hypothesis that it reveals itself in what we can call the "theology of resistance," and that in turn, this theology is expressed in a narrative of its own, with a marked "counter-discourse" character. In my opinion, these elements, which can be clearly seen in the evolution of Chaadaev's thought, continue to determine the Russian Christian discourse, as can be demonstrated with an examination of the thought of the current Patriarch, Kirill (Vladimir Mikhaylovich Gundyayev).

First, in the section "Theology and Resistance," we will present a concise outline of the fundamental features of the theological sphere. As we see with the Chaadaev example, the philosophical discourse is determined from the center of this sphere. Konstantin Antonov recently noted that "the fundamental category in [Russian] religious philosophy, which begins with

1. This publication was generously supported by a grant, "Science, Religion and Politics in the Russian Philosophical Thought," from the National Science Center, Poland, no. 2014/15/B/HS1/01620.

Chaadaev, is the category of original sin,"[2] and therefore, it is more than justified (and necessary) for us to try to understand the basis for interpretation offered by the Russian Orthodox legacy in order to even make an attempt at understanding the discourses born and crafted within the scope of broadly understood Russian culture. In order to see how this is manifested in practice in the effort to structure this theology into a discourse that reflects the identity it has formed, we will conclude this analysis—in the section "Narrative of Resistance"—with a number of quotes taken from speeches made by the current Patriarch of the Russian Orthodox Church, Kirill, and with some commentaries and conclusions.

Theology and Resistance

The "religious character" of the Russian tradition is a particular differentiating feature thereof. In order to better understand what this character consists of, we will start our analysis with the well-known presentation of the differences in how the East and West understand salvation because those differences determine how we understand modern secular power with its soteriological claims. This explanation summarizes the prevailing opinion among specialist theologians:

> The goal of life for Christians in the Byzantine tradition is divinization; for Christians in the West, it is the attainment of holiness . . . According to the Orthodox, the Word became flesh in order to restore to man his likeness with God that was lost through Adam and to divinize him. According to the Latins, he became man to redeem humanity . . . and to pay the debt owed to God's justice.[3]

It is generally noted that Orthodox soteriology, that is, teaching on salvation, is summed up in the ontological view of divinization, and Latin soteriology in St. Anselm's juridical theory of atonement due to sin. Thus, for the Orthodox, the principal purpose of baptism is not to eliminate sin, but rather to free man from the overall power thereof, to restore the lost image of God, and for the child to put on the New Adam, or Christ. In Orthodox culture, theology, spirituality, and mysticism are united; there is no idea of a theology that is not also mystical, that is to say, experiential. The same does not hold in the West, where, even in the teachings and especially

2. Antonov, "Politecheskoye izmierenie," 290.

3. Bardy, *Dictionnaire de spiritualité*, 1389.

with the arrival of Scholasticism, mysticism and spirituality have occupied a different realm than dogmatics.

The Orthodox are more interested in the person of Christ than in his works, more interested in his being than in his actions. Man created as a physical being represents the arena for the restoration of the lost unity with God. This union is verified through covenants, God's promises, and is expressed in narratives and practices that shape the community. These narratives and practices influence and even determine the ways the community's internal and external relations are understood and built. Communities with developed models of relations always have a political dimension, and the entire spectrum of the life of a political community is determined by some type of cult (in the sense of worship or a system or community of religious worship and liturgy, rather than in the colloquial sense of an extremist sect).

Father Pavel Florensky precisely defined the location of the center of culture as a phenomenon of the search for the meaning of life and of the world. In his well-known work *Philosophy of Cult*, in the second chapter[4] he explains that culture, arising from cult, is "the activity through which and in which man first makes himself man,"[5] but under the condition of the truth of the cult, which is the center of the culture.[6] And it is within the cult that "the primary activity" (*pervodeyatelnost'*) appears and takes place; this primary activity is the result of the encounter with the Word made flesh,[7] due to which man, in an anthropological sense, is *homo liturgus*,[8] because the heart of all human activity is in the liturgy. It is there where the *pervodeyatelnost'*, that "primary activity," takes place.[9] The rite of the cult is what brings the community together, and is the source of culture. Florensky was also aware that man could reject the cult, and that this decision appeared at the core of modern culture. The decisive figure in the genesis of the thought that gave rise to this culture for Florensky (as for Chaadaev) was Kant: "Kant did not want to know anything about cult. The only significant reality for him was himself and his placement at the absolute center of the universe, and that was the essence of the spirit of the new times in Western Europe."[10]

This relationship between cult and culture, which is the political community's forum for the continual search and rediscovery of its identity,

4. Florenskiy, *Filosofiya kul'ta*, 51.
5. Ibid., 55.
6. Ibid., 58.
7. Ibid., 55.
8. Ibid., 59.
9. Ibid., 60.
10. Ibid., 104.

establishes the fundamental principles for the community's *politeia*. In the specific *politeia* of Christian communities, that is to say, in the *ekklesioteia*, the nature of man as a being created by God and, what is more, as a physical, carnal, sexual being, is a decisive principle. But this characteristic is not just proper to the Orthodox tradition; rather, it belongs to the entire Judeo-Christian legacy.

For our analysis, the events described in the Books of the Maccabees represent a paradigmatic example from the Jewish tradition.

Antiochus IV Epiphanes, descendant of the Seleucid dynasty, was an exemplary student and stubborn promoter of the Hellenic way of understanding the world. The crowning moment in his attempts to subordinate Judea to his interests (and coffers) was the proclamation of an edict in the year 167 BC that in practice eliminated Judea's "autonomy," prohibited "ancient religious practices" like circumcision, and made it mandatory to eat pork during public celebrations. The idea was to thereby hellenize the Jewish identity, to reorganize space and time, with new centers of power, new festivals, a new calendar: to not only conquer the territory but also to colonize its history and tradition and the way its people understood themselves and the world around them.

The *gymnasia* and the *ephebeia* were the institutions (instruments) designed to fulfill the objective of this cultural colonization and the transformation of the elite young people of Judea according to Greco-Macedonian principles.[11] There, the future citizens were submerged in Hellenic culture, in how that culture understood the *polis*; there, they exercised their minds, souls, and bodies to serve that culture and prepared themselves to give their lives for the empire. They no longer belonged to the community from whence they had come; they were no longer participants in the genealogy of their own people; they became subjects of the law imposed by the basileus, a law that controlled the world around them.

The athletic, naked bodies of the participants in the exercises and youth games became an advertisement, a declaration of principles of the new culture, granting and attesting to a new identity. The torsos covered in oil bespoke the new order. The oil was no longer an element of worship of the One God, fruit of the harvest and a sign of his blessing and presence in daily life, but became an expensive and coveted present. The body appeared as the image of a new ideal of man. An ideal in which, however, a small detail was awry: it was circumcised. This detail, though small, nevertheless took on the importance of what it symbolized: faithfulness to

11. Kyle, *Sport and Spectacle*, 232–34.

the Covenant,[12] the Covenant embodied in a genealogy, in a specific, carnal history. This detail, furthermore, was such a serious obstacle to public and social life during the Antiochian hellenization that not a few *fecerunt sibi præputia*, undergoing medical intervention so as to adapt to the demands of the dominant culture.[13]

But there were also those who did not surrender, preferring to die rather than defile themselves with the foodstuff and break the holy covenant, like the seven brothers whose deaths are described in 2 Maccabees: one after the other they were tortured to death, with their mother encouraging their refusal to eat pork.

It is no coincidence that from the beginnings of Christianity the Maccabean brothers have been granted a cult worthy of the Christian saints, as for Christians, the carnal dimension, the body, holds the same if not greater importance. But we have allowed ourselves to linger on this piece of Jewish history for another reason as well. The Books of the Maccabees offer us a foundational example of the way in which Christian theology approaches the body of man, while simultaneously providing an example of a very specific narrative: the narrative of counterdiscourse. A counterdiscourse in which we participate due to our bodily nature understood in light of Judeo-Christian anthropology, a counterdiscourse that articulates new parameters of thought and action, a counterdiscourse about which theoreticians of resistance are writing today.[14]

If we agree with Florensky's affirmation that cult prefigures culture, it would seem legitimate to affirm that behind every culture there is some type of cult. Therefore, the Kantian rejection of cult, which Florensky himself points out, left an "empty space" in which "the Western European spirit" of modernity established a cult specifically of its own that was fundamental to its culture. Despite its dominance, this Western culture, created around its specific cults, also faces resistance, counterdiscourses; this mechanism is as appropriate for the era of Hellenic domination as it is for the dawn of Christianity and the beginning of the modern age.

St. Ephrem, for example, one of the Church Fathers, perfectly understood the Manichean context of Bardaisan's thought and the complexity of the theological and philosophical premises that shaped the worldview that appears in his work *The Book of the Laws of the Countries*. Ephrem understood that the descriptions of the countries and how they were organized politically reflected a metaphysics and an anthropology that were much

12. Gen 17:9–14.

13. 1 Macc 1:15.

14. Terdiman, *Discourse/Counter-Discourse*, 59.

more important than the description of the external "geo-political panorama" that described the dominant culture. For St. Ephrem, as well as for other Church Fathers, the awareness of creation's orientation toward Christ, of the unity of design between creation and redemption, which modern Westerners have lost, takes on a decisive character.[15]

The objective of this description of the laws of the countries, which tends to be very interesting for historians, is to prove the fundamental thesis: that although nature and fortune can influence man's fate in different ways, "we have free-will in ourselves to avoid serving physical nature and being moved by the control of the powers."[16] The relationship between the corporeal and the law that appears in Bardaisan's *Book of the Laws* is derived from the idea of the flawed nature of the body, and therefore, of the continuous need for the body to be corrected and controlled by will and by the law as the expression of will. In *Prose Refutations*, Ephrem clearly indicates that false views about the origin of evil make the law an absurdity or make good akin to evil.[17] In the second discourse he states that the doctrine of Bardaisan, Mani, and Marcion according to which "body was made by evil one" leads to the false interpretation "that the body is a prison-house for the soul."[18] For St. Ephrem, therefore, a good understanding of the significance of man's bodily reality and consequently, of the nature and meaning of marriage, was vitally important. And in order to reach this type of good understanding, it was necessary to first set down the event of the Incarnation and Resurrection of Jesus Christ as a foundation.

This is a line of theological development characteristic of patristics; it has marked the history of the theological thought rooted in the experience of the Orthodox churches and was the foundation for theology and the *ekklesioteia* in the era of the Byzantine Empire.

Today we know that the history of the church has been marked by questions, debates, and heresies since St. Ephrem's time. Fifteen centuries later, the Russian philosopher Vladimir Soloviev, in *The Great Controversy and Christian Politics* (1883), gave a summarized description of the history of the church as a series of debates and christological heresies, above all Arianism and Manicheism. He thus wrote: "The principal theoretical and practical errors of the first sects therefore resulted from their rejection of the

15. Martinez, "Nota del editor," xxi.

16. Bardesan, "Dialogue on Fate," 15.

17. Ephraem Syrus, "First Discourse to Hypatius," xii–xiii.

18. Ephraem Syrus, "Second Discourse to Hypatius," xxxi.

true intermediation between creation and the divine in the true godmanhood of Christ incarnate."[19]

Soloviev, like St. Ephrem, also decides to respond to the specific ideas of some important authors of his time, to those ideas that were transforming society's way of life in the middle of the nineteenth century, or perhaps not so much that were transforming it, but rather that reflected certain processes that even today continue to mark modernity. Soloviev certainly espouses a counterdiscourse.

In the last decade of the nineteenth century, and at the end of his life, Soloviev appeared to clearly distance himself from his theocratic ideas. At the beginning of this period he wrote *The Meaning of Love* (1892–1894). The clear objective of *The Meaning of Love* was to set forth the (practical) Christian methodology as a response to, above all, two authors whose thinking and its consequences have given rise to a lively debate in Russian society. We refer, of course, to Arthur Schopenhauer and his *Die Welt als Wille und Vorstellung*, and to Leo Tolstoy and above all his *The Kreutzer Sonata*. In the face of Schopenhauer's pessimism and Darwinism and Tolstoy's abstract moralism and reduction of love to unhealthy egoism, Soloviev tries to explore the significance of physical, bodily, conjugal love in the context of a full Christian understanding of man and woman. This understanding is based on discerning the aspects of subjectivity and materiality typical of humanity and which are grounded on the truth of the Incarnation and on the existential experience and vocation of *theosis*.

Thus, today Metropolitan Hilarion writes: "The Holy Fathers, relying on the Bible, teach that the soul and the body are not strangers that come together in the individual only for a time; rather they are simultaneously and permanently given to man in the very act of creation: the soul 'is married' to the body and cannot be separated from it."[20] Further on he adds: "According to the teachings of the Fathers of the Eastern Church, the purpose of man's life is 'divinization' (*theosis*)."[21] In this way we can understand not only the essence of Orthodox theology, but the entire arena of man's existence, his spiritual-bodily reality, the entire culture born from the Orthodox cult that shapes the identity of a people, of a political and eschatological community, the central element of the *ekklesioteia* of the Russian Orthodoxy. This idea of *theosis* has been the key issue in Eastern religious life and all of the dogmatic, ethical, and mystical questions revolve around it.[22]

19. Soloviev, "Velikiy spor i khristianskaya politika," 37.

20. Ilarion, *Tainstvo very*, 107.

21. Ibid., 99.

22. Popov, "Ideya obozheniya," 213.

"Confessing the true faith, fulfilling the commandments, praying, receiving the sacraments . . . all of these are altogether necessary in order to achieve divinization, which is precisely in what the salvation of man consists."[23] This is the essence of Russian cultural identity, and even if unconsciously or when rejected, it has shaped and continues to define a specific way of thinking and understanding itself.

The Narrative of Resistance

In order to be able to interpret the events and narratives that shape them, we must perform an in-depth search for the profound reasons behind them; only by doing so will we be able to find points to support us in our efforts to not only understand the past and the present but also to predict the future. Because "the future is always around us—just like the past. Events leave a long shadow. The past leaves its footprints: the future speaks through signs. Only it is very difficult to understand its language," as Georgy Fedotov wrote in his article entitled "Carmen Saeculare," published in the journal *Put'* in 1928.[24]

Analyzing what yesterday has in common with today, and with tomorrow as well, will undoubtedly help us understand the past and interpret the signs of the future. And what unites the accounts of the examples we examined above, from Judea in the second century BC to modern Russian Christian thought, what these accounts share, is their nature as practices and narratives that can be understood as resistance, as counterdiscourse. In addition to the more trivial definitions of resistance that emerge from Max Weber's thought, the ones put forth by Klass Van Walraven and Jon Abbink are relevant for our case: in these definitions, resistance as such is understood to mean "intentions and concrete actions taken to oppose others and refuse to accept their ideas, actions, or positions for a variety of reasons, the most common being the perception of the position, claims, or actions taken by others as unjust, illegitimate, or intolerable attempts at domination."[25] We should also keep in mind Douglas Haynes and Gyan Prakash's definition, in which "intention" is not considered to be a necessary component: "Resistance, we would argue, should be defined as those behaviours and cultural practices by subordinate groups that contest hegemonic social formations, that threaten to unravel the strategies of domination; 'consciousness' need

23. Ilarion, *Tainstvo very*, 306.

24. Fedotov, "*Carmen Saeculare*," 101, see also Mrówczyński-Van Allen "Fedotov's *Carmen Saeculare*."

25. Walraven and Abbink, "Rethinking Resistance," 8.

not be essential to its constitution."[26] In order to complete our basic overview of the concept of resistance, we still need to explain just what it rises up against. Timothy Mitchell's presentation of the summary of Gramsci's concept of "hegemony" is especially useful to that end: "non-violent forms of control exercised through the whole range of dominant cultural institutions and social practices, from schooling, museums, and political parties to religious practice, architectural forms, and the mass media."[27]

And as Anathea Portier-Young indicates, the articulation and proclamation of a counterdiscourse are the first forms of resistance:

> In each case articulating and promulgating resistant discourse accompanies other forms of resistance, including embodied practices such as fasting, prayer, fighting, or the acceptance of martyrdom . . . The very binary nature of the hegemonic construction of reality . . . (inside/outside, center/periphery, good/bad, civilized/barbaric, normal/aberrant) also creates the possibility for resistance to hegemony through critical inversion, wherein categories are retained but the hierarchy of values or assignment of value is turned upside down . . . A frequently touted example of the latter is the Christian transformation of the cross from an instrument of torture and symbol of imperial coercive power into a symbol of nonviolence, self-giving, and divine redemptive power.[28]

In my opinion, we can thus see that starting with Chaadaev, the narrative of Russian Orthodox identity has had the character of a counterdiscourse *vis-à-vis* the West. Therefore, we can now move on to an examination of specific examples of the current-day counterdiscourse proper to Russian Christian thought. To that end, below we will cite extensive examples from the thought of the current patriarch, Kirill, from when he was Metropolitan of Smolensk and Kaliningrad and the representative of the Department for External Relations of the Russian Orthodox Church. We will look at sections of some of his speeches in which we can already undeniably discern a counterdiscourse character. These speeches were made prior to the Ukrainian crisis, and therefore cannot be discredited by the accusation that they are merely topical or instrumental in view of recent events.

May this passage of the text that originally appeared in the newspaper *Izvyestiya* in 2006 serve as a first step for us:

26. Haynes and Prakash, "Entanglement of Power," 3.

27. Mitchell, "Everyday Metaphors of Power," 553.

28. Portier-Young, *Apocalypse Against Empire*, 12–14.

The exclusion of sin from daily life and from the sphere of intellectual debate leads to the disappearance of the boundaries of good and evil from man's conscience. Man is only prohibited from acting a certain way if by doing so he would be restricting the freedom of another human being. In other words, legal regulations must be respected, but moral ones, not necessarily. This is precisely why today religious ethics, which insist on the primacy of moral values, are gravely attacked and are branded old-fashioned, as if they were an obstacle to progress. At best they are tolerated, so long as they do not contradict the proposed principles of liberalism.

So it is that we cannot ignore the existence of major contradictions between the religious and secular views of human dignity. The Russian Orthodox Church has been the first to lay out this problem and to transfer it to the international stage . . . Like it or not, Russia belongs to the European sphere because of its culture, geography, history, politics, and psychology. In the ongoing processes of integration, however, we must not let ourselves be swayed nor unquestioningly accept the liberal models of behavior or the moral values that were formulated without our participation. Russia, with its millennial spiritual, cultural, theological, and intellectual tradition, must not carelessly accept without critical analysis the ideas that have emerged in the Western European cultural context.

Unfortunately, our intention of objectively analyzing and understanding this set of ideas is frequently rebuffed. What is more, any position critical of secular liberalism, the model that currently plays the role of an ideological guarantee in the process of integration into the new Europe, is rejected. At the same time, we can regrettably observe signs that reveal the efforts made by some liberal circles towards the deliberate use of force in the fight against religious values and traditions . . . Europe and Russia already experienced an unforgettably difficult and dramatic period in which all classes and social groups defended their values through the use of force, depriving others of the right to express their beliefs. In cases like this, the victory of an ideology demands, if not the physical extermination of those who think differently, than their moral submission.

For us it is clear that the primacy of human rights and freedoms in the context of international relations must be based on a broad consensus that includes all of the interested parties, and not on arbitrary and selective interpretations that, worse yet, sometimes serve particular political or ideological groups.

> The principal issue, I believe, lies in the extent to which the proposed new world order corresponds to religious principles. That is why I consider this situation—a situation in which an attempt is made to contain and conquer the vast diversity of God's world with the help of certain ideas that were formulated in the philosophical and political context of Western Europe without the true participation of Muslims, Buddhists, Jews, Orthodox Christians, or many Catholics—to be wrong and even dangerous. Furthermore, the overall majority of the population has its own ancient, native culture. These cultures did not participate in creating the value system that is currently being consolidated worldwide as the universal model, sometimes through the use of force.
>
> There is a danger that the people who cannot adequately respond to this pressure will choose violent forms of resistance. It is not difficult to incite a religious person to an act of sacrifice, to convince him to defend what he holds sacred, even at the cost of his own life. We cannot exclude the possibility that people with evil aims may use believers hidden but real resistance to the aggressive wave of liberalism in order to stir up violence.[29]

In this article we can easily find the same position that we saw in the Peter Chaadaev example with which we started these reflections. We also find the apocalyptic character typical of Judeo-Christian theological counternarratives. During his time at the head of the Department for External Church Relations of the Russian Orthodox Church, the current patriarch Kirill studied the nature of the relationships between the church and secular power in depth, both within political communities as well as at the international level. In the domestic context, he followed the development of the concept of the "symphonious" relationship between the Patriarchate and the government of the Russian Federation, trying to establish a specific *ekklesioteia* for the Russian Orthodox tradition.

Therefore, given the clear need to establish a narrative capable of entering into the debate with the dominant discourse, the church must define its own position. This will provide the community's political representatives and leaders with a resource to reference, a meta-narrative that will establish the counterdiscourse that is part of the identity aspect of the community they represent. Of course, the way the true political and economic powers will turn to this discourse (which can obviously be manipulated, made into an instrument, or rejected) no longer depends entirely on the church.

29. Kirill, *Svoboda i otvetstvennost'*, 125–28.

In his speech on human rights and moral responsibility at the Tenth World Russian People's Council in 2006, Kirill asked if human rights are truly universal in their modern formulation, and then continued, establishing the linchpin of his answer in the most Orthodox position of the cultural and theological tradition:

> The Incarnation bears witness to the extremely high value of the nature of man, which was accepted by Jesus Christ and included in the life of the One and Triune God. After man was created, he did not only have value in the eyes of God: his very life shared that value; in other words, had dignity . . . Although the fall into sin did not change this mission, it did make it impossible without God's help. [And therefore] not all of man's acts can be considered to be in compliance with the regulations that God established during Creation, and consequently, there are actions may not be included among man's rights and liberties . . . On the one hand, personal freedom must be guaranteed, and on the other, people must be helped to follow moral norms. It would probably be wrong to establish criminal sanctions for gambling, euthanasia, or homosexuality, but they cannot they be accepted as lawful norms or, more importantly, as socially accepted ones.[30]

The current Patriarch of Moscow and all Russia thus clearly sees totalitarian features in the imposition of a dominant and exclusive discourse. After suffering the experience of Communist totalitarianism, Kirill can affirm in no uncertain terms that a society "in which the state has all of the rights over man is indisputably inhumane; so too is the society in which human rights are turned into an instrument for the development of instincts, in which the concepts of good and evil mix."[31] That is to say, Western society.

We can thus conclude with the following clear and illuminating words, when Kirill uses the analysis of political commentator Alexander Tsipko to expose his own thinking:

> We are willing to engage in dialogue with the West, but only under equality of conditions, because the truth is that today we are allowed to say and preach anything on the condition that we do not touch the fundamental grounds of that way of thinking. Its followers have claimed the right to evaluate everything based on their own scale of moral values, and earnestly desire to adapt the world's diversity to their model. I am completely convinced

30. Kirill, "Vystupleniye mitropolita."

31. Ibid.

> that today Russia must defend the idea of a multipolar world . . . whose foundation cannot be faceless unity in the context of a forcibly implemented model that will obviously lead to a catastrophe of civilization.[32]

As we have already noted, if we accept Father Pavel Florensky's principle that culture is born out of cult, we can also affirm that by observing a culture we can discover the cult or cults that form it, its theology. With this aim, rather than imposing our own paradigms of interpretation, we must at least listen to others, be attentive to their counterdiscourses, come closer to the ontology, anthropology, and historiosophy that beat in the heart of a people and make it live, that make it live in a particular, unique way, whether in the case of Russia or of so many other peoples and cultures that are resisting modern colonization by the dominant and prevailing discourse of secular modernity.

But we must also bear in mind that the uniqueness of Chaadaev's thought consists in a certain dichotomy, an awareness of human frailty that Russian literature has masterfully been able to show us: an awareness that the human heart, just like human history, is a true battleground between truth and lies; an awareness, beginning in a unique way with Chaadaev and furthered by Patriarch Kirill, that although the specific Russian cultural legacy may have the character of a counterdiscourse, it is written into the history of Europe on equal terms. On November 10, 2014, at the inaugural address for the Eighteen Russian Universal Popular Council, the Patriarch said that

> we cannot agree with those who reduce our history to only a few dark and heavy pages. Similar episodes also took place in the histories of neighboring civilizations. Even a pro-Westerner as radical as Peter Chaadaev, who saw in our past only a bleak and cloudy existence, said: *I am certainly not claiming that there are only vices among us and only virtues among Europeans, God forbid!*[33]

In directly quoting this passage from Peter Chaadaev's "First Philosophical Letter,"[34] the Patriarch not only clearly reveals his belonging to the tradition of counterdiscourse initiated thereby, but also makes it possible to interpret his entire religious-cultural discourse in this key. In conclusion, we can therefore dare to state that not only is the figure of Peter Chaadaev

32. Kirill, *Svoboda i otvetstvennost'*, 106–7.

33. Kirill, "Slovo Glavy VRNS."

34. Chaadaev, "Philosophical Letters," 24.

present in the minds of all Russian intellectuals, but so too do his reflections surprisingly "foreshadow" Russian thinkers, including the representatives of the Orthodox Church from the nineteenth and early twenty-first century. We see that in this same letter quoted by the Patriarch, Chaadaev audaciously affirmed the premise that seems to summarize Kirill's counterdiscourse and thought, and the continuity of this specifically Russian narrative:

> Peoples are moral beings just as individuals are. It takes centuries to educate them, just as it takes years to educate a person. In a sense, it can be said that we are an exceptional people. We are one of those nations which do not seem to form an integral part of humanity, but which exist only to teach some great lesson for the world. The lesson which we are destined to provide will assuredly not be lost, but who knows when we shall find ourselves once again amid humanity and how much misery we shall experience before the fulfillment of our destiny?[35]

Bibliography

Antonov, Konstantin. "Politecheskoye izmierenie russkoy religioznoy filosofii." *Gosudarstvo, Religia, Tserkov'* 3 (2014) 264–94.

Bardesan. "Dialogue on Fate: The Book of the Laws of the Countries." In *Spicilegium Syriacum*, edited and translated by William Cureton, 1–34. London: Rivington, 1855.

Bardy, Gustave. *Dictionnaire de spiritualité, ascétique et mystique*. Vol. 3. Paris: Beauchesne, 1937.

Chaadaev, Peter. "The Philosophical Letters Addressed to a Lady." In *Philosophical Works of Peter Chaadaev*, edited by Raymond T. McNally and Richard Tempest, 18–101. Dordrecht: Springer, 1991.

Ephraem Syrus. "First Discourse to Hypatius." Translated by Charles W. Mitchell. In *S. Ephraim's Prose Refutations of Mani, Marcion, and Bardaisan*, 1:i–xxviii. London: Williams and Norgate, 1912.

———. "Second Discourse to Hypatius." Translated by Charles W. Mitchell. In *S. Ephraim's Prose Refutations of Mani, Marcion, and Bardaisan*, 1:xxix–xxixi. London: Williams and Norgate, 1912.

Fedotov, Georgy. "*Carmen Saeculare*." *Put'* 12 (1928) 101–15.

Florenskiy, Pavel. *Filosofiya kul'ta*. Moscow: Mysl', 2004.

Haynes, Douglas, and Gyan Prakash. "The Entanglement of Power and Resistance." Introduction to *Contesting Power*, edited by Douglas Haynes and Gyan Prakash, 1–22. Berkeley: University of California Press, 1991.

Illarion (Alfieyev). *Tainstvo very*. Moscow: Eksmo, 2010.

35. Ibid., 22.

Kirill (Gundyayev). "Slovo Glavy VRNS, Svjatejshego Patriarkha Moskovskogo i Vsey Rusi Kirilla na XVIII Vsemirnom Russkom Narodnom Sobore." http://vrns.ru/documents/79/3403/#.V3po9NSLTys.

———. *Svoboda i otvetstvennost': v poiskah garmonii*. Moscow: Izdatel'stvo Moskovskoy Patriarkhii, 2014.

———. "Vystupleniye mitropolita Smolenskogo i Kaliningradskogo Kirilla na X VRNS." http://vrns.ru/documents/63/1190/#.V3pqXdSLTys.

Kyle, Donald G. *Sport and Spectacle in the Ancient World*. Oxford: Blackwell, 2007.

Martinez, Javier. "Nota del editor." In *Divina Economía*, by Stephen D. Long, xiii–xxviii. Granada: Nuevo Inicio, 2006.

Mitchell, Timothy. "Everyday Metaphors of Power." *Theory and Society* 19 (1990) 545–77.

Mrówczyński-Van Allen, Artur. "Georgy Fedotov's *Carmen Saeculare*: A Reflection on Culture as a Judgment of Modernity from the Philosophy and Theology of Some Nineteenth- and Twentieth-Century Russian Thinkers." In *Apology of Culture: Religion and Culture in Russian Thought*, edited by Artur Mrówczyński-Van Allen, Teresa Obolevitch, and Paweł Rojek, 43–52. Eugene, OR: Pickwick, 2015.

Popov, Ivan. "Ideya obozheniya v drevnevostochnoy Tserkvi." *Voprosy filosofii i psikhologii* 97 (1906) 165–213.

Portier-Young, Anathea E. *Apocalypse against Empire. Theologies of Resistance in Early Judaism*. Grand Rapids: Eerdmans, 2011.

Solov'yev, Vladimir. "Velikiy spor i khristianskaya politika." In *Sobranie sochinieniy*, 4:3–103. Bruxelles: Zhizn' s Bogom, 1966.

Terdiman, Richard. *Discourse/Counter-Discourse: The Theory and Practice of Symbolic Resistance in Nineteenth Century France*. Ithaca: Cornell University Press, 1985.

Walraven, Klass, and Jon Abbink. "Rethinking Resistance in African History: An Introduction." In *Rethinking Resistance: Revolt and Violence in African History*, edited by Klass van Walraven, Mirjam de Bruijn, and Jon Abbink, 1–40. Leiden: Brill, 2003.

4

"The Madman" Appeals to Faith and Reason

On the Relationship between Fides and Ratio in the Oeuvres of Peter Chaadaev[1]

Teresa Obolevitch

Peter Chaadaev (1797–1856) is widely known in the first place as one of the founding fathers of original Russian thought who dealt mainly with philosophy of history and was a precursor of the Westernizers intellectual movement. Nevertheless, in his papers one could distinguished a number of other topics concerning metaphysics, epistemology, philosophy of religion, etc. In particular, "the madman" from Basmannaya Street, as the Tsar Nicholas I had labeled Chaadaev,[2] paid much attention to the role of reason and faith in human life as well as interaction between them. A brilliant historian of the Russian philosophy, Fr. Vasilii Zenkovsky even suggested that Chaadaev's views on Russia are simply "logical deduction from his general ideas in the philosophy of Christianity."[3] According to

1. This publication was generously supported by a grant, "Science, Religion and Politics in the Russian Philosophical Thought," from the National Science Center, Poland, no. 2014/15/B/HS1/01620.

2. See Tempest, "Madman or Criminal" and "La démence de Čaadaev."

3. Zenkovsky, *History of Russian Philosophy*, 153. Nowadays the similar view is shared, i.e., by Richard Pipes, Konstantin Antonov, Lev Shaposhnikov and Alexander Fedorov or Leszek Augustyn. See Pipes, *Russian Conservatism and Its Critics*, 103; Antonov, *Filosofiya religii v russkoy metafizike*, 37; Shaposhnikov and Fedorov, *Istoriya russkoy religioznoy filosofii*, 173; Augustyn, "O religii, tradycji i wolności," 3.

Andrzej Walicki, this opinion is exaggerated,[4] but even so, one could not deny that both "philosophical" and private letters of Chaadaev as well as his notes are dedicated, among others, to the issue of reason itself and its connection to Christian faith. Perhaps it was one of the cases for which the "Sixth" and the "Seventh Philosophical Letter" were not included in the Soviet edition of Chaadaev's works in 1935.[5] It is worth considering the problem of his religious philosophy, in particular, the possibility and necessity of harmony between rational activity and belief in God. After all, Chaadaev himself in his letter to Princess Sofiya Meshcherskaya (May 27, 1839) wrote that he was "merely a Christian philosopher" and "the whole object" of this epistle was only to refute the error that "faith and reason have nothing in common with each other."[6]

The Concept of Reason

Before beginning the analysis of relationship between faith and reason it is important to establish how Chaadaev understood the last notion. In order to better explore the background of the author of *Philosophical Letters*, let us start with the observation that he was knowledgeable about his contemporary philosophy, including the most influential French and German idealism, as well as empirical science. As a witness to this, one can observe that two libraries of the Russian thinkers contained the writings of Kant, Fichte, Hegel, and the so-called neo-Catholic thinkers, Hugues-Félicité-Robert de Lamennais, Louis-Gabriel-Ambroise de Bonald, Joseph de Maistre, and others.[7] Besides, Chaadaev himself was considered by Alexander Turgenev, the Russian statesman and historian, as "the Moscow Lamennais."[8] Like the later, he claimed that the origin of all ideas is God speaking to man. This issue will be detailed below.

Chaadaev also personally got to know and conducted a correspondence with Schelling. In his first letter addressing to the German idealist in 1832 he confessed:

4. Cf. Walicki, *Slavophile Controversy*, 87; Copleston, *Philosophy in Russia*, 40.

5. Cf. Lossky, *History of Russian Philosophy*, 49.

6. Chaadaev to Schelling, 1832, Chaadaev, "Fragments," 177.

7. See McNally, *Chaadayev and His Friends*, 164–95; Walicki, *Flow of Ideas*, 148; Grechaninova, *Katalog biblioteki Chaadayeva*; Veselovskiy, "Chaadayev i frantsuzskaya mysl'"; Riasanovsky, "On Lamennais, Chaadaev and the Romantic Revolt," 1173; Tarasov, *Neprochitannyy Chaadayev*, 15–16; Obolevitch, *La philosophie religieuse russe*, 85.

8. See Tempest, "Chaadaev and Tiutchev," 385; Tarasov, *Neprochitannyy Chaadayev*, 33.

> You will permit me, I believe, to say to you, that the study of your works has opened a new world to me; by the light of your spirit I have been able to see imperfectly into the domain of spacial thought which had been entirely hidden from me, this study has been a source of fertile and delicious meditations for me.[9]

Under the inspiration of Schelling the Moscow thinker tried to elaborate a kind of synthesis of philosophy and religion. In his other letter (May 20, 1842) Chaadaev even expressed hope that the philosophy of Schelling would bring a breakthrough in the development of Russia: "The destinies of a great nation depend in a certain way on the success of your system."[10] In turn, the German thinker recognized Chaadaev as "one of the most remarkable men not only in Russia but in Europe,"[11] shared with him his plans and discussed about the forthcoming "philosophy of revelation."

However, according to Mary-Barbara Zeldin, it was Kant who wielded the most influence on Chaadaev.[12] Indeed, on the margin of his copy of *Critique of Practical Reason* (purchased in Dresden in 1826) he noted in German: "*Es war nicht das Licht, sondern das erzeugte von dem Licht*"[13]—"He was not the light, but came to bear witness about the light" (John 1:8). Namely, Kant inspired Chaadaev to explore the nature of reason, even if the result of his investigation was quite different. As the Russian thinker claimed, so-called pure reason reflected by modern philosophy was in fact "an artificial" or "fallen" reason.[14] In this sense Kant "was not the light," even if he gave a witness to the limitation of human reason. Nicolai Lossky noticed that "in reading Kant's *Critique of Pure Reason* Chaadaev scratched out the title and wrote instead: *Apologete adamitisher Vernunft*. He evidently meant that Kant expounded the doctrine not of pure reason but of reason distorted by sin."[15]

According to metaphysical and epistemological conception of Chaadaev, the primordial source of all beings is God—the supreme, absolute

9. Chaadaev, "Fragments," 153. Cf. Bezwiński, "Czaadajew i Schelling."

10. Chaadaev, "Fragments," 184.

11. McNally and Tempest, "Commentaries," 280.

12. See Zeldin, "Influence of Kant," 111; Zeldin, "Chaadayev's Quarrel with Kant," 277.

13. Chaadayev, "Zametki na knigakh," 612. Although Chaadaev referred to the biblical text, he apparently used the metaphor of light which was very popular at the Age of Enlightenment.

14. The concept of "fallen" or submitted reason (*raison soumise*) was proclaimed by French neo-Catholic philosophers.

15. Lossky, *History of Russian Philosophy*, 49. Cf. Smirnova, "Chaadayev i nemetskiy idealizm," 210.

Reason (*raison suprême, raison absolue*) revealed in Christ. On the next stage of the ontological ladder there exist the universal reason (*raison universelle, générale*) or common intelligence (*unique intellegence*)—"the sum of all the ideas which live on in man's memory"[16] which manifests in the empirical world (i.e., in the shape of the laws of nature as well as throughout history and tradition). Finally, each man has an individual, subjective, finite, "Adamic," fallen, artificial, and evil reason (*raison artificielle, factice, mauvaise*).[17] "If it is true that in the higher or objective reality, man's reason is really only the perpetual reproduction of God's thought, then it is also certain that his present reason or subjective reason is only the reason made by man's reason itself thanks to his free will."[18] And besides,

> this artificial reason, which we willfully substituted for the portion of universal reason bestowed upon us in the beginning . . . *which so often distorts objects under observation, which makes us see them differently from what they really are does not, however, obscure the absolute order of things so as to deprive us of the ability to recognize the primacy of subordination over that of freedom and the dependency of our selfmade laws upon the general law of the world.*[19]

Therefore, all human rational activity is a result of participation in the divine mind (*l'esprit de Dieu*), "all scientific discoveries are ultimately to be traced to God's illumination given to man through the gift of intuition."[20] It is drafted into man and governed or "directed from the outside by a higher power."[21] In his letter to Ivan Yakushkin from 1838 Chaadaev clearly suggested: "Reason or rather spirit is one in heaven and on earth; the continuous invisible emanations from the upper world into the lower, from the first moment that the two worlds were created."[22] In this connection, the revealed truths concern not only the sphere of faith, but the entire domain of cognition:[23] "Our thinking and our knowledge, indeed our very nature, are dependent on God."[24] As Andrzej Walicki noted with remarkable clarity,

16. Chaadaev, "Philosophical Letters," 61–62.
17. See ibid., 43–44; Goerdt, *Russische Philosophie*, 280–85.
18. Chaadaev, "Philosophical Letters," 64.
19. Ibid., 43–44.
20. Drozdek, "Chaadaev and the Principle of Unity," 52.
21. Mrówczyński-Van Allen, *Between the Icon and the Idol*, 53.
22. Chaadaev, "Fragments," 176.
23. Cf. McNally, "Quelques idees glanées," 292.
24. Zeldin, "Chaadayev's Quarrel with Kant," 279.

> In this way Chaadaev combined the traditional theistic conception of a transcendent God with pantheistic emphasis on God's immanent presence in the world. This was in tune with Christian Neoplatonism (which reached Chaadaev through the esoteric tradition in Freemasonry, as well as through Schelling, whom he personally met in 1825) and with the panentheistic religious ideas of the German Romantics.[25]

For Chaadaev the human reason is a divine gift, "a finite, limited form of infinite and omnipotent divine reason"[26] and is obliged to be subordinated to the later: "The well-made mind gravitates towards a belief, towards a submission just as naturally as the badly-made mind pushes away all belief, resists against all submission."[27] Dmitry Shakhovskoy, the grandson of Chaadaev's cousin-in-law and an outstanding researcher and publisher of his writings, even concluded that the individual consciousness does not exist; it is nothing but the product of the world's collective mind; furthermore, this conception is the most important idea of "the Moscow Lamennais" and a key to the whole Russian philosophy.[28] This interpretation seems to be too strong, although it is true that Chaadaev was convinced that "human reason does not achieve its most positive knowledge purely by its own inner power but must be perpetually set in motion from the outside."[29] In "Fifth Philosophical Letter" one can read the following description of the origin of our faculty of reasoning: "On the day when man was created God spoke with him, and man heard and understood him: this is the true genesis of human reason; psychology will never find a more profound explanation."[30] "The divine thought" is also a primordial source of human language: "Verb is the acting word, the creating word."[31] In his letter to Princess Meshcherskaya Chaadaev noticed that the divine word, "in order to make itself understood by human reason" in the process of transfer of Revelation, "had to utilize human language and, as a

25. Walicki, "Chaadaev," 6. Cf. Chaadaev, "Philosophical Letters," 58: "Undoubtedly, an absolute unity exists among all beings: this is the very thing which we are attempting to demonstrate as best we can; furthermore, in that lies the credo of ever healthy philosophy. But this unity is objective unity, completely outside the reality which we sense; an immense fact which throws an extraordinary light on the great All and forms the logic of cause and effect, but which has nothing in common with the sort of pantheism professed by the majority of contemporary philosophers, a sad teaching which colors all contemporary philosophic systems with its false tint."

26. Smirnova, "Problem of Reason," 11.

27. Chaadaev, "Fragments," 137.

28. Cf. Shakhovskoy, "Stat'i i nabroski," 124–25, 138–39.

29. Chaadaev, "Philosophical Letters," 45.

30. Ibid., 63.

31. Chaadaev, "Fragments," 130.

consequence, to submit to the imperfections of this language."[32] Hence, as divine reason is subordinated to the tools of human language, so must human reason be obedient to its Creator.

Some scholars held that Chaadaev had been not consistent in his deliberations about reason. For instance, Frederick Copleston claimed: "To the present writer at any rate it is none too clear how his theory of 'universal intelligence' should be understood."[33] Indeed, sometimes he wrote in a Platonic manner that it is the locus of all universal ideas, and another time thought that the universal reason concerns merely moral ideas and ideas about spiritual reality which had been communicated to people by God and transmitted by tradition. At any rate, Chaadaev elaborated his quite sophisticated hierarchical and dialectical concept as a reaction to a "simplified" model of Kant who had thought about only the human type of reason which supposed to be active, synthetic, and self-sufficient. The Moscow thinker emphasized that

> the most profound and most productive of all the known systems is the one which strives to construct conscientiously an absolutely abstract intelligence, an exclusively intelligent nature, in order to take the intellectual phenomenon into account without going back to the very source of the spiritual principle. But, since it is always man in his present state who furnishes the materials from which this system constructs its model, it happens that this system shows us artificial reason again, but not original reason.[34]

The chief questions of Kant were sounded: "What can we know?" or "How knowledge is possible?" and their solution did not refer to the Christian Revelation. As an alternative, Chaadaev posed the most fundamental questions that could be formulated in a following manner: "How reason is possible?" and "What reason must subordinate itself?" However,

> both Chaadaev and Kant see reality as consisting of two realms, a physical and a mental one. For Chaadaev the former exists in itself but is known only in terms of mental constructs, whereas for Kant it is similarly known, but, since the forms by which it is known are not objectively in it—not God-given primitive ideas traditionally handed down—but rationally imposed categories,

32. Ibid., 176–77.

33. Copleston, *Philosophy in Russia*, 34.

34. Chaadaev, "Philosophical Letters," 65.

> it is known only as a common but merely phenomenal world, never as a world real in itself.[35]

It should be added that a distinction between "original" and "artificial" reason (which somehow distorts the divine truth) corresponds to a differentiation between *Logos* and *ratio* proclaimed, i.e., by Alexei Losev or Vladimir Ern[36] (as well as Nikolai Berdyaev's doctrine of "great mind" and "little mind"[37]). To some extent, it is a common element of the entire Russian philosophical tradition.

Fides Quaerens Intellectum and *Intellectus Quaerens Fidem*

Having briefly exposed the concept of reason of Chaadaev, it is possible to move on to the analysis of its relation to faith. One can remember that the thought of the Russian philosopher (including his reflection about the reconciliation of *fides* and *ratio*) has evolved through his life journey. In *Philosophical Letters* faith and reason were treated as two reliable paths representing feeling (of a temporary nature) and reasoning (which is more constant and stable) respectively and both leading to God. Yet reason itself is deficient. In the spirit of the Greek Fathers Chaadaev wrote: when "reason tries to know God all by itself, it makes a God with its own hands."[38] The mistake of the contemporary philosophers consists in the matter that they "are only able to explain man by man: thus, they separate him from God and inspire in him the idea that he is self-sufficient."[39] As a consequence, they purely misrepresent the objective reality. Meanwhile, "there is no human knowledge capable of replacing divine knowledge."[40] Even Pythagoras, Socrates, Zoroaster, and Plato—the philosophers illuminated by "an extraordinary reflection"—"could not rise to the knowledge of the genuine characteristics in absolute truth."[41] Therefore, religious (theistic) justification or interpretation should end any philosophical question.

Chaadaev argued that the more reason is subordinated to the supreme principle, the stronger it is. The task of philosophy is nothing else

35. Zeldin, "Influence of Kant," 116.

36. See Lossew, "Die russische Philosophie," 203–4; Ern, "Nechto o Logose," 78–80.

37. See Berdyaev, "Filosofiya svobody," 35–36. Cf. Shestov, "In Praise of Folly," 42.

38. Chaadaev, "Fragments," 135.

39. Chaadaev, "Philosophical Letters," 39.

40. Ibid., 40.

41. Ibid., 41.

but demonstrate that principle and show "the origins of this light which should guide us in life."[42] For instance, in the process of cognition of the material world reason cannot break the rules of logic and mathematics. It should, however, strive to find a foundation which serves as a source of the whole knowledge as well as moral behavior, in other words—God: "Divine reason is the cause of everything . . . man's reason is only an effect."[43] That is why the significance of Christianity for the nineteenth-century philosophy is difficult to overestimate:

> It is time for modern reason to acknowledge that all its power is due to Christianity. It is time for it to learn that it is only through the extraordinary means furnished by revelation and through the living clarity which Christianity was able to spread to all objects of human reflection that the majestic structure of the new science was built.[44]

Christianity is of a rational character and can be compared with philosophical systems: "Christianity exists . . . not only as religion, but also as science, as religious philosophy,"[45] since "the first element of Christianity is faithfulness to truth."[46] Philosophy and Christian Revelation represent two forms of knowledge and the difference between them concerns only the degree to which it is measured.

On the other hand, reason should be able to rely on its own forces, because "an idea which is thought out never leaves us, no matter what our spiritual mood may be, whereas the idea which is only felt escapes us ceaselessly and changes instantaneously, depending upon whether our heart beats more or less rapidly."[47] Subsequently, faith also demands the confirmation of reason: "no matter how strong faith may be, it is beneficial for the intellect to realize how to gain support from the powers found within it."[48] It means that theology and philosophy—like in Schelling's system—are complementary disciplines:[49] reason provides understanding the truth of

42. Ibid., 44.

43. Ibid., 51.

44. Ibid., 98.

45. Chaadaev, "Fragments," 146. Cf. Chaadayev, "Zametki na knigakh," 587.

46. Shakhovskoy, "Pis'ma i zametki," 547.

47. Chaadaev, "Philosophical Letters," 42.

48. Ibid.

49. Cf. Chaadaev's letter to Schelling from 1832: "In reading you, that a religious philosophy was bound to flow from your system one day, but I cannot tell you how happy I have been to learn that the most profound thinker of our time, has arrived at this great idea of the fusion of philosophy with religion. From the first moment when

Revelation, whereas Christian faith clarifies the origin and process of human knowledge.

> The questions which the human spirit has posed since time immemorial, questions which Christianity resolved in its own way, with the instruments of faith but which have not yet been resolved with those of reason. Thus, one can say that its [philosophical—T. O.] work is the work of Christianity.[50]

In his notes (published as "Fragments and Various Thoughts" only in the twentieth century) Chaadaev slightly changed his view on the role of faith. In contrast to *Philosophical Letters* he examined faith "not only as feeling, which helps the process of knowledge, but also as an aspect of the process itself."[51] Faith is recognized as a specific faculty which permits an act of reasoning. As Chaadaev put it,

> Faith is thus only a moment or an epoch of human knowledge and nothing more. So, that candidly and without mental reservations, to make of religion and science two absolutely distinct regions is to return to scholasticism before Abelard . . . Then who today ignores the fact that faith is one of the most powerful and most fruitful agents of thought? . . . Knowledge always implies a certain degree of faith, just as faith always implies a certain degree of knowledge.[52]

Faith is now gaining the universal significance and is not reducing to the religious belief: "the human spirit has admitted from time immemorial certain truths such as articles of faith, *a priori* truths, elementary truths, without which all operation of the mind is unimaginable."[53] This position is akin to the conception of Clemens of Alexandria who identified faith (*pistis*) in the religious sense with faith as a presumption (Aristotelian "conjecture") which precedes and founds the process of cognition: "no one shall learn anything without faith, since no one [learns anything] without preconception."[54] Also in the eyes of Chaadaev faith (in the wide meaning of this word) is the beginning and the end of any rational activity.

I began to philosophize, this idea occurred to me as the beacon and the goal of all my intellectual work." Chaadaev, "Fragments," 153.

50. Chaadaev, "Fragments," 122.

51. Smirnova, "Problem of Reason," 10.

52. Chaadaev, "Fragments," 114.

53. Ibid.

54. Clement of Alexandria, *Stromata*, II, 4.

In my opinion, faith and reason might be also seen as two cultural types or paradigms: the Eastern and Western one correspondingly. It is no secret that Chaadaev's respect for reason was strongly connected with his pro-Catholic sympathy.[55] For him, one of the greatest achievements and an attribute of European civilization is "the Western syllogism" that allows one to consider "each natural phenomenon"[56] and which is unfamiliar in Russia.[57] At any rate it was the attitude of the secular, "abstract" rationalism in the sense that will be later on critiqued by Vladimir Soloviev. Still, Chaadaev (and many others Slavs, including the Polish poet and messianic thinker Adam Mickiewicz) appreciated the significance of Christian faith, although, unlike the latter, was far from any kind of fideism.[58] In 1838 he persuaded his friend Yakushkin that the divine Wisdom need be worshiped in a rational manner: not adapting an attitude of pietistic silence, but "with deep thought in the soul and living word in the month."[59]

To sum things up, Chaadaev maintained the moderate position and stressed the role of a holistic conception of reality and the coincidence faith and reason in the process of knowledge (both concerning its origin from the "universal mind" and the individual perception of truth) that seems to overcome the alleged opposition between the Western and Eastern mentality, Catholic and Orthodox approach to cognition. One may say, therefore, that the problem of the relationship between *fides* and *ratio* has not only methodological and epistemological, but also social and ecclesiastical load and implications. What is more, for Chaadaev the question of integration of faith and reason, religion and philosophy and shaping of the universal Christian system served as one of the condition of realization of the kingdom of God on earth.[60] In agreement with it, "the progress of the human spirit does not consist in imposing laws of its invention on the world, but in

55. Chaadaev did not considered himself as a "true Catholic." In his letter to Alexander Turgenev from 1820 he wrote: "You see that my religion isn't exactly that of theologians, and you'll perhaps tell me that it's not even that of the people . . . If I had found such a completed religion around me, when I was seeking one of them, I would have assuredly taken it up; but not having found any, I was forced to embrace the community of the Fenelons, the Pascals, the Leibnitzes, and the Bacons." Chaadaev, "Fragments," 163. Cf. McNally, "Revelations in Chaadaev's Letters to Turgenev," 325.

56. Chaadaev, "Philosophical Letters," 50; cf. Chaadaev, "Fragments," 128.

57. See Chaadaev, "Philosophical Letters," 23.

58. Cf. O'Connor, "*Adveniat Regnum Tuum*," 401, 406–7.

59. Chaadaev, "Fragments," 129.

60. See Chaadaev, "Philosophical Letters," 101; McNally, "Chaadaev's Major Ideas," 14; Antonov, *Filosofiya religii v russkoy metafizike*, 41.

approaching incessantly towards the more perfect knowledge of those laws which govern the world."[61]

Science and Theology

As already shown above, Chaadaev—presumably under the influence of Schelling—was interested in empirical science: physics, mechanics, astronomy, and other disciplines. Even the title of his most important work (*The Philosophical Letters*) contains an obvious allusion to *Lettres philosophiques* of Voltaire composed during his stay in England where the French thinker "became convinced that his home culture needed to appreciate and embrace the institutions and attitudes of British empiricism."[62] By all means, the context and content of these papers were quite different: while Voltaire laid stress on the significance of the Age of Reason and scientific rationality, Chaadaev aimed at the Age of Faith. Nonetheless, the Moscow thinker shared the conviction that empirical experience is of a great importance for the understanding of reality. As he pointed out in his letter to Yakushkin (October 19, 1837), "The natural sciences are moreover far from being hostile to religious beliefs to day."[63] Between science and theology not only there is no contradiction; what is more, the scientific discoveries are in tune with religious truths: "All the recent discoveries of science, of electricity notably, came to the support of Christian traditions, confirming the cosmogonic system of the Bible."[64] As we can see, Chaadaev's way of relating science and religion is a version of concordism, or an attempt to align and harmonize Revelation with science.

Simultaneously, Chaadaev opposed materialism and such a newly established philosophical direction as positivism. It was one of the reasons for which Alexander Herzen (who in general admired Chaadaev)[65] in his essay entitled "Buddhism in Science" (as a part of the work *Dilettantism in Science*, 1843) struggled against idealistic German Romanticism and perhaps conducted a covert polemic with Chaadaev. Herzen composed a paean to progress, "the fearlessness of reason, to the energy of the individual who, in his determined drive toward a 'sober knowledge' of life, destroys all the ramshackle prejudices, illusions, and myths of the superhuman mainsprings

61. Chaadaev, "Fragments," 116.

62. Peterson, "Civilizing the Race," 557. Cf. McNally, "Chaadaev's Letters to Vyazemsky," 76.

63. Chaadaev, "Fragments," 168.

64. Ibid., 169.

65. See Herzen, "Young Moscow," 531.

and forces that govern the world,"[66] whereas Chaadaev was attached to the religious conviction about the Supreme Being and could not accept a naturalistic conception of science. Indeed, as we have seen, for the author of *Philosophical Letters* the laws of nature merely express the divine reason, therefore, to know them means to know God's providence.

In the opinion of Chaadaev, the view that science is restricted to the empirical world constitutes both its strong and weak sides. "In what way has natural science achieved its great certitude?"—Chaadaev asked and answered: "By reducing reason to a completely passive, completely negative activity," "because it places the human spirit before nature in the humble position appropriate to it."[67] Science uses the symbolic language. It does nothing but approach the cognition of reality. Even mathematics (which implies the most universal laws) does not grasp reality as such. Chaadaev's God (unlike Plato's vision) is not a great mathematician:

> If there were complete certitude in mathematics, a number would be something real . . . We who seriously believe in God, are absurd when we dare to arm the hand of the Creator with a compass. We forget that measure and limit are the same thing, that infinity is the first attribute of divinity, that which forms, so to say, all its divinity; so that if we make the Supreme Being into a geometrician, we deprive him of his eternal nature and bring him down to our level . . . It is not true that number exists in divine thought; creations flow from God like the waters of a torrent, without measure and without end. But man needs a point of contact between his limited intelligence and God's infinite intelligence, which are separated by immensity, and that is why he loves to imprison divine power in the dimensions of his own nature.[68]

In addition, "all the perfection of . . . sciences, all their might flows from their ability to restrict themselves wholly to their legitimate circle."[69] We can conclude that Chaadaev at first glance proclaimed the principle of methodological naturalism, according to which science studies the world without taking into account any supernatural factors, thus is limited to the empirical reality. But the more detailed examination shows that in the opinion of the

66. Gurvich-Lishchiner, "Chaadaev—Herzen—Dostoevsky," 13. Cf. Herzen, "Dilettantism in Science," 73: "Science demands that man abandon himself unhesitatingly and without reservations and be rewarded by the heavy cross of sober knowledge."

67. Chaadaev, "Philosophical Letters," 44.

68. Ibid., 50–51.

69. Ibid., 52.

Russian thinker science is by no means religiously neutral. After all, it has its primordial (and ultimate) source in the divine reason, since all physical phenomena could be utterly explained only in this light. For instance, according to Newton, the most general law of nature is "attraction or universal gravity." However, there is another "force, without which gravity would be worthless, is the initial impulse or thrust,"[70] and which is given by God. Empirical theory at best "only verifies certain phenomena in our nature; however, as for the general phenomenon, it does not take that into account at all."[71] These words express the conviction that the task of science—*contra* positivistic views—is not just to explore the external connection between empirical data, but strive to find their genuine cause (i.e., mechanics—the "first mover"). In this fashion "the mechanistic model of the physical world served Chaadaev as a mode of religious explanation of consciousness as not subordinated to the mechanical laws of nature but communicated by the divinity."[72] In this reflection one can notice some inconsistency and even error from the scientific side (namely, Chaadaev seemed to recognize the Aristotelian cosmological model in the post-Newtonian era), but the message is crystal clear: for the Russian thinker only a believing scientist deserves the title of authentic expert. Like philosophy, science leads to the Creator: "Religion is the knowledge of God, science is the knowledge of the universe. But it can be said with even more reason that religion learns to know God in his being and science in his works. In this way both end at God."[73]

It is worth adding that the preceding statement does not refer to the Eastern-Christian distinction between the unknowable divine essence and divine energies: it was basically unfamiliar in Chaadaev's days. The above quotation rather articulates the view, according to which the scientific and religious ways of cognition are different, but the result is the same. As an illustration one put the following words from his already mentioned letter to Princess Meshcherskaya:

> The divine founder of Christianity never planned to impose a dumb and myopic faith on the world . . . since Christianity is the word and the light *par excellence*, it should naturally provoke the word and disseminate the greatest daylight possible on all the objects of man's intellectual vision that, far from contradicting the facts of science, Christianity supported them with its lofty authority, while science in its turn daily came to confirm the

70. Ibid., 53; cf. ibid., 60. Cf. Tarasov, *Chaadayev*, 174.

71. Chaadaev, "Philosophical Letters," 55–56.

72. Kamensky, "Pyotr Chaadayev," 136.

73. Chaadaev, "Fragments," 251.

> Christian truths by its discoveries . . . Christianity had furnished new and numerous instruments to the human spirit by means of the immense exercise which it was made to undergo . . . the most illustrious saints of the church were at the same time the greatest philosophers of their age; finally . . . Christianity had demonstrated that the most fertile epochs in the history of the human spirit were those in which science and religion clasped hands together.[74]

As Chaadaev held, to proclaim "the old" opposition between science and religion—which was established in the eighteenth century and which "neither the Fathers of the Church, nor the doctors of the Middle Ages, those giants of religious thought, conceived of at all"[75]—is not a philosophical approach any more.[76]

As a Way of Conclusion

It is common knowledge that the thought of Chaadaev triggered heated debates in Russia; the most famous were conducted between Slavophiles and Westernizers. In this context it is important to add that also his investigations on the relationship between faith and reason were analyzed and reflected by his followers. For one thing, one could notice the figure of the Russian Schellingist, Ivan Yastrebtsov (1797–1869). He supposed to be the only "direct pupil" of Chaadaev and the author of the book entitled *Concerning the Systems of Sciences Proper Today for Children Belonging to the Most Educated Classes in Society* (1833) as well as the articles "On reason" (1837) and "On feeling" (1838).[77] Yastrebtsov denied the principal "epistemological axiom of Chaadaev," according to which reason has to gain support from the powers found within it. As a consequence, he abolished philosophy, science and even reason itself stepping—contrary to Chaadaev—on the way of fideism.[78]

It seems that the author of *Philosophical Letters*, if not initiated, deepened the research on a special capacity or function uniting faith and reason. As Mary-Barbara Zeldin appositely observed, this type of reflection "is rare in modern Western philosophy":

74. Ibid., 178.

75. Ibid.

76. Ibid., 127.

77. See McNally, *Chaadayev and His Friends*, 27; Sapov, "Ucheniki Chaadayeva," 150, 155, 161.

78. See Sapov, "Ucheniki Chaadayeva," 162.

> St. Augustine's "*credo ut intellegam*" and St. Anselm's "*fides quaerens intellectum*" suggest a cognitive faculty of faith which is dropped as philosophy becomes secular in the Renaissance and thereafter . . . On the other hand, Russians, in general, posit a faculty called "integral reason," "free willing reason," "reason in its wholeness" by Khomiakov; "intuition," "faith," "mystical knowledge," "mystical perception," "immediate experience," "direct perception," by Soloviev; "spiritual experience," by Berdiaev—which directly intuits the thing-in-itself.[79]

Notably, Chaadaev's tendency to a harmonious correlation between faith and reason will be taken out by Vladimir Soloviev (1853–1900) in his conception of so-called integral knowledge. In the writings of both thinkers one notice the evident parallels between their search for union *fides* and *ratio* and aspiration of overcoming (although in a different way) the cultural antagonism between the East and West, Russian "apophatic silence" and modern occidental philosophy,[80] or—as Semen Frank suggested—between the Eastern ascetic Christianity which watches over the purity of the faith and the Western social engaged attitude.[81]

It is plain, then, that the problem of the relationship between faith and reason in the oeuvres of Chaadaev, even supposing this was not the major topic, by no means could be seen as accidental or marginal. Even his "most historiosophical" "First Letter" appeared as a reply to the epistle of Mrs. Ekaterina Panova who had asked him for advice concerning the religious issues.[82] Moreover, Chaadaev took a view that also philosophy of history (within which he taught about the heritage and destiny of Russia) concerns the universal reason that expresses in the world. As the title of this volume suggests, Chaadaev had two loves:[83] fatherland (a special topic of his "First Philosophical Letter" and *Apologia of a Madman*) and the truth or, more precisely, the absolute Truth that might be perceived not only by faith but also by reason. Chaadaev disputed both with the secular rationalism of the Enlightenment and a fideistic inclination of Orthodoxy trying to find a successful compromise between them. Some of Chaadaev's reflections in this field seem to be immature or eclectic, nonetheless, his manifest of the religious renewal (and *ipso facto* restoration of the whole human life, including

79. Zeldin, "Chaadayev as Russia's First Philosopher," 478, cf. 475.

80. Cf. Aizlewood, "Revisiting Russian Identity," 23; Kuznetsov, "Metafizicheskiy Nartsiss," 744; Zlatopol'skaya, "Shakhovskoy," 114.

81. See Frank, "Chaadaev," 33.

82. See Gershenzon, *Chaadayev*, 66–67.

83. "Love of the fatherland is certainly a very beautiful thing, but there is one thing better than that; it is the love of truth." Chaadaev, "Apologia of a Madman," 102.

cognition) proclaimed in the Golden Age of Russian culture, found resonance in the original Russian philosophy of so-called Silver Age. It worth adding that the name of Chaadaev was mentioned by John Paul II in his encyclical letter *Fides et Ratio* as an example of the "fruitful relationship between philosophy and the word of God."[84]

Bibliography

Aizlewood, Robin. "Revisiting Russian Identity in Russian Thought: From Chaadaev to the Early Twentieth Century." *Slavonic and East European Review* 78 (2000) 20–43.

Antonov, Konstantin. *Filosofiya religii v russkoy metafizike XIX—nachala XX veka*. Moscow: Izdatel'stvo Pravoslavnogo Svyato-Tikhonovskogo Gumanitarnogo Universiteta, 2013.

Augustyn, Leszek. "O religii, tradycji i wolności. Religijny wymiar myśli Piotra Czaadajewa." *Studia Religiologica* 1 (2016) 1–19.

Berdyaev, Nikolay. "Filosofiya svobody." In *Filosofiya svobody. Smysl tvorchestva*, 12–250. Moscow: Pravda, 1989.

Bezwiński, Adam. "Czaadajew i Schelling—o korespondencji dwóch myślicieli." *Studia Filologiczne. Filologia Rosyjska* 7 (1980) 47–53.

Chaadaev, Peter. "Apologia of a Madman." In *Philosophical Works of Peter Chaadaev*, edited by Raymond T. McNally and Richard Tempest, 102–11. Dordrecht: Springer, 1991.

———. "Fragments and Various Thoughts." In *Philosophical Works of Peter Chaadaev*, edited by Raymond T. McNally and Richard Tempest, 112–255. Dordrecht: Springer, 1991.

———. "The Philosophical Letters Addressed to a Lady." In *Philosophical Works of Peter Chaadaev*, edited by Raymond T. McNally and Richard Tempest, 18–101. Dordrecht: Springer, 1991.

Chaadayev, Petr. "Zametki na knigakh." In *Polnoe sobranie sochineniy i izbrannye pis'ma*, 1:582–626. Moscow: Nauka, 1991.

Clement of Alexandria. *The Stromata*. Translated by William Wilson. http://logoslibrary.org/clement/stromata/204.html.

Copleston, Frederick. *Philosophy in Russia: From Herzen to Lenin and Berdyaev*. Notre Dame: University of Notre Dame Press, 1986.

Drozdek, Adam. "Chaadaev and the Principle of Unity." *Slavia Orientalis* 1 (2008) 47–60.

Ern, Vladimir. "Nechto o Logose, russkoy filosofii i nauchnosti." In *Sochineniya*, 71–108. Moscow: Pravda, 1991.

Frank, Semen. "Chaadayev." *Logos i Ethos* 43 (2016) 28–33.

Gershenzon, Mikhail. *P. Ya. Chaadayev. Zhizn i myshlenie*. Saint Petersburg: Tipografiya M. M. Stasyulevicha, 1908.

Goerdt, Wilhelm. *Russische Philosophie: Grundlagen*. Munich: Verlag Karl Alber, 2002.

Grechaninova, Vera S., ed. *Katalog biblioteki P. Ya. Chaadayeva*. Moscow: Pashkov dom, 2000.

Gurvich-Lishchiner, Sophia. "Chaadaev—Herzen—Dostoevsky: Individual and Reason in the Creative Mind." *Russian Studies in Literature* 43 (2007) 6–54.

84. John Paul II, *Fides et Ratio*, 74.

Herzen, Alexander. "Dilettantism in Science." In *Selected Philosophical Works*, 15–96. Translated by Lev Navrozov. Moscow: Foreign Languages, 1956.

———. "Young Moscow." In *Selected Philosophical Works*, 507–45. Translated by Lev Navrozov. Moscow: Foreign Languages, 1956.

John Paul II. *Fides et Ratio*. Encyclical letter. September 14, 1998.

Kamensky, Zakhar. "Pyotr Chaadayev." In *A History of Russian Philosophy: From the Tenth through the Twentieth Centuries*, edited by Valery A. Kuvakin, 1:131–39. Buffalo, NY: Prometheus, 1994.

Kuznetsov, Pavel V. "Metafizicheskiy Nartsiss i russkoe molchanie: P. Ya Czaadayev i sud'ba filosofii v Rossii." In *Petr Chaadayev. Pro et contra: Lichnost' i tvorchestvo Petra Chaadayeva v otsenke russkikh mysliteley i issledovateley. Antologiya*, edited by Aleksandr Ermichev and Anna Zlatopol'skaya, 729–52. Saint Petersburg: Izdatel'stvo Russkogo Khristianskogo Gumanitarnogo Universiteta, 1996.

Lossew, Alexis. "Die russische Philosophie." In Elena A. Takho-Godi, *Aleksey Losev v epokhu russkoy revolyutsii: 1917–1919*, 191–233. Moscow: Modest Kolerov, 2014.

Lossky, Nicolai O. *History of Russian Philosophy*. New York: International University Press, 1951.

McNally, Raymond T. "An Analysis of Chaadaev's Major Ideas." In *Philosophical Works of Peter Chaadaev*, edited by Raymond T. McNally and Richard Tempest, 14–17. Dordrecht: Springer, 1991.

———. "Chaadaev's Letters to Vyazemsky." In *The Golden Age of Russian Literature and Thought: Selected Papers from the Fourth World Congress for Soviet and East European Studies, Harrogate, 1990*, edited by Derek Offord, 76–83. New York: St. Nartin's, 1992.

———. *Chaadayev and His Friends: An Intellectual History of Peter Chaadayev and His Russian Contemporaries*. Tallahassee, FL: Diplomatic, 1971.

———. "Quelques idees glanées dans les ouvrages inédits de Pierre Čaadaev." *Revue des études slaves* 55 (1983) 299–304.

———. "Significant Revelations in Chaadaev's Letters to A. I. Turgenev." *Studies in Soviet Thought* 32 (1986) 321–39.

McNally, Raymond T., and Richard Tempest. "Commentaries and Notes to Fragments, Articles, and Other Letters." In *Philosophical Works of Peter Chaadaev*, edited by Raymond T. McNally and Richard Tempest, 278–309. Dordrecht: Springer, 1991.

Mrówczyński-Van Allen, Artur. *Between the Icon and the Idol: The Human Person and the Modern State in Russian Literature and Thought; Chaadayev, Soloviev, Grossman*. Translated by Matthew Philipp Whelan. Eugene, OR: Cascade, 2013.

Obolevitch, Teresa. *La philosophie religieuse russe*. Translated by Maria Gawron-Zaborska. Paris: Cerf, 2014.

O'Connor, Mark. "*Adveniat Regnum Tuum*: Chaadaev, Mickiewicz, and the Kingdom of God on Earth." *Studies in Soviet Thought* 32 (1986) 397–409.

Peterson, Dale E. "Civilizing the Race. Chaadaev and the Paradox of Eurocentric Nationalism." *Russian Review* 56 (1997) 550–63.

Riasanovsky, Nicholas V. "On Lamennais, Chaadaev, and the Romantic Revolt in France and Russia." *American Historical Review* 82 (1977) 1165–86.

Sapov, Vadim. "Ucheniki Chaadaeva." In *Novye idei v filosofii. Ezhegodnik Filosofskogo obshchestva v SSSR*, edited by Ivan Frolov et al., 149–63. Moscow: Nauka, 1991.

Shakhovskoy, Dmitriy. "Pis'ma i zametki." In *Petr Chaadayev. Pro et contra: Lichnost' i tvorchestvo Petra Chaadayeva v otsenke russkikh mysliteley i issledovateley. Antologiya*, edited by Aleksandr Ermichev and Anna Zlatopol'skaya, 517–53. Saint

Petersburg: Izdatel'stvo Russkogo Khristianskogo Gumanitarnogo Universiteta, 1996.

———. "Stat'i i nabroski." In *Filosofskiy vek. Al'manakh*, vol. 26, *Istoriya idey v Rossii: materialy i issledovaniya*, edited by Tat'yana Artem'eva and Mikhail Mikeshin, 118–45. Saint Petersburg: Sankt-Peterburgskiy Tsentr istorii idey, 2004.

Shaposhnikov, Lev, and Aleksandr Fedorov. *Istoriya russkoy religioznoy filosofii*, Moscow: Vysshaya shkola, 2006.

Shestov, Lev. "In Praise of Folly: On the Occasion of Nikolai Berdiaev's Book *Sub Specie Aeternitatis*." *Russian Studies in Philosophy* 39 (2000) 36–53.

Smirnova, Zinaida V. "P. Ya. Chaadayev i nemetskiy idealizm kontsa XVIII – pervoy poloviny XIX veka." In *Istoriko-filosofskiy ezhegodnik'98*, edited by Nelly Motroshilova, 207–25. Moscow: Nauka, 2000.

———. "The Problem of Reason in Chaadaev's Philosophical Conception." *Russian Studies in Philosophy* 38 (1999) 8–24.

Tarasov, Boris. *Chaadayev*. Moscow: Molodaya gvardiya, 1986.

———. *Neprochitannyy Chaadayev, neuslyshannyy Dostoevskiy (khristianskaya mysl' i sovremennoe soznanie)*. Moscow: Academia, 1999.

Tempest, Richard. "Chaadaev and Tiutchev." *Studies in Soviet Thought* 32 (1986) 383–95.

———. "La démence de Čaadaev." *Revue des études slaves* 55 (1983) 305–14.

———. "Madman or Criminal: Government Attitudes to Petr Chaadaev in 1836." *Slavic Review* 43 (1984) 281–87.

Valitskiy, Andzhey. "Chaadayev, Petr Yakovlevich (1794–1856)." *Filosofskoe obrazovanie* 2 (2012) 3–17.

Veselovskiy, Aleksey. "Chaadayev i frantsuzskaya mysl'." In *Petr Chaadayev. Pro et contra: Lichnost' i tvorchestvo Petra Chaadayeva v otsenke russkikh mysliteley i issledovateley. Antologiya*, edited by Aleksandr Ermichev and Anna Zlatopol'skaya, 184–88. Saint Petersburg: Izdatel'stvo Russkogo Khristianskogo Gumanitarnogo Universiteta, 1996.

Walicki, Andrzej. *The Flow of Ideas: Russian Thought from the Enlightenment to the Religious-Philosophical Renaissance*. Translated by Hilda Andrews-Rusiecka and Jolanta Kozak. Frankfurt am Main: Peter Lang, 2015.

———. *The Slavophile Controversy: History of a Conservative Utopia in Nineteenth-Century Russian Thought*. Translated by Hilda Andrews-Rusiecka. Notre Dame: University of Notre Dame Press, 1989.

Zeldin, Mary-Barbara. "Chaadayev as Russia's First Philosopher." *Slavic Review* 37 (1978) 473–80.

———. "Chaadayev's Quarrel with Kant: An Attempt at a Cease-Fire." *Revue des études slaves* 55 (1983) 277–85.

———. "The Influence of Immanuel Kant on Peter Yakovlevich Chaadayev." *Studies in Soviet Thought* 18 (1978) 111–19.

Zenkovsky, Vasilii V. *A History of Russian Philosophy*. Vol. 1. Translated by George L. Kline. London: Routledge, 2006.

Zlatopol'skaya, Alla. "D. I. Shakhovskoy—istorik russkoy filosofii i obshchestvennoy mysli." In *Filosofskiy vek. Al'manakh*, vol. 26, *Istoriya idey v Rossii: materialy i issledovaniya*, edited by Tat'yana Artem'eva and Mikhail Mikeshin, 111–17. Saint Petersburg: Sankt-Peterburgskiy Tsentr istorii idey, 2004.

5

Peter Chaadaev's Ideas on the Unity of Nations and the Crisis of Post-National Europe

Olga Tabatadze

But seek first the kingdom of God and his righteousness, and all these things will be added to you.

—Matthew 6:33

In this chapter I would like to discuss the ideas of Peter Chaadaev concerning nations and the foundations of their unity, as expressed by the author in his *Philosophical Letters* (1829–1831) and *Apologia of a Madman* (1837) and to reflect on why, in our opinion, those ideas show a potential way to overcome the crisis that the post-national Europe is going through today; moreover, behind them we can find, undoubtedly, man's crisis of understanding.

Before examining the ideas of our first Russian religious philosopher we want to remind the reader that the concept of "nation" has not always been understood in the same way. We must not forget that in its traditional meaning the term "nation" designated, first, a real ethnic community. But in modern times, with the birth of the modern states, the term "nation" started to be understood as an institutionalized form of the group identity that explains the existence of the modern national state. In 1989, in an interview with Jean-Marc Ferry on the national and post-national identity, Jürgen Habermas announced the existence of a "post-national" identity that developed into the universal principles of the rule of law and democracy, typical of the European countries after World War II and which was also the way to overcome the nationalisms of modern national states.[1]

Let us return to Peter Chaadaev's ideas about nations and, concretely, the European nations. Using this concept in its traditional meaning, in both of his works mentioned above, the author underlines repeatedly that Christianity was the unifying principle of all European nations, their "common physiognomy," the "family resemblance" that joined all European nations as a whole, allowing them to move, hand in hand and along the same path, from one century to another, in spite of the differences in their histories and traditions, established—according to Chaadaev—by their own ideological legacy. "Not very long ago all of Europe was called Christendom . . . For a number of centuries this society [Europe—O. T.] formed a genuine federal system, or rather a single people and . . . this system was dissolved only by the Reformation."[2]

Chaadaev remarks that the disagreement in the idea of unity brought about the division of the unity of society. In this regard, the Lutheran interpretation of the doctrine of the two kingdoms actually "broke" the medieval metaphor of the two swords.

However, in our opinion, the Russian thinker was wrong in thinking that this break was caused only by the Reformation. The rise and consolidation of the modern national state that took place in parallel to the Reformation and was hastened by it, contributed to this division. In his book *Theopolitical Imagination*, the contemporary American theologian William T. Cavanaugh points out that Martin Luther, in his attempt to separate the civil and the ecclesiastical powers, contributed to the myth of the state as the savior in the wars of religions; he reminds us also of the change in the perception of the state before the Reformation:

> In the medieval period, the term *status* had been used either in reference to the condition of the ruler (*status principis*), or in the general sense of the condition of the realm (*status regni*). With Machiavelli we begin to see the transition to a more abstract sense of the state as an independent political entity, but only in the works of sixteenth-century French and English humanists do there emerge the modern idea of the state as "a form of public power separate from both ruler and the ruled, and constituting the supreme political authority within a certain defined territory.[3]

1. Habermas, "Ethics, Politics and History," 436–37.
2. Chaadaev, "Philosophical Letters," 22–23, 75.
3. Cavanaugh, *Theopolitical Imagination*, 22.

In the secularization process that started at that time, a new meaning was given to the concepts of "religion" and "politics," Theology was separated from politics, and the church started to be considered only as a group of faithful that meet to nourish their souls with faith, being excluded from the pseudo-neutral discourse, ruled by the civil powers. The Christian unity of the European nations, that lived in the church and whose source is the Eucharist, would be replaced by the newly created centralized national states.

Returning to the ideas of Peter Chaadaev on the Christian unity of the nations of Europe, we would like to emphasize that the thinker noted the fact that, in spite of the division, Europe was still Christendom, and even though it was in a different state from that of its age of youth and faith, it would certainly never return to the historical state, but he hoped that one day "the lines which separate Christian people will be obliterated once again and that the original principle of modern society will become manifest more energetically than ever under a new form."[4]

Peter Chaadaev's hope regarding the future Christian unity of the European nations lay, in our opinion, in his conviction that both the history of a particular person and of a whole nation develops according to the divine idea and that it is the "providence or a perfectly wise intellect" that unites its past with its future over the course of events. The thinker understands history just as "a providence which dominates the centuries and leads humanity to its final destinies"[5] and he claims to realize that "human reason is not simply constituted by the force which it has in the narrow present, but that there is another force in it which, by integrating both past and future into a single thought, forms its true being and places it in its genuine activity."[6] As said by Hans Urs von Balthasar, the history of mankind is embodied in Christ's life and it is the history of men's salvation, and Christ is the beginning and the end of this history.[7]

Actually, the memory of the influence of the divine idea in the history of a nation and the memory of this nation in its past for the correct interpretation of its future are important enough in Chaadaev's understanding. Pointing out the shortcomings of the traditional history that focuses its attention only on man, the thinker remarks that for a correct interpretation of the history man cannot exclude the action of providence that really leads the course of events and unites the past with the future. Chaadaev points

4. Chaadaev, "Philosophical Letters," 75.

5. Ibid., 68.

6. Ibid., 69.

7. Balthasar, *Theology of History*, 49–75.

out that the "vain erudition" of the present narrative history explains all this amazing intertwining of centuries, languages and ideas

> by using its favorite theory . . . the natural development of the human spirit without any traces of providence, without any cause other than the mechanical force of its own nature . . . This philosophy considers the human spirit nothing more than a snowball which grows by rolling, that is all. Besides, from its one point of view this philosophy either sees progress and a natural perfection everywhere as a something inherent in human nature or else simply finds a motiveless, meaningless movement.[8]

The intellect of past times and the role of the real people in them, and not a simple chronological verification of the events, would help, according to the Russian thinker, to establish the perception of the destiny they are called to achieve in the consciousness of the living nations.

> Each nation should perceive its present actual existence through a clear understanding of the different epochs in its past life and should be able to predict somewhat the course of its own future development. In this way, the people's genuine national consciousness would be composed of a certain number of positive ideas, evident truths deduced from their recollections, strong convictions which would more or less dominate all their minds and would urge them along towards a similar goal. In that case the nationality groups, which have simply divided men up to now, would combine with one another in order to produce one harmonic and universal result, since they would be divested of their blindness and their impassioned interest; then all people would link arms and march together towards a single goal.[9]

This single goal is, as half a century later Vladimir Soloviev would say in his work *The Russian Idea*, the participation of the nations in the life of the Universal Church.[10]

Summing up his ideas, Chaadaev concludes that "as the masses, as individuals, in order to fulfill their destinies in the world, both have to look back upon their past lives and discover their future in the past."[11] Remembering Cicero's words, the Russian thinker underlines that for the man to understand the sense of human life and so that the memory of "the past" is

8. Chaadaev, "Philosophical Letters," 70.

9. Ibid., 72.

10. Solovyov, *Russian Idea*, 24.

11. Chaadaev, "Philosophical Letters," 73.

not alien to himself he must link the present with the past, and besides not only with yesterday's past, but much further into the past. Chaadaev asserts that it is indeed history the one that explains the nations and that "it is in man's nature to lose himself when he does not find the means of referring his condition to what preceded and what follows him; then all consistency, all certitude escapes him; without the feeling of continuity to guide him, he discovers that he has wandered aimlessly in the world."[12]

It is interesting to point out that the opinion of French thinker and Religion historian Ernst Renan, whose idea of the unity of the nation was exposed in his famous work *What Is a Nation?*, read in Paris in May 11, 1882,[13] and that is still perhaps one of the most popular and up-to-date treatises on the concept of nation, is very different from Chaadaev's. As is well-known, this lecture was a reaction of the thinker to the Treaty of Frankfurt that ended the Franco-Prussian War (1870–1871), as a result of which the French Regions of Alsace and Lorraine were annexed to Germany. With this lecture, the aim of the French philosopher was to persuade the listeners at the Sorbonne that these regions were politically French, because their inhabitants felt they were French and not German. Renan understood the term "nation" in a modern way:

> Nations . . . are something fairly new in history. Antiquity was unfamiliar with them; Egypt, China and ancient Chaldea were in no way nations . . . Neither in Egypt nor in China were there citizens as such. Classical antiquity had republics, municipal kingdoms, confederations of local republics and empires, yet it can hardly be said to have had nations in our understanding of the term.[14]

He identified the formation of the nation with the formation of the modern national state, precisely in the terms expressed by William Cavanaugh, that is, as the process of the achievement of the symbolic power of the Monarch over the other Princes, centralizing the power in his hands. Renan wrote:

> If one were to believe to some political theorists, a nation is above all a dynasty, representing an earlier conquest, one which

12. Ibid., 23.

13. It is interesting the fact that six years later, on May 23, 1888, again in the French capital and in French, Vladimir Soloviev read his lecture *The Russian Idea*, in which, talking about his book *Russia and the Universal Church* he presented, for the first time, the Russian Idea as a closed philosophical system (as it is known, the concept of the Russian Idea was first introduced by Fyodor Dostoevsky in 1861).

14. Renan, "What Is a Nation?," 9.

> was first of all accepted, and when forgotten by the mass of the people. According to the above-mentioned theorists, the grouping of provinces effected by a dynasty, by its wars, its marriages, and its treaties, ends with the dynasty which had established it. It is quite true that the majority of modern nations were mad by a family of feudal origin, which had contracted a marriage with the soil and which was in some sense a nucleus of centralization.[15]

The French thinker considers that the unity of nations contemporary to his time is achieved by oblivion and a historical mistake:

> Forgetting, I would even go so far as to say historical error, is a crucial factor in the creation of a nation, which is way progress in historical studies often constitutes a danger for [the principal of] nationality. Indeed, historical inquiry brings to light deeds of violence which took place at the origin of all political formations, even of those whose consequences have been altogether beneficial. Unity is always effected by means of brutality; the union of northern France with the Midi was the result massacres and terror lasting for the best part of the century. Though the king of France was, if I may make so bold as to say, almost the perfect instance of an agent that crystallized (a nation) over a long period; though he established the most perfect national unity that there has ever been, to searching a scrutiny had destroyed his prestige. The nation which he had formed has cursed him, and, nowadays, it is only men of culture who know something of his former value and of his achievements.[16]

Nevertheless, according to Renan, there is another way to achieve the unity of the nation or the unity of nations. Using Switzerland or the United States of America as an example, the author concludes that this new method has no dynastic basis, but it is based on national rights.[17] Reflecting on the different criteria on which the national law—race, language, religion,[18] community of interests or geography—is based, the author concludes that these criteria are not enough.

15. Ibid., 12.

16. Ibid., 11.

17. Ibid., 12.

18. Here, the concept of "religion" is also used in its modern and secularized meaning. The process of transformation of the meaning of the term "religion" is very well developed by William T. Cavanaugh, *Theopolitical Imagination*, 31–42.

> Nation is a spiritual principle, the outcome of the profound complications of history; it is a spiritual family . . . Two things, which in truth are but one, constitute this soul or spiritual principle. One lies in the past, one in the present. One is the possession in common of a rich legacy of memories; the other is present-day consent, the desire to live together, the will to perpetuate the value of the heritage that one has received in an undivided form . . . A heroic past, great men, glory (by which I understand genuine glory), this is the social capital upon which one basis a national idea. To have common glories in the past and to have a common will in the present; to have performed great deeds together, to wish to perform still more—these are the essential conditions for being a people.[19]

Finally, the author concludes: "We have driven metaphysical and theological abstractions out of politics. What then remains? Man, with his desires and his needs."[20] In the last phrases of his articles, Renan expresses his hope that, in the future, this way of understanding the concept of "nation" might find its embodiment: "Human wills change . . . The nations are not something eternal. They had their beginnings and they will end. A European confederation will very probably replace them. But such is not the law of the century in which we are living."[21]

Actually, nineteenth-century law was not like that; but the European nations, that survived two world wars in the first half of the twentieth century, would not only be witnesses to such a confederation, but they would become its immediate members when, on May 9, 1950, the French Foreign Minister Robert Schuman suggested for the first time the idea of the creation of a European Coal and Steel Community, that eventually would become the European Union that we know. It is not the task of this essay to deepen into the development of this inter and supranational European unity, that started giving its first steps with the union of six countries and that today is formed by twenty-eight European states; we only want to say that the idea of the "father of Europe"[22] lay in the reestablishment of peace and the elimination of the centuries-old opposition between France and Germany without which,

19. Renan, "What Is a Nation?," 19.

20. Ibid., 20.

21. Ibid.

22. It is interesting to mention that Robert Schuman had much to do with the French regions of Alsace and Lorraine that, due to the Treaty of Frankfurt, were annexed to Germany. Thus, being the son of a Lorrainer, he was a German citizen; but when in December 8, 1918, Alsace and Lorraine were returned to France, he accepted the French citizenship, see Lejeune, *Schuman*, 72–73.

according to Schuman, the unity of Europe would have been impossible. As a unifying factor he chose the French-German production of coal and steel, achieved under the direction of the highest organ of this international organization, open to the other European countries. This solidarity in the production should demonstrate that the war between Germany and France was not only unthinkable, but materially impossible. It is obvious that the economic unity and organization of the "United States of Europe" necessarily included political unity and organization.

As Chaadaev, Schuman repeatedly pointed out the Christian roots of the European countries, emphasizing that democracy owed its existence to Christianity,[23] as he believed that only one "Lord of the history who definitely guides men's destiny according to his plan exists: he is the Almighty that choses his instruments among men of goodwill."[24] "We are all imperfect instruments of Providence, that uses them to achieve his great plan that exceeds us," wrote Schuman in his book *For Europe*.[25] In his service to the state he saw the service to God.[26]

However, at the same time, Schuman was heir to the Enlightenment with his account of the secularization that takes for granted "that directly politicized theology is inherently dangerous service for peace in separating power from religion."[27] And it is precisely for this reason, in our opinion, and guided by his goodwill, that the "father of Europe" divided the area of action of the church from that of the state: "the actions of the church and the state must complement themselves, but not oppose themselves or get mixed up. Society is not a theocracy and there is no place for the implementation of materialist or positivist points of view, open for the enemy power of Christianity."[28]

The principles on which a united Europe is based—which are the result of the reflection of Robert Schuman—found their practical expression in the *Convention for the Protection of Human Rights and Fundamental Freedoms*, signed by him on behalf of France in Rome on November 4, 1950. This document proclaims the inalienable civil, political, economic, social,

23. Schuman, *Por Europa*, 42 and Lejeune, *Schuman*, 84, 166. According to Schuman, "Democracy will be Christian or it will not be democracy. An anti-Christian democracy is a caricature that will fail and become a tyranny or an anarchy." Lejeune, *Schuman*, 236, and Schuman, *Por Europa*, 48.

24. Schuman made this statement in a meeting in 1946. See Lejeune, *Schuman*, 148.

25. Ibid.

26. Ibid., 134.

27. Cavanaugh, *Theopolitical Imagination*, 5.

28. Lejeune, *Schuman*, 104. This same idea can be found in Schuman, *Por Europa*, 44–45.

and cultural rights of man and forces the signatory countries to guarantee these rights to each person under their jurisdiction. According to Schuman's idea, united Europe should be an example to all mankind.

Going back to Habermas's terminology mentioned at the beginning of this chapter, we can really state that we are talking of a post-national Europe founded in the universal principles of the rule of law and democracy, and united by common economic and political interests.

Nevertheless, taking into account that in the last years practically all members of the European Union, to a greater or lesser extent, are facing an economic, political and humanitarian crises such as, for example, unemployment and nationalism, national and individual identity crisis, crisis in the value of human life, family and refugee crisis, etc., we wonder if this current post-national Europe, based on the principles of democracy and human rights, can offer a real answer to these problems. In our humble opinion, it cannot.

And it cannot—we think that the comparison of Chaadaev's and Schuman's ideas allow us to reach this conclusion—because it has forgotten that the course of history is guided by Providence, and not by man's thought about himself and the destiny of every nation; because he does not remember that to understand the meaning of his future in the right way he cannot forget his past, insisting only on the civil proposals of remaining united; because it has been forgotten that the meaning of the unity of nations consists of the participation of the nations in the Universal Church, and that it's not only men who decide the destinies of nations; and, most importantly, because he has erased from his horizon the fact that the true body of human society is not the modern state, born from the desire of the civil power to rule over the ecclesiastical one, but the church, the mystical body of Christ, formed by all the faithful of the past, present and future, gathered around the Eucharist in different places of the world and, at the same time, in the same one: around the Eucharist.[29] According to us, only in the church, that is a real nation of nations, and only thanks to the Eucharist, is the gathering of people as a true community possible, in which the particular and the group interests are surpassed by mutual participation, in which the logic of power is transformed by the logic of gift, and where economic equality flourishes with justice and with help for the needy.

29. Cavanaugh describes this idea as "the world in a wafer" and develops it in his *Theopolitical Imagination*, 112–16.

Bibliography

Balthasar, Hans Urs von. *A Theology of History*. London: Sheed and Ward, 1964.

Cavanaugh, William T. *Theopolitical Imagination*. New York: T. & T. Clark, 2004.

Chaadaev, Peter. "Apologia of a Madman." In *Philosophical Works of Peter Chaadaev*, edited by Raymond T. McNally and Richard Tempest, 102–11. Dordrecht: Springer, 1991.

———. "The Philosophical Letters Addressed to a Lady." In *Philosophical Works of Peter Chaadaev*, edited by Raymond T. McNally and Richard Tempest, 18–101. Dordrecht: Springer, 1991.

Habermas, Jürgen. "Ethics, Politics and History: An Interview with Jürgen Habermas Conducted by Jean-Marc Ferry." Translated by Stephen K. White. *Philosophy and Social Criticism* 14 (1988) 433–39.

Lejeune, René. *Robert Schuman. Padre de Europa (1886–1963)*. Madrid: Ediciones Palabra, 2000.

Renan, Ernest. "What Is a Nation?" Translated by Martin Thom. In *Nation and Narration*, edited by Homi K. Bhabha, 8–22. New York: Routledge, 1990.

Schuman, Robert. *Por Europa*. Madrid: Ediciones Encuentro, 2006.

Solovyov, Vladimir. *The Russian Idea*. Translated by John P. Ricket. North Charleston, SC: Createspace, 2015.

6

Individual and "Supra-Individual" in Chaadaev's *Philosophical Letters*[1]

Daniela Steila

The polarity between the universal and the particular, between the individual and the supra-individual, between the singular and the collective, has been widely considered as a peculiar character of Russian philosophical thought. For example, if we look in the history of Russian thought, the classical scheme elaborated by the Slavophiles appears particularly compelling. According to it, the opposition between Western and Russian cultures consisted exactly in a different attitude toward separation and integrity, individual and community. As Ivan Kireyevsky famously wrote:

> In the West we find a dichotomy of the spirit, a dichotomy of thought, a dichotomy of learning, a dichotomy of the state, a dichotomy of estates, a dichotomy of society, a dichotomy of familial rights and duties, a dichotomy of morals and emotions, a dichotomy of the sum total and of all separate aspects of human being, both social and individual. We find in Russia, in contrast, a predominant striving for wholeness of being, both external and inner, social and individual, intellectual and workaday, artificial and moral.[2]

On the opposite side, Westernizers generally maintained the rights of individual reason and a person's ethical autonomy. Belinsky, for instance, was

1. This essay is a part of a wider research project on individual subjectivity and the collective in Russian thought in nineteenth and twentieth century, carried on during a visiting fellowship at the Aleksanteri Institute, University of Helsinki, September 2015.

2. Kireevsky, "On the Nature of European Culture," 229.

ready to give up the chance to be "on top of the stairs of development," if he could not receive a full account of "all the victims of the circumstances of life and history, all the victims of casualties, superstition, Inquisition, Philipp II etc. etc."[3] Although it would be a simplification to interpret the opposition between the Slavophiles and Westernizers in terms of super-individual versus individual perspectives, the theme as such has had a major role within their discussions. Chaadaev, who is usually found in the general surveys of the history of Russian thought in the chapter before the outburst of the contrast between Slavophiles and Westernizers, and who has somehow anticipated characters from both these currents of thought, had some very original views on the relationship between individual and super-individual.

In contrast to the philosophers of the Enlightenment, Chaadaev criticizes the idea of the human being as a free and autonomous individual. According to him, the human being is actually inclined to subordinate himself, both in nature and society, to the physical order and to the moral one. As Andrzej Walicki summarized:

> His true inclination is to subordinate himself, being is hierarchical in structure and the natural order is based on *dependence*. Human actions are directed from outside by a force transcending the individual, and the power of man's reason is in direct proportion to his obedience, submissiveness, and docility. The individual is nothing without society; his consciousness and knowledge flow from a social, supra-individual source. The mind of the individual is anchored in the universal mind and draws its nourishment from it.[4]

The Role of the Individual in the Structure of Being

First of all, let us briefly discuss Chaadaev's views on the individual and his role within the structure of being. In his *Philosophical Letters*, Chaadaev traced a general hierarchy of being, at the basis of which is nature. Chaadaev considers the world as consisting of two realms: the physical realm of nature and the mental realm of morality and intellect. Both are created by God and guided by Providence. In the physical realm, Providence appears as the law of gravitation, which acts in terms of centripetal and centrifugal forces, following an initial divine impulse. In the moral realm, mental events also

3. Belinsky to Vasiliy Botkin, 30 December 1840 (22 January 1841), Belinskiy, "Pis'ma 1841," 171.

4. Walicki, *Flow of Ideas*, 148.

descend from the initial impulse of ideas that were impressed by God on the mind of the first man, and were therefore transmitted from generation to generation through traditions and social intercourse. In the moral realm, the two forces that are simultaneously combined in the action are "the one force which we are aware of, our *free choice*, our will, the other, which dominates us without our knowing it, the action of an *exterior force* upon our being."[5] In both realms the aim of the development is a wider unification. In the "Fifth Letter," Chaadaev explains:

> Just as bodily collision in nature serves to continue this first thrust, imparted to matter, intellectual collision likewise continues spiritual motion; just as in nature everything is linked with all that goes before it and follows it, so each individual human and each human thought are linked with all human beings and with all human thoughts, those which precede and those which follow; and, since nature is one, so, according to the picturesque expression of Pascal, also the whole *succession of men is one man, who always exists*, and each one of us participates directly in the intellectual work which is being completed throughout the centuries. Finally, just as a certain plastic and perpetual work of the material elements or atoms, the generation of physical beings, constitutes material nature, so also then a similar work of intellectual elements or ideas, the generation of spirits, constitutes spiritual nature; and just as I conceive of all tangible matter as one whole, then I must also conceive of the succession of intelligences as a single and sole intelligence.[6]

From such a perspective, individual consciousness has to acknowledge its submission to the external action of tradition and history, inasmuch as the body is submitted to the laws of the natural world. "If we were deprived of contact with other intelligent beings, we would eat grass instead of speculating on our nature,"[7] Chaadaev writes. As a consequence, the thoughts of a single human being must be identified with the thought of the whole human species: "As in the rest of the created world, so in the intellectual world nothing can be understood as perfectly isolated, as if it were self-sufficient."[8] Any idea, any thought is meant to be communicated to other people, to combine with other thoughts, to become a "common good" of humankind. Chaadaev explains:

5. Chaadaev, "Philosophical Letters," 53.

6. Ibid., 60–61.

7. Ibid., 64.

8. Ibid.

> A thousand of invisible ties unite the thoughts of one reasonable being with those of another; our most intimate thoughts discover every means possible for reproducing themselves outside; when they are disseminated, when they cross on another, they fuse together, they unite, they pass from one spirit to another, they sow, they fertilize, they engender universal reason.[9]

Chaadaev asks himself: "Is there anything more absurd than the supposition that each human individual begins his species anew, like the beast?"[10] These views have important consequences on the philosophy of history, as we will see in the following pages. As for the hierarchical structure of being, it can be said that, in Chaadaev's view, the moral world of individual consciousness is placed above nature, and it only exists as such thanks to a common space that depends on God, which is the supreme principle of the oneness of the universe.[11] God's speech creates human reason, and his words keep working within history through human thoughts and traditions:

> On the day when man was created God spoke with him, and man heard and understood him: this is the true genesis of human reason; psychology will never find a more profound explanation. Later, he partially lost the ability to hear the voice of God; this was a natural consequence of the gift of unlimited liberty which he had obtained. But he did not lose his recollections of God's first words which resounded in his ear. Then this same word from God, addressed to the first man and trasmitted from generation to generation, strikes the child in the crib and introduces him into the intellectual world and really makes him into a thinking being. The same method which God used in order to create man from nothing, He utilizes today in order to create every new thinking being. It is always God who speaks to man through the intermediary of his fellow men.[12]

This view of the individual as a specific part of the hierarchical structure of being has many important implications within epistemology, ethics and philosophy of history.

9. Ibid., 61.
10. Ibid., 63.
11. Cf. Walicki, *Flow of Ideas*, 149.
12. Chaadaev, "Philosophical Letters," 63.

Epistemology

According to Chaadaev, our thinking and our knowledge depend on God. But, after Adam's transgression, human reason has been damaged. Chaadaev therefore distinguishes two kinds of reason. First comes the primordial reason that was given to Adam by God; it is objective and possesses a true knowledge of reality, since it derives directly from God and comprises his original words to his creatures. This "truly pure" reason was weakened by the human Fall, and thus reason became individual, i.e., limited by time and place, by one's own experience and character, different in everyone, and divisive among human beings.[13] Without primordial reason, humans could not achieve a common world, neither physical, nor moral. Knowledge can be achieved only through tradition, revelation, social intercourse, and the ideas of certain enlightened persons or nations. Human, "artificial" reason can be successful if it is obedient, passive to the superindividual contents and inspirations, whereas it falls into either intellectual or moral error every time it acts independently, according to its own free will. In Chaadaev's words: "the real principle of our intellectual power is in reality nothing more than a kind of *logical abnegation*, identical with moral abnegation and originating from the very same law."[14] According to Chaadaev, human being can be rescued from the Fall not through individualistic self-perfection and asceticism, but only through the sphere of super-individual consciousness. In the "Seventh Letter," it can be read that "man's whole aim on earth consists in annihilating his personal existence and substituting a completely social or impersonal one for it."[15] Walicki observes that "Chaadaev's emphasis on sociality did not preclude a defense of social hierarchy or an espousal of a typically aristocratic, elitist theory of knowledge."[16] It is the church that mediates the human relationship with God, and Chaadaev's criticism of the Reformation is founded mainly on the latter's individualistic egalitarianism.

The Fall itself and the consequent corruption of human reason are explained by Chaadaev as the separation of the egoistic *ego* from the divine order of the world, from the "great All."[17] The goal of the historical development of human thought is therefore to go back to divine reason, which is embedded in tradition and social intercourse. In the "Fifth Letter," Chaadaev explains his views as follows:

13. Cf. Zeldin, "Chaadaev's Quarrel with Kant," 279.
14. Chaadaev, "Philosophical Letters," 45.
15. Ibid., 86.
16. Walicki, *Flow of Ideas*, 150.
17. Cf. Smirnova, "Problem of Reason," 11.

> All that exists in the world of ideas comes from a certain number of notions which have been transmitted traditionally, and which do not belong to any intellectual individual any more than the forces of nature belong to any physical individual. *Archetypes* of Plato, *innate ideas* of Descartes, *a priori* of Kant, all these diverse elements of thought, which were necessarily recognized by all profound thinkers as in advance of any kind of operation by the soul, as preceding all experimental knowledge and all the appropriate activity of the mind, all these pre-existing seeds of reason without which man would simply be a two-legged and two-armed mammal—no more, no less . . . Once this is established, the study that we still have to do is simple: we only have to investigate the movement of these traditions throughout the history of humanity, in order to see how and where the idea, originally put into the heart of man, was preserved in its wholeness and purity.[18]

Ethics

In Chaadaev's views, the realization of the unity on earth depends on the moral progress of humankind, and requires not only the divine primitive impulse, but also human free will. "The proper activities of man" should be considered "as an *accessory* principle (*principe occasionel*): as a force which works only insofar as it is united with another superior force, just as the force of gravity works only along with the force of initial thrust."[19] The discussion about the theme of freedom and responsibility obviously includes the tension between individual and super-individual principles, since Chaadaev has to consider the ethical consequences of the relationship between single free will and the submission of the single subject to the providential designs of the order of the world. The solution expressed in the "Fourth Letter" is based on the circumstance that the external force that moves every human being moves him or her in terms of knowledge: "The great problem of free will, no matter how abstruse it may be, would certainly not offer any difficulties, if only men understood how to become permeated with the idea that the nature of intelligent being consists only in awareness and that, insofar as intelligent being is aware, it loses nothing of its own nature, no matter how awareness comes to it."[20] Chaadaev explains:

18. Chaadaev, "Philosophical Letters," 66.
19. Ibid., 54.
20. Ibid., 55. Cf. Zeldin, "Influence of Kant," 114.

> Man is constantly stimulated by a force, which he does not sense at all, it is true, but this exterior action has an influence upon him by means of his awareness; consequently, no matter how the idea which I find in my head reaches me, I find it there only because I am aware of the idea which I find there. But to become aware is to act. Therefore, I really and unceasingly act at the same time that I am dominated by something more powerful than myself. *I am aware* of it. One factor does not destroy the other, they occur without negating each other, and one is just as demonstrable as the other.[21]

If my freedom consists in the fact that I determine my will according to my principles, the fact that the ultimate source of these principles is external does not imply any loss of freedom. On the contrary, I am really free only by submitting myself to the external power, since freedom consists in acting on God-given ideas. In Zeldin's words: "*How* I receive ideas is irrelevant: they are, when I have them, *mine*; since I always act in terms of ideas and since my self consists of what I know, it is *I*, wholly I and not something external to me, that acts; hence I am free."[22] If, on the contrary, I refuse to submit myself to a divine power and decide to follow my individual inclinations instead, I cease thereby to self-determine myself, and so I lose my freedom. As a result, if the human being acts according to his own individual and arbitrary will, he will not actually be free, since he would therefore give up his own nature as an intelligent being, and would end up in isolation and divisiveness:

> A man's proper activity is genuinely so only when it corresponds to the law. Every time that we act contrary to the law it is no longer we ourselves who determine ourselves, but it is our environment which determines us. When we abandon ourselves to these outside influences, when we go beyond the law, we annihilate ourselves.[23]

As we have seen, reason can achieve knowledge only by submission to divinely given ideas. Similarly, morality consists of submission to an external law, which is also given, and is the source of all our moral ideas (the ideas of good, duty, virtue, etc.).[24] The human mind longs to obey and, as a result, to join the divine mind; our true freedom consists in the fact that

21. Chaadaev, "Philosophical Letters," 55.

22. Zeldin, "Chaadaev's Quarrel with Kant," 283. Cf. also her "Influence of Kant," 114.

23. Chaadaev, "Philosophical Letters," 56.

24. Cf. Zeldin, "Chaadaev's Quarrel with Kant," 282.

we don't feel our dependence. No wonder Chaadaev prefaced his "Fourth Letter" with a quotation from Spinoza. According to him as well as Spinoza, the maximum of freedom requires giving up one's personal liberty. But this does not entail passive subordination to the cosmic order, as it happens with the physical atom, but instead the acknowledgment and the choice of such an order. In his "Third Letter" Chaadaev asks:

> Now let us see what would happen if man could push his own submission to the point of complete forfeiture of his own freedom . . . it is clear that this would be the highest level of human perfection . . . Instead of this individual, isolated idea, which permeates him at this moment, instead of this personality which isolates him from all around him and clouds up everything before his eyes and which is not at all the necessary condition of his particular nature, but solely the consequence of his violent alienation from universal nature, in surrendering the fatal present *ego*, would he not recover the idea and also the comprehensive personality, as well as the whole power of pure intelligence in its original link with the rest of things?[25]

Without such a basic harmony in the world, any arbitrary action might lead to destruction. On the premise of the parallelism between moral and natural world, Chaadaev observes: "Assume that one single molecule of matter would make an arbitrary movement once, for example, instead of tending towards the center of its system, it would deviate a little from the radius in which it is located. What would happen? Would not the whole order of the world be disturbed at once?"[26]

God decided to take the risk of our freedom, when he created humans in his image and likeness, but "how is it possible to doubt that, since He decided to give us this surprising power which seems to clash with the whole order of the universe, He did not also decide to give it rules and to let us know how we should use it?"[27]

At the beginning Adam understood God's original word, then God illuminated some chosen men, and finally he sent the God-man to reveal "to us all that we can know about the divine mystery."[28] Christianity represents, according to Chaadaev, a decisive passage in the process that would lead to the defeat of individuality.[29] In the "First Letter," it can be read that:

25. Chaadaev, "Philosophical Letters," 46.

26. Ibid., 56.

27. Ibid.

28. Ibid.

29. Cf. Gurvich-Lishchiner, "Chaadaev—Herzen—Dostoevsky," 15.

> Wherever Christ's name is pronounced, this mention alone sweeps men along, no matter what they may do. Nothing demonstrates the divine origin of this religion better than this character of absolute universality, which allows it to infuse itself into men's souls by every possible means and makes it seize men's minds without their knowing it; even when they seem to resist it most it dominates and subjugates them by introducing into the intellect some truths which were not there before, by causing the heart to experience emotions it had never felt, by inspiring us with sentiments which place us, without our knowing it, in the general world-order. So the function of each individual is determined by Christianity which makes everyone strive towards a single goal.[30]

Philosophy of History

However, divine action wants to respect human freedom. Therefore, it has appeared during the course of history in different ways and different grades. Chaadaev writes: "It is evident that individuality and freedom exist only insofar as there is diversity of intelligence, moral powers, and knowledge."[31] The universal intelligence, which enables both knowledge and morality, develops over time, within history. Individuals and nations, endowed with what Chaadaev called supra-individual "moral personalities," are the instruments of history, in its path toward universality.[32] No single individual belongs directly to humankind, he actually belongs to a nation: "One must work within the domestic circle in which one is placed and have an effect upon one's natural, social family, in order to have an effect upon men; one must address oneself to one's nation, in order to speak distinctly to mankind; otherwise one will not be heard, and nothing will be accomplished."[33] Nations, as "moral personalities," are free in the same sense in which single individuals are free: they can choose to conform themselves to the objectivity of the universal law and become truly free, or they can choose to accept the false freedom of the arbitrary free will, which condemns nations to division and isolation. Chaadaev's social utopia has been defined "collectivist

30. Chaadaev, "Philosophical Letters," 29–30.

31. Ibid., 68.

32. Cf. Walicki, *Flow of Ideas*, 150–51; Dobieszewski, "Chaadaev and the Rise of Modern Russian Philosophy," 29–30.

33. Chaadaev, "Philosophical Letters," 89.

and internationalist,"[34] since every nation as well as every single individual develops its own consciousness within history and becomes part of the general movement of humankind toward an ideal unity. "Peoples are moral beings just as individuals are. It takes centuries to educate them, just as it takes years to educate a person."[35]

The unfortunate example of Russia itself clearly shows that without history no collective consciousness can develop. From such a point of view, the most famous statement in the "First Letter" concerning Russia means much more than a mere condemnation of Russian backwardness:

> Isolated by a strange destiny from the universal development of humanity, we have absorbed nothing, not even traditional ideas of mankind. It is upon these ideas, however, that the life of people is based; it is from these ideas that the future of people unfolds and from them comes their moral development. If we wish to take up a position similar to that of other civilized people, we must, in a certain sense, repeat the whole education of mankind.[36]

In the "Sixth Letter," Chaadaev explicitly discusses the plurality of peoples within history: "in our hopes for future happiness and definite perfection we could not initially isolate the great individual nationalities any more than their less important composite parts. We must accept them as principles and means for reaching a perfect state. Thus, the cosmopolitan future of philosophy is only an idle dream."[37] Exactly in the same way it is with individuals, who should not isolate themselves in order to affirm their true nature, but who should on the contrary overcome their singularity by obeying the universal design, so different peoples deteriorate if they separate themselves from the human family and become closed in themselves. Chaadaev asks in his "Seventh Letter":

> Could man ever allow the extremely personal, individual consciousness now found within himself to be supplanted by this general consciousness which would make him constantly feel himself to be part of the great moral totality? Yes, without doubt. Men must realize that besides the feeling of our personal individuality we also cherish a feeling of our relationship to the fatherland, the family, and the community of opinion to which we belong. This latter feeling is often even stronger than the former.

34. Kamenskiy, "Paradoksy Chaadayeva," 41.
35. Chaadaev, "Philosophical Letters," 22.
36. Ibid., 21–22.
37. Ibid., 72–73.

> Men must also notice that the germ of a superior consciousness resides within us in a very genuine way and forms the essence of our nature, and that the present *ego* is not imposed upon us by an inevitable law but has been created by ourselves. Then men will see that man's whole aim on earth consists in annihilating his personal existence and substituting a completely social or impersonal one for it.[38]

The final goal of history, according to Chaadaev is the realm of God on earth, that is to say "*the accomplished moral law*. All the work of the ages in man's intellectual life is meant to produce this definite result which is the end and goal of all things, the last phase of human nature, the dénouement of the universal drama, the great apocalyptic synthesis."[39]

Chaadaev and Kant

It seems clear that the relationship between individual and super-individual plays a major role in different aspects of Chaadaev's thought. Chaadaev's attitude toward Kant might shade some light on such a tension between individual and super-individual, as it appears in Chaadaev's work. On this topic, there is a specific, though not very wide, literature. As Teresa Obolevitch reminds us in her own contribution to the present volume,[40] Mary-Barbara Zeldin, at the end of the seventies wrote that "the major Western influence on his [Chaadaev's] views is not Schelling and certainly not, as some maintain, Hegel, but Immanuel Kant."[41] A little less forcefully, Petr Toropygin in 1994 deemed that Kant had a decisive influence on Chaadaev's philosophy of history.[42] Without entering here this specific discussion, we will just take into consideration the undoubted fact that Kant has been a very important discussant for Chaadaev when he was developing his reflections on the theme of individual and super-individual.

Chaadaev directly knew some of the major works of Kant. While he was still serving in the army, he famously complains in a letter to a friend that he could not obtain a copy of Kant's first *Critique* in Saint Petersburg.[43] For sure, the first and second *Critiques*, in German, both heavily underscored and annotated, appear in the catalogue of Chaadaev's second library,

38. Chaadaev, "Philosophical Letters," 86.

39. Ibid., 101.

40. Obolevitch, "'The Madman' Appeals to Faith and Reason," 57.

41. Zeldin, "Influence of Kant," 111.

42. Toropygin, "Chaadayev i Kant."

43. Chaadaev to Dmitriy Obleukhov, 1812, 7.

which he built after his coming back from Europe (he had sold his first to a cousin-in-law in 1821).[44]

Chaadaev's high opinion of Kant is declared in the well-known passage of the "Fifth Letter" where the author acknowledges that "assuredly the most profound and most productive of all the known systems is the one which strives to construct conscientiously an absolutely abstract intelligence, an exclusively intelligent nature, in order to take the intellectual phenomenon into account without going back to the very source of the spiritual principle."[45] Chaadaev immediately emphasizes a limit in Kant's thought: "But, since it is always man in his present state who furnishes the materials from which this system constructs its model, it happens that this system shows us artificial reason again, but not original reason."[46] And as a matter of fact, on the title page of his copy of the *Kritik der reinen Vernunft*, Chaadaev crossed out the title and wrote over these words: *Apologete adamitischer Vernunft*.[47]

According to Chaadaev, Kant's basic misunderstanding of the real nature of human reason prevented him to raise to the only point of view, from which one can properly understand both the human being and the world: "the profound thinker, the author of this philosophy, did not see that there was no point in representing an intelligence which would only will to seek out and evoke supreme intelligence; an intelligence with a mode of perfectly legitimate activity, as everything which exists, and intelligence whose power would consist only in an infinite tendency to fuse with this other intelligence."[48] Such a deep standpoint would have saved Kant from what Chaadaev considered his worst mistake: to confuse the human reason after the Fall with the "truly pure" reason and to reach, in consequence, "the false teaching about the *autonomy* of human reason" and "another, even more arrogant philosophy, the philosophy of the omnipotence of the human ego."[49]

In spite of these "mistakes," Chaadaev acknowledges that Kant deserves his respect:

> We owe all the healthy ideas in the world today to the movement which he gave to philosophical knowledge; and we ourselves are nothing but a logical consequence of his idea. He traced the limits of human reason with steadfast hand; he made it clear that

44. McNally, "Books in Chaadayev's Libraries," 498.
45. Chaadaev, "Philosophical Letters," 65.
46. Ibid.
47. Chaadayev, "Kommentariy," 768.
48. Chaadaev, "Philosophical Letters," 65.
49. Ibid.

> reason had to accept its two most profound convictions without being able to prove them, namely: the existence of God and the unlimited continuity of its own being; he taught us that a supreme logic exists, which cannot be fitted under our measurements and which is imposed upon us despite ourselves, and that there is a world which is contemporary and different from the one on which we move and that our reason must recognize this world, because of the opposite danger of falling into nothingness, and that from this we should draw all our knowledge, in order then to adapt our knowledge to the real world.[50]

Kant represented for Chaadaev a sort of John the Baptist, as he announced a new philosophical Messiah. On his copy of the *Critique of Practical Reason* he actually wrote down in German: "*Er war nicht das Licht, sondern das erzeugte von dem Licht*."[51] Chaadaev acquired Kant's two *Critiques* in 1826 in Dresden, where he probably found some new thoughts he had been waiting for, presumably the same he wrote about in his letter to Pushkin in 1831: "Man will come bearing the secret of time . . . the movement that will conclude the destinies of mankind will begin."[52]

According to Zeldin, "the real disagreement between Chaadaev and Kant is not a matter of autonomy as such; it lies in their concern for the other two objects 'to which all the speculation of reason . . . is directed,' the existence of God and the immortality of the soul."[53] Their difference being that Chaadaev accepts revelation, while Kant does not, at least as far as epistemology is concerned. But another clear element of disagreement consists once again in the nature of reason and its use as the instrument for obtaining knowledge. In the "Fifth Letter," Chaadaev wrote:

> Note how the most certain, the most positive, the most strict philosophy of our time proceeds. It begins with the establishment of the fact that, since our reason is the given instrument of knowledge, it is necessary first of all to study how to know our reason. Without that, the philosophy says, there is no way of making suitable usage of reason. After that, this philosophy attempts to dissect and to analyze this reason as best it can. But how does this philosophy perform this preliminary work, this indispensable work, this anatomy of intelligence? Is it not by means of this reason itself? Thus, since in this, its most primary and most important operation, this philosophy is forced to

50. Ibid., 65–66.

51. John 1:8; Chaadayev, "Zametki na knihakh," 612; "Kommentariy," 706.

52. Chaadaev, "Fragments," 151.

53. Zeldin, "Chaadaev's Quarrel with Kant," 285.

> utilize an instrument which by its own admission it still does not know how to use, how can it come to the knowledge which it seeks? This is impossible to understand.[54]

Kant wanted to employ an artificial or abstract reason, without considering its origins and its history. But, according to Chaadaev, both in the sphere of knowledge and in the moral world, Kantian reason proves to be limited and powerless, since without God human beings are disabled both in theory and in practice. Without God, they cannot obtain any knowledge, and without his support they cannot behave according to morality.

Although she admits this basic disagreement, Mary-Barbara Zeldin tried to single out some important analogies between Kant and Chaadaev, in order to make her thesis about Kant's influence on Chaadaev more consistent. The comparison sometimes seems to be a little arbitrary, for instance when Zeldin emphasizes that, for both thinkers, moral law is "a law which man must recognize before he can attain true personality,"[55] while in point of fact the recognition happens in opposite ethic frames: the dignity of the autonomy of reason in Kant, and the passivity of obedience to the divine order in Chaadaev. But, from our point of view, it is very interesting that Zeldin emphasizes a possible relationship between the two philosophers exactly as regards the idea of "unity" as the furthest horizon of morality and, at least for Kant, on the transcendental level, of human knowledge as well: for both, according to Zeldin, "there is, and for both, there ought to be, an ultimate union of the natural and moral realms into a kingdom of God on earth."[56]

Second, concerning the destiny of humankind, Zeldin observes that "for Chaadaev the moral progress involved in achieving the kingdom of God is inherited by succeeding generations and individuals; for Kant the progress exists only for mankind as a whole, not for the individual person, that is, it exists only in the sense in which, for Chaadaev, all men form but one single man."[57]

Finally, in regard to the relationship between the individual and the whole, Zeldin recalls that "generalized, for both Kant and Chaadaev, determination according to moral law will result in the achievement of a moral world, the kingdom of God or the kingdom of ends, a world in which each person has absolute value in a systematically organized whole."[58]

54. Chaadaev, "Philosophical Letters," 59.

55. Zeldin, "Influence of Kant," 117.

56. Ibid., 116.

57. Ibid.

58. Ibid.

One might argue that such positions do not correspond exactly to what Kant might have thought. But what is interesting to us here is that Chaadaev might have read Kant in such a perspective. As Toropygin suggests at one point, a sort of "Kantian" element in Chaadaev's views on individual and the whole can shade some light on the differences between Chaadaev's "collectivism" and the Slavophiles' perspective.[59] For the Slavophiles, considered roughly as a whole in spite of all their differences, the proper relationship between individual and totality was realized first of all in a historical community, in this case in the Russian past. Chaadaev wanted to sketch a complete picture of the world and its history, where the relationship between individual and totality defines itself within history, but according to an *a priori* design, which represents the meaning of both history itself and the world.

Translated by Lucia Pasini

Bibliography

Belinskiy, Vissarion. "Pis'ma 1841." In *Polnoe sobranie sochineniy*, vol. 12, *Pis'ma. 1841–1848*, 169–87. Moscow: AN SSSR, 1956.

Chaadaev, Peter. "Fragments and Various Thoughts." In *Philosophical Works of Peter Chaadaev*, edited by Raymond T. McNally and Richard Tempest, 112–255. Dordrecht: Springer, 1991.

———. "The Philosophical Letters Addressed to a Lady." In *Philosophical Works of Peter Chaadaev*, edited by Raymond T. McNally and Richard Tempest, 18–101. Dordrecht: Springer, 1991.

Chaadayev, Petr. "Kommentariy i primechaniya k tekstam na russkom yazyke." In *Polnoe sobranie sochineniy i izbrannye pis'ma*, 1:690–769. Moscow: Nauka, 1991.

———. Letter to Dmitriy Obleukhov, 1812. In *Polnoe sobranie sochineniy i izbrannye pis'ma*, 2:7. Moscow: Nauka, 1991.

———. "Zametki na knigakh." In *Polnoe sobranie sochineniy i izbrannye pis'ma*, 1:582–626. Moscow: Nauka, 1991.

Dobieszewski, Janusz. "Petr Chaadaev and the Rise of Modern Russian Philosophy." *Studies in East European Thought* 54 (2002) 25–46.

Gurvich-Lishchiner, Sophia. "Chaadaev—Herzen—Dostoevsky: Individual and Reason in the Creative Mind." *Russian Studies in Literature* 4 (2007) 6–54.

Kamenskiy, Zakhar A. "Paradoksy Chaadayeva." Preface to Petr Chaadayev, *Polnoe sobranie sochineniy i izbrannye pis'ma*, 1:9–85. Moskow: Nauka, 1991.

Kireevsky, Ivan. "On the Nature of European Culture and on Its Relationship to Russian Culture." Translated by Valentine Snow. In *On Spiritual Unity: A Slavophiles Reader*, edited by Boris Jakim and Robert Bird, 187–232. New York: Lindisfarne, 1998.

McNally, Raymond T. "The Books in Petr Ja. Chaadaev's Libraries." *Jahrbücher für Geschichte Osteuropas* 14 (1966) 495–512.

59. Toropygin, "Chaadayev i Kant," 36–37.

Obolevitch, Teresa. "'The Madman' Appeals to Faith and Reason: On the Relationship between *Fides* and *Ratio* in the Oeuvres of Peter Chaadaev." In *Peter Chaadaev: Between the Love of Fatherland and the Love of Truth*, edited by Artur Mrówczyński-Van Allen, Teresa Obolevitch, Paweł Rojek, 55–72. Eugene, OR: Pickwick, 2018.

Smirnova, Zinaida G. "The Problem of Reason in Chaadaev's Philosophical Conception." *Russian Studies in Philosophy* 38 (1999) 8–24.

Toropygin, Petr G. "P. Ya. Chaadayev i I. Kant." *Kantovskiy sbornik* 18 (1994) 28–37.

Walicki, Andrzej. *The Flow of Ideas: Russian Thought from the Enlightenment to the Religious-Philosophical Renaissance.* Translated by Jolanta Kozak and Hilda Andrews-Rusiecka. Frankfurt am Main: Peter Lang, 2015.

Zeldin, Mary-Barbara. "Chaadayev's Quarrel with Kant: An Attempt at a Cease-Fire." *Revue des études slaves* 55 (1983) 277–85.

———. "The Influence of Immanuel Kant on Peter Yakovlevich Chaadayev." *Studies in Soviet Thought* 18 (1978) 111–19.

PART II

Contexts

7

Some Reflections upon Russian Literary Prose

and the Chaadaev/Pushkin/Custine/Mickiewicz Node

Bernard Marchadier

This chapter has two parts. The first one is devoted to some linguistic dimensions of Chaadaev's *Philosophical Letters*, the second one to some of the philosophical and political echoes of his thoughts.

The Language of Chaadaev

Chaadaev is without doubt a Russian thinker. From a number of perspectives, he can even be considered as the very first *Russian* thinker. He did not write extensively; but whatever he, as a Russian thinker, wrote was not in Russian; it was in French. That fact is not without great importance and I would like to devote some time to considering it, following step by step the development that made such a situation both possible and necessary.

As the saying goes, in the tenth century, Russia was "christened but not educated" (*kreshchena no ne prosveshchena*). The monks Cyril and Methodius and their disciples translated the liturgy, the Psalter, the Gospel and a few books by the Church Fathers from Greek into the old Bulgarian language (called here "Church Slavonic"), but the people spoke another language: old Russian. There were two languages in use: one was South Slavic (high style) and the other Eastern Slavic (low style). The situation evolved along the centuries, as Church Slavonic tended to take on more and more Eastern Slavic features, but on the whole the country remained for centuries in a state of "diglossia," a term coined by the American linguist Charles Fergusson to describe a situation "in which, in addition to the primary dialects of the language (which may include a standard or regional standards), there is a very divergent, highly codified (often grammatically more complex) superposed variety, the vehicle of a large and respected body of written literature."[1]

Diglossia is a very common phenomenon in all civilizations, but the specific problem of Russia was not only that its "high style" language was not really understood by the great majority of the people, but that, apart from being the language of liturgy and prayer, it did not give access to greater culture. Until the seventeenth century, the translations from Greek or Latin into Slavonic were very scarce.

In the Byzantine world and in Europe the situation was quite different as educated people could have direct access to the universe of higher learning and classical literature, through languages (Greek and Latin) that were evolved enough to be powerful instruments of thought and exchange. It was not the case in Russia, which, as Chaadaev put it, was originally cut away from the *idées traditives* bequeathed by God to guide men. "We have not been affected by the universal education of mankind."[2]

It is worth noting that, especially in Western Russia, there developed an administrative (*kantselyarskiy*) and commercial language half way between high and low languages. But, for lack of proper connotations, that middle of the road *prosta mova* ("simple tongue") was not deemed prestigious enough to be the vehicle of higher learning. Typically enough, in the second half of the sixteenth century, Prince Andrey Kurbsky, who had fled abroad to avoid Ivan the Terrible's wrath and who had founded in Lithuania a modest but epoch-making centre of learning and printing, thought impossible to publish Cicero's works in *prosta mova* which anybody would have understood, and chose to have them translated into high style Slavonic.

In the early eighteenth century, Emperor Peter the Great imposed a simplified "civil" (*grazhdanskiy*) alphabet, closer to European types, that made both printing and reading easier. He also introduced into the language a lot of foreign words (mostly German and Latin). Russia was becoming a major European power, and the tools of her might were not only of a political, military, and industrial nature, they had also to be linguistic and cultural. Just like Peter had Russians shave their beards and don English greatcoats, he had them use a Europeanized language. But if there was a Russian poetry (poetry always exists, in all the dialects and at all the stages

1. For a study of diglossia in Russia, see Uspenskiy, *Kratkiy ocherk istorii.*

2. Chaadaev, "Philosophical Letters," 20.

of development of any people as it cannot be separated from man), Russian prose was still *in statu nascendi* as the language of conversation and novel writing had not yet appeared.

The works of Vasily Tredyakovsky (1705–1769)[3] mark a very important moment in the birth of the Russian literary language, especially his *Treatise on Eloquence* (*Slovo o vitiystve*). Tredyakovsky had lived for some time in Paris and had followed closely the polemics between the Jesuits and the Jansenists, which had, among others, a linguistic dimension. In their respective schools, the Jesuits taught in Latin and the Jansenists in French. Tredyakovsky transposed that discussion on Russian soil, paralleling Slavonic and Latin on one side with Russian and French on the other. He suggested obtaining a synthesis of Slavonic and Russian in order to make the former understandable by everyone and to gentrify the latter. He called that hybrid *slavianorossiyskiy*, which, in his view, would be the exclusive language of neither learned monks nor merchants, but the language of "good society," a language which ladies—the *spiritus movens* of European sociability—could understand and would not fear to speak.

Unlike Mikhail Lomonosov (or, to take a contemporary example, Aleksandr Solzhenitsyn), Tredyakovsky insisted that language grows and becomes more accurate not by drawing from the springs of the past and of old usage but by being in contact with foreign languages. Languages enlarge, whet and fine-tune each other and hence the importance of translation as a groundbreaking enterprise. Chaadaev will take up this argument in his "Fifth Letter": "If we were deprived of contact with other intelligent beings, we would eat grass instead of speculating on our nature."[4] By nature, man mixes and discusses not only with his neighbors but with whomever he happens to be in contact with, be they representatives of other countries and worlds. We are meant to grow and flourish inside the sphere of conversation. And translation is one of the forms of conversation.

It is no surprise, then, that the first novel ever published in Russian was a translation from the French, made by Tredyakovsky himself: that of abbé Paul Tallemant's *Voyage de l'Isle d'Amour*, a seventeenth-century allegorical tale. After Tredyakovsky's translation, a very important landmark in the early history of Russian literature was the publication of Nikolai Karamzin's sentimental novel *Poor Liza* and his *Letters of a Russian Traveller*. Both books were based on European models. And both are perfectly and pleasantly readable to this day: Russian literary prose had been born.

3. On Tredyakovski, see the remarkable studies of Breuillard, *Derrière l'histoire*, 57–85.

4. Chaadaev, "Philosophical Letters," 64.

Such is, very sketchily, the genealogy of Russian literary prose, which could appear only because it was founded on examples drawn from European literatures and more particularly on French literary models. It is interesting to note that Pushkin did not see in gallicisms a corruption of his mother tongue but a way to enrich it and an instrument of thought. In a letter to his friend Peter Vyazemsky, he wrote: "You did well in openly coming out in defence of Gallicisms. Sometime is must be said aloud that the Russian metaphysical language is still in a savage condition with us. God grant that some day it be formed similar to the French (the clear, precise language of prose, i.e., the language of ideas)."[5]

Vladimir Nabokov once noted that, if Pushkin wrote in Russian and not in French, it was because he was first and foremost a poet. Russian was his true language even when, in prose, he followed not so much Karamzin (who belonged to the generation before his) as French models like Voltaire or Mme de Staël. That is also why Chaadaev himself recommends to him to write not in French, but in Russian: "You must speak in no other language but the language of your vocation as poet."[6] But Pushkin will continue writing to him in French: "My dear friend, I shall speak to you in the language of Europe; I am more at home in it than in ours."[7]

Chaadaev's case is quite different from Pushkin's. He is a thinker, he writes essays and letters, and, in those days when Russian prose was only very recent, he prefers to make himself clear in French. For decades Russian will still seem too rugged, too unpolished, too un-European to express problems accurately and to convey the intimate secrets of the heart. French will remain the language of private letter-writing till almost the end of the nineteenth century, at least until its seventies. Not only Pushkin and Chaadaev, but also Aleksey Tolstoy, Alexander Herzen, Ivan Turgenev, Afanasiy Fet, Fedor Tyutchev will leave a rich correspondence in French.

French is also the language of well-educated ladies. In his novel in verse *Eugene Onegin*, Pushkin will pretend that Tatiana's letter to Eugene was originally written in French, and that the Russian version in the novel is a translation:

> Another hindrance I foresee:
> saving the honour of my native land,
> undoubtedly I'll be obliged
> Tatiana's letter to translate.

5. Pushkin to Peter Vyazemsky, 13 July 1825, *Letters of Alexander Pushkin*, 229.
6. Chaadaev to Pushkin, 27 June 1831, 68.
7. Pushkin to Chaadaev, 6 July 1831, *Letters of Alexander Pushkin*, 500.

She knew Russian badly,
did not read our reviews,
and expressed herself with difficulty
in her native tongue;
hence wrote in French.
What's to be done about it! I repeat again;
as yet a lady's love
has not expressed itself in Russian,
as yet our proud tongue has
to postal prose not got accustomed.[8]

To sum up our point here, we shall they that Chaadaev's *Philosophical Letters* were written in French because they are *philosophical*, because they are *letters*, and because they are addressed to *a lady*. At that stage of the development of Russian culture it is possible to contribute to improving mores and consolidating civilization only through women and through the French discourse of feminine salons. Or, at least, salons from which women are not excluded and where genteel *bon ton* is the rule.

Pushkin, Mickiewicz, and de Custine

Chaadaev's style perfectly fits into the French literary models of those days. It is abundant, clear, rhythmical, and energetic; it is beautiful French prose, not pages written by a foreigner who happens to know French well, it is the language of such masters as Chateaubriand, Tocqueville, or de Maistre whom Chaadaev knew personally and read. One can say that Chaadaev is a French classical author.[9] Unlike Pushkin, he is a prose writer, and that is the reason why his natural language is not Russian but French. He also wants to address the whole of Europe, and in those days French is the language of the élites throughout the whole continent.

Chaadaev was six years older than Pushkin. They met for the first time when the poet was seventeen years old. Pushkin was still a high school student, and Chaadaev an officer in a hussar regiment. For Pushkin, Chaadaev became a sort of mentor, who taught him to think. In 1820, when tsar Alexander condemned Pushkin to banishment, Chaadaev and Karamzin intervened so that their young protégé would not be sent to the

8. Pushkin, *Eugene Onegin*, 162.

9. Another Russian "French writer" would be Fedor Tyutchev, whose *La Russie et la revolution* (1848) and *La Question romaine* (1850) are superb samples of political prose.

Solovki penitentiary or to Siberia, but to more cheerful Southern places like Moldavia and Odessa.

It has been surmised, on the basis of some elements of Pushkin's *Eugene Onegin*, that the description of the hero in the novel is a portrait of Chaadaev. Isn't Onegin introduced to the reader as "a good friend" of the author, doesn't he speak and write "impeccably in French," doesn't he master the art of epigrams to perfection? And above all there is this passage:

> My Eugene, a second [Chaadaev]
> being afraid of jealous censures,
> was in his dress a pedant
> and what we've called a fop.
> He three hours, at the least,
> in front of mirrors spent,
> and from his dressing room came forth
> akin to giddy Venus
> when, having donned a masculine attire,
> the goddess drives to a masquerade.[10]

But it would be too hasty a conclusion. Already in his youth, Chaadaev was a living legend and his name—almost a common noun. So "a second Chaadaev" would mean no more than "a second Byron" or "a second Brummell." Like Onegin, he was, as we have seen, a dandy. But (and this is not unimportant), unlike him (and young Pushkin), Chaadaev was anything but a ladies man (no woman is known to have won his heart or stirred his senses). Of course, like Onegin, Chaadaev was also a hypochondriac, but it does not really argue for the former being the portrait of the latter, as hypochondria was a fashionable disease in those days, when literary heroes (Chateaubriand's René, Byron's Childe Harold, Constant's Adolphe, etc.) were all splenetic. It seems then that, if Onegin has obviously a few important features in common with Chaadaev, he could hardly be considered as his "portrait."

The July 1830 Revolution in Paris, followed in November by the Polish uprising, was a terrible shock to Chaadaev, who bewailed "the death of an entire world . . . this general clash of all of the elements in human nature," adding: "As for me, tears fill my eyes when I see the vast calamity that has befallen that ancient, my ancient, society; this general catastrophe, which befell Europe in such an unforseen manner, has doubled my own

10. Pushkin, *Eugene Onegin*, 106.

unhappiness."[11] Chaadaev was particularly incensed by what he heard about the Polish insurrection, "that insane enterprise," and, strangely enough, this most European of Russians started using arguments that were soon to be those of the Panslavists and Slavophiles: "As a people, the Poles are Slavs and they must share the fate of their brother, the Russian people, who can bring into the lives of both of them so much strength and prosperity."[12]

As a traditionalist and a legitimist, Chaadaev could not condone nor excuse any revolution against a legitimate sovereign. And both France's Charles X and Russia's Nicholas I *were* legitimate in his eyes. Pope Gregory XVI, in his encyclical letter *Cum Primum* (1832), also condemned unambiguously the Polish November Insurrection.

More surprisingly, at least at first glance—in spite of his attachment to the Byronic tradition to which he owed so much, and in opposition to his political liberal friends (Peter Vyazemsky, Alexander Turgenev, Alexander Herzen) not to mention his poet friend Adam Mickiewicz—Pushkin condemned the Poles in a famous poem, *Klevetnikam Rossii* ("To the Slanderers of Russia"):

> What do you raise an outcry over, national bards?
> Why do you threaten Russia with Anathema?
> What stirred you up? The throes of Lithuania?
> Desist: this is a strife of Slavs among themselves,
> An old domestic strife, already weighed by fate,
> An issue not to be resolved by you.
> . . . .
> Leave us alone: you have not read
> Those bloody tablets;
> To you is unintelligible, to you is alien
> This family feud;
> Mute to you are the Kremlin and Praga;
> Unthinkingly you are beguiled
> By the valour of a desperate struggle—
> And you hate us.[13]

Pushkin's poem delighted Chaadaev:

11. Chaadaev to Pushkin, 18 September 1831, Chaadaev, "Fragments," 150–51.
12. Chaadaev, "Un mot sur la question polonaise."
13. Pushkin, "To the Slanderers of Russia," 248.

> Never have you given me such pleasure. At last, you are a national poet; you have finally divined your vocation. I cannot express to you the satisfaction that you made me feel. We shall talk about this another time, and at length. I don't know whether you understand me correctly. The poem addressed to the enemies of Russia is especially admirable; it is I who tell you this: It contains more ideas than were expressed and implemented in this country in the last one hundred years . . . I feel the urge to say: here at last is our Dante . . . perhaps one that is too precocious.[14]

Pushkin has been accused of being unfaithful to his freedom-loving ideals and, worse, of having written that poem out of cringing servility.[15] It is most probably not so. He was genuinely outraged against the Polish insurgents, as appears in his December letter (of course, in French) to Elizabeth Khitrovo: "The news of the Polish insurrection has bowled me over. So our old enemies, then, will be exterminated, and thus nothing Alexander did will remain, because nothing is based on the real interests of Russia, and all rests only on considerations of personal vanity, of theatrical effects, etc."[16]

Another element has to be taken into account if we want to understand Pushkin's reaction; as he once wrote to his friend Vyazemsky: "I despise my country from its head to its toes, but I am angry when a foreigner shares my feeling."[17]

About Pushkin's poem, Wacław Lednicki quotes a very interesting judgement by Alexander Turgenev in a letter to his brother Nicholas:

> Your conclusion about Pushkin is just; there is, indeed, still some barbarity in him, and Vyazemsky harassed him in Moscow for the sake of Poland . . . He is a barbarian only in his attitude towards Poland. As a poet, he thinks that without Russian patriotism, such as he understands it, one cannot be a poet, and for poetry's sake he does not want to abandon barbarity.[18]

When Pushkin published his poem, Chaadaev's "First Philosophical Letter" had no yet been published in the journal *Teleskop*, but his friends had all read it. The French and Polish events had a strong influence on Chaadaev's views; not only his political views, but also his historiosophical views. He started to see Russia differently. Of course, the country had

14. Chaadaev to Pushkin, 18 September 1831, 152–53.

15. This is what Mickiewicz infers in his poem *To My Russian Friends*.

16. Pushkin to Elizaveta Khitrovo, 9 December 1830, *Letters of Alexander Pushkin*, 446.

17. Quoted after Lednicki, *Russia, Poland and the West*, 72.

18. Ibid., 88.

no past, but it is precisely for that reason, argued Chaadaev, that it might have a promising feature. It was like a blank sheet of paper, ready to receive whatever God's finger would wish to write on it.[19]

But Chaadaev's philosophy could not be one of sanguine expectations, and that moment of patriotic passion or hope against all odds did not last.[20] In 1854—on the eve of the Crimean war—he wrote an article which he pretended had been published by the French catholic journal *L'Univers* and which, as far as the nature of Russia is concerned, sounded exactly like his "First Letter." Its concluding paragraph is as follows:

> In speaking about Russia people always believe that they are speaking about a political power like others. But that is not so at all. Russia is an entire world obeying the will, the caprice, the fantasy of only one man, whether he is called Peter or Ivan, no matter, it's always an incarnation of arbitrariness. Russia is a country which, contrary to all the laws of human societies, advances only towards its own enslavement and those of the people who are neighbours. Hence it is as much in its own interest and that of other nations that it would be useful for Russia to pursue a new path.[21]

After the Insurrection had failed, Adam Mickiewicz, who was one of the targets of his friend Pushkin's poem (the "Lithuanian bard threatening Russia with anathema": that's him), emigrated to Dresden and then to Paris. The dialogue between Pushkin and Mickiewicz was not interrupted by the tragic events in Poland; in fact, Pushkin's *Bronze Horseman*, in which he tries to justify national and individual sacrifices for the sake of Russia's grandeur, can be considered as an indirect answer to Mickiewicz's *Statue of Peter*

19. Unlike Chaadaev, Pushkin never accepted the "blank page" idea and strongly affirmed the historicity of Russia. See Pushkin to Chaadaev, 19 October 1836, *Letters of Alexander Pushkin*, 779–80.

20. Lednicki could not believe that Chaadaev was sincere in praising Pushkin's poem and suspected in him either fear of censorship or "devilish irony." Lednicki, *Russia, Poland and the West*, 82–83. It is interesting to note that the addressee of the *Philosophical Letters*, Ekaterina Panova, was on the side of the Polish insurgents and that she admitted that she "prayed to the Lord to send victory to the Poles because they fought for freedom." Ibid., 87.

21. "En parlant de la Russie, on croit toujours parler d'une puissance comme une autre: mais ce n'est pas du tout cela. La Russie est tout un monde obéissant à la volonté, au caprice, à la fantaisie d'un seul homme, qu'il s'appelle Pierre ou Jean, n'importe, c'est toujours une incarnation de l'arbitraire. La Russie est un pays qui, contrairement à toutes les lois des sociétés humaines, n'avance que vers son propre asservissement et celui des peuples qui l'avoisinent. C'est donc autant dans son propre intérêt que dans celui des autres nations qu'il serait utile de lui faire prendre une voie nouvelle." Published for the first time by François Rouleau, "La lettre de Tchaadaiev."

the Great. And, in 1834, Pushkin will compose a poem called *To Mickiewicz*, full of regret for the loss of his great Polish friend: "He lived among us . . . He cherished in his soul no bitterness against us, and we loved him . . . But our peaceful guest became our enemy."[22]

Like Chaadaev, Mickiewicz had his "Slavophile" period. When, invited by Jules Michelet and Edgar Quinet, he will give between 1840 and 1844 his famous Collège de France lectures, he will prophesy a brilliant future for the Slavs (not only Russians, of course), as "peoples of the Word" (*Slavianie/Slovo*), whose hour has come at last to say their word (*slovo*) in the history of mankind.

Chaadaev and Mickiewicz most certainly knew each other: a famous painting by Grigoriy Myasoyedov shows the Polish bard improvising in the salon of Princess Zinaida Volkonsky, and Chaadaev, the philosopher who said "*ty*" to no one, leaning against a pillar with his arms crossed at the other end of the room, staring at him. In the assistance, we recognize Pushkin, Vyazemsky, Khomyakov, Pogodin and Shevyrev.[23] All those great names belonged to the same circle. What is most striking, however, is not the fact that Chaadaev and Mickiewicz probably met, but the fact that, although neither of them mentions the other, some of their judgements about Russia are so similar, both in substance and in tone. If we take Mickiewicz's *Ustęp* ("Digression") in part 3 of his verse drama *Dziady* ("The Forefathers"), composed in 1832, we read passages like:

> This land is so large and almost void of inhabitants
> Broad-chested, great of strength, a stalwart band;
> And, like the trees and creatures of the North,
> They pulse with life and health that knows no pain;
> But every face is like their home, a plain,
> A waste on which no inward light shines forth.
> Their hearts, like underground volcanoes, throw
> Upon the cheeks no flame of fierce desire.
> Their moving lips reflect no ardent glow;
> No wrinkled brows fade with the dying fire
> Seen of men's foreheads in more favoured lands,
> O'er which have passed, through many weary years,
> Such strong traditions, sorrows, hopes and fears
> That in each face a nation's history stands.

22. Pushkin, "To Mickiewicz," 245–46.

23. See the reproduction in Lednicki, *Russia, Poland and the West*. The reader will find in that book many quotes suggesting parallels between Chaadaev and Mickiewicz.

> And here the eyes of men are large and clear,
> Like their unstoried towns; no storm-tossed heart
> Makes anguished glances from their pupils dart
> Or hopeless sorrow in their depths appear:
> But near at hand, empty and desolate.[24]

And now, let's take Chaadaev:

> Even in our expressions I find that there is something strangely vague, cold, uncertain, resembling somewhat the features of people placed at the lowest rung of the social ladder. In foreign lands, especially in the South, where physiognomies are so lively and so expressive, I often compared the faces of the inhabitants to those of my compatriots and I was struck by the sullenness in ours.[25]

Or Mickiewicz again:

> Each body is a web, a coarse-spun roll,
> In which there sleeps a caterpillar's soul
> Ere it transforms its tiny breast for flight
> And weaves and tints its wings to fairy guise.
> But when the sun of liberty shall rise,
> What kind of insect then will greet the light?
> Will a bright butterfly soar from the earth,
> Or a dull moth of dark, uncleanly birth?[26]

Astolphe de Custine will draw from that same source of images and judgements to write his *La Russie en 1839*, published in 1843. As George Kennan noted, comparing Chaadaev's "First Letter" with Custine's book:

> Such comparison suggests that the similarity exists not so much in point of content as in tone. It is Chaadaev's sorrowful cadences, constituting as they did a sort of lyrical lament for Russia—her unhappy history, her wasted opportunities, her underdevelopment, the futility in the lives of her gifted people—that suggest most strongly the negative quality of Custine's subsequent work.[27]

24. Mickiewicz, "Road to Russia," 483.
25. Chaadaev, "Philosophical Letters," 24.
26. Mickiewicz, "Road to Russia," 483–84.
27. Kennan, *Marquis de Custine and His "Russia in 1839,"* 40.

Although Alexander Turgenev, in Paris, had asked Vyazemsky to introduce Custine to Chaadaev when in Moscow, we do not know for sure if the two men met (but the mysterious interlocutor Custine comes across in the English Club[28] could be him). In any case, Custine was bound to have heard about the 1836 *Teleskop* scandal and most certainly had read the "First Letter" (maybe before going to Russia, through Alexander Turgenev). It is impossible not to hear a "pre-custinian" ring in the following lines of Chaadaev's "First Letter":

> We grow but we do not mature; we advance but in an oblique line, i.e., in a line which does not lead to any goal. We resemble children . . . all their knowledge lies on the surface of their existence, their whole soul exists outside themselves . . . It would seem that in our case the general law of humanity has been revoked. Alone *in* the world, we have given nothing *to* the world, taken nothing from the world, bestowed not even a single idea upon the fund of human ideas, contributed nothing to the progress of the human spirit, and we have distorted all progressivity which has come to us. Nothing from the first moment of our social existence has emanated from us for man's common good; not one useful idea has germinated in the sterile soil of our fatherland; we have launched no great truth; we have never bothered to conjecture anything ourselves, and we have adopted only deceiving appearances and useless luxury from all the things that others have thought out . . . In order to call attention to ourselves, we had to expand from the Bering Straits to the Oder.[29]

Conversely, quite a few pages in Custine's book (especially the XXVIII letter) bear the strong imprint of Chaadaev's views.[30]

28. See *La Russsie en 1839*, letters XXVII and XXVIII.

29. Chaadaev, "Philosophical Letters," 22, 25; italics are mine. Michel Cadot notes that such ideas about Russia were already spreading before Chaadaev and Custine, and quotes as an example a passage from Charles-François Philibert Massons's *Mémoires secrets sur la Russie sous les règnes de Catherine II et de Paul 1er*: "Le Russe est un peuple nouveau sur lequel toutes les nations ont plus ou moins influé. Il a reçu de l'étranger des arts, des sciences, des vices et peu de vertus. Le génie du gouvernement et le caractère particulier de l'autocrate s'impriment sur toute la nation, comme sur un seul homme, et la religion grecque, la plus absurde de toutes les sectes chrétiennes, achève de la dénaturer. On peut dire du Russe que son gouvernement l'avilit, que sa religion le déprave et que sa prétendue civilisation l'a corrompu." Cadot, *La Russie*, 188. On Masson, see de Grève, *Le Voyage en Russie*, 1258–59.

30. See examples in Cadot, *La Russie*, 200–203.

In Russia, Custine's book met with a *succès de scandale* just as resounding as Chaadaev's "First Letter." But Custine was not only a beneficiary of the advice and information about Russia which his liberal Russian friends (Piotr Kozlovsky, Alexander Turgenev, etc.) gave him for writing his book; in a way, he also became their spokesman. They had helped him, but he helped them in return. Unless they were ready to share Chadaev's fate and be declared insane, *they*, as Russian subjects, could not say publicly about Russia what he said. *He* could. And he did.

Custine had predicted that people would object to his book: "Trois mois de voyage, il a mal vu." And he had prepared his answer: "Il est vrai: j'ai mal vu, mais j'ai bien deviné." If he guessed so well, it is because he was guided—before, during, and after his journey—by friends who told him how to read the reality of Russia. It is interesting to note that Custine's *La Russie* is less a travelogue (like, for instance Alexandre Dumas's *Voyage en Russie*) than a series of conversations about Russia in Russia as a sequel to the conversations about Russia he had had in Paris. As if it was the same conversation going on. In any case, Custine had guessed so well that, as soon as 1843, Fedor Tyutchev admitted to his German friend Varnhagen von Ense:

> The book made a tremendous impression in Russia; the whole of our cultivated élite more or less agrees with its judgements; almost nobody is indignant. They praise the style. Even General Benkendorf frankly said to the Emperor: "M. de Custine has only formulated ideas about us that have long been shared by everybody, including by us!"[31]

Custine most certainly also knew of Mickiewicz, as in Paris he was very close to the Polish émigré milieu; he had probably attended some of his public lectures in the Collège de France on Slavic literatures and quite a few passages from *La Russie* betray an attentive reading of Mickiewicz's *Digression*.[32]

Who influenced whom? Who borrowed from whom? Who had read whom? I am sure this remains a rich field for scholars and researchers to explore. But it is very important never to forget that, while researching who (de Maistre,[33] Pushkin, de Custine, Mickiewicz, Chaadaev, Turgenev,

31. Ibid., 210.

32. See Kennan, *Marquis de Custine*, 28. The first French translation of Mickiewicz's works appeared in Paris in 1841, as Custine was composing his book. As Kennan notes: "The similarity will be found not so much in individual passages, although there are one or two striking instances of this nature, but rather in the spirit of the two works, and in the frequent identity of theme." Ibid.

33. In his chapter, I have not mentioned Joseph de Maistre, in whose *Soirées de Saint-Pétersbourg* or *Quatre chapitres inédits sur la Russie* we would have found many

Griboyedov,[34] or others) influenced whom, borrowed from whom or opened whose eyes, one also has to consider that all those people knew each other quite well and that they met, discussed and argued in the same milieu. To put it very simply: it is not because one of them put forward an idea that it is to be considered as definitely *his* idea. It takes a lot of attention and finesse to get the proper feel and to find the relevant dividing lines of a past world. Thus only can one avoid committing the historian's worst deadly sin: intellectual anachronism. Nor should one forget that, concerning Russia, the works of Chaadaev, Pushkin, Custine and Mickiewicz draw from a common fount of opinions—fed, directly or indirectly, by an on-going conversation and by images about Russia—all of which were transmitted, developed and enriched both in letter-writing and in the salons of ladies like Princess Volokhonsky or Countess Rostopchin in Moscow or, in Paris, of Mme de Circourt (née Anastasia Khliustina),[35] Princess Czartoryska, or Mme Svétchine.

Bibliography

Breuillard, Jean. *Derrière l'histoire—la langue: études de littérature, de linguistique et d'histoire (Russie et France, XVIIIe—XXe siècle)*. Paris: Institut d'études slaves, 2012.

Cadot, Michel. *La Russie dans la vie intellectuelle française 1839–1856*. Paris: Fayard, 1967.

Chaadaev, Peter. "Fragments and Various Thoughts." In *Philosophical Works of Peter Chaadaev*, edited by Raymond T. McNally and Richard Tempest, 112–255. Dordrecht: Springer, 1991.

———. "The Philosophical Letters Addressed to a Lady." In *Philosophical Works of Peter Chaadaev*, edited by Raymond T. McNally and Richard Tempest, 18–101. Dordrecht: Springer, 1991.

Chaadayev, Petr. Letter to Pushkin. 27 June 1831. In *Polnoe sobranie sochineniy i izbrannye pis'ma*, 2:67–68. Moscow: Nauka, 1991.

———. "Un mot sur la question polonaise." In *Polnoe sobranie sochineniy i izbrannye pis'ma*, 1:278–81. Moscow: Nauka, 1991.

Custine, Astolphe de. *La Russie en 1839*. Paris: Solin, 1990.

Grève, Claude de. *Le Voyage en Russie*. Paris: Robert Laffont, 1990.

---

of the themes already examined here. But it would have required a study of its own. De Maistre most certainly knew Chaadaev and Mickiewicz, whom he met at least in masonic circles. And Custine had obviously read the *Soirées*.

34. It has been argued that Chaadaev was the prototype for Chatsky, the hero of Griboyedov's play *Sorrow from Wit*.

35. Her husband, Adolphe de Circourt, was a close friend of Alexis de Tocqueville. Mickiewicz had courted her before her marriage and she was a personal friend and admirer of Chaadaev. See Cadot, *La Russie*, 77.

Kennan, George. *The Marquis de Custine and His "Russia in 1839."* London: Hutchinson, 1972.

Lednicki, Wacław. *Russia, Poland and the West*. London: Hutchinson, 1954.

Mickiewicz, Adam. "The Road to Russia." Translated by Marjorie Beatrice Peacock and George Rapall Noyes. *Slavonic and East European Review* 13 (1935) 481–86.

Pushkin, Alexander. *Eugene Onegin: A Novel in Verse*. Translated by Vladimir Nabokov. Vol. 1. Princeton: Princeton University Press, 1990.

———. *The Letters of Alexander Pushkin*. Translated by J. Thomas Shaw. Los Angeles: Schlacks, 1997.

———. "To Mickiewicz." In *Adam Mickiewicz, 1798–1855: In Commemoration of the Centenary of His Death*, 245–46. Zurich: UNESCO, 1955.

———. "To the Slanderers of Russia." Translated by Walter Arndt. In *Pushkin Threefold: Narrative, Lyric, Polemic and Ribald Verse*, 248. New York: Dutton, 1972.

Rouleau, François. "La lettre de Tchaadaiev à *L'Univers*." *Cahiers du monde russe et soviétique* 15 (1974) 410–13.

Uspenskiy, Boris A. *Kratkiy ocherk istorii russkogo literaturnogo yazyka (XI–XIX vv.)*. Moscow: Gnozis, 1994.

8

Peter Chaadaev and St. Innocent of Kherson

The New Contours of Tradition[1]

Fr. Pavel Khondzinskiy

At first glance, Peter Chaadaev and St. Innocent of Kherson have little in common. Apparently, they didn't know each other and in texts by Chaadaev, there are two references to the name of the saint by which it is difficult to define his attitude toward him, it is clear only that he had read at least some of his sermons. St. Innocent doesn't mention Chaadaev anywhere and yet there is something that allows us to put them side by side and compare their views.

First of all, they belonged to the same generation—St. Innocent was six years younger than Chaadaev and lived only a year longer than him. However, these six years of difference between them meant a lot. Chaadaev participated in the war of 1812, while the future saint was twelve when it started. And yet, for all the differences in origin, social class, education, life experience, etc., both of them belonged to those whose views were shaped by the era of Alexander I, but who themselves became known in the following, Nicholas, era, more precisely, in its first two decades, when the intellectual environment began to actively assimilate the ideas of classical German philosophy. And while all Chaadaev's younger contemporaries and friends were interested in the spiritual and academic environment, St. Innocent,

1. This chapter was prepared within the project *Genealogy of a Theological Personalism (on Material of the Russian Religious Thought of Nineteenth through the Beginnings of the Twentieth Century)* with assistance of Fund of development of St. Tikhon's Orthodox University in Moscow.

perhaps, was the first major author, whose works significantly reflected the new direction. The latter is quite natural, since he graduated from the Kiev Theological Academy which introduced the study of the German authors in its historical and philosophical courses earlier than others. Thus a comparison of the texts by Peter Chaadaev and St. Innocent should show the first fruits and the impact of the new concepts and terminology perception, respectively, in the Russian philosophical and theological tradition of the first half of the nineteenth century.

Peter Chaadaev

As to the first one, there is no doubt that Chaadaev was significantly influenced in this regard by the ideas of Count Joseph de Maistre and it is easy to see their traces in his historiosophical constructions. It is the Catholic Church, the church-kingdom,[2] that is seen by Chaadaev as the beginning and the foundation of the social system, "which must make truth reign among men."[3] And it cannot be otherwise, as Christianity is historical by definition and should, consequently, bring its fruits in history, on the earth.[4] Of course, this kingdom is different from the earthly kingdoms, but even if it is like them, we must remember that such a dispensation of the church in the West was once again the result of historical reasons and could not be otherwise.[5] Whatever it was, it was the church that has become the foundation and the guarantor of civilization[6] in the West: European nations were looking for *the kingdom of God* and the rest *followed* them, "they found well-being and freedom."[7]

The anthropology of Chaadaev is in a way adjacent to his philosophy of history, one of the main ideas of which is considered to be the idea of parallelism of the physical and moral world in a sense of the immutability of the laws that are governing them. Hence, Chaadaev's idea about the necessary

2. De Maistre, *Du pape*, 19.

3. Chaadaev, "Philosophical Letters," 19.

4. Ibid.

5. See Chaadaev to Princess Ekaterina Dolgorukova, 22 January 1848, Chaadaev, "Fragments," 220.

6. See Chaadaev to Princess Sofiya Meshcherskaya, December 1841, Chaadaev, "Fragments," 181. Cf. Chaadaev to Alexander Turgenev, October-November 1841, Chaadayev, "Pis'ma," 100.

7. Chaadaev to Sergey Stroganov, 8 November 1836, Chaadayev, "Pis'ma," 113.

subordination of the individual mind to the divine one, which should also eventually lead to social reconstruction.[8]

It is more difficult to describe Chaadaev's ideas about the structure of a human personality.

First of all, it should be noted that he didn't think of it in the classical categories of Christian anthropology, which stemmed from the philosophical anthropology of antiquity. It is hard to find in his works, with no violence to the text, the ideas about nature and hypostasis, the three forces of the soul, the interaction and correlation of the spiritual, mental and physical. However, they contain a concept of the image of God, its substantial damage in the fallen humanity and restoration in Jesus Christ. For Chaadaev, this image first of all reveals itself in freedom, an essential feature of which is the ability to know when "we oppose our own creator,"[9] i.e., to recognize those divine laws and our avoidance of them. This ability is obviously a remnant of the divine knowledge (direct communion with divine reason) available for Adam before the Fall. In his face, Christ returns "the divine mind" to a man.[10] Joining this mind in Christ means abandoning the "fatal present *ego*" and finding "the comprehensive personality."[11] The latter, however, does not mean the loss of freedom:

> In our submission to divine power, we are never fully conscious (*conscience*) of this power, therefore, it can never encroach upon our freedom. Thus, our freedom consists only in the fact that we do not sense our dependency: this is enough for us to consider ourselves as perfectly free and liable for everything which we do, for each idea which we think.[12]

It is easy to assume that the concept, which so definitely puts an emphasis on the category of *reason*, gives an important place to the category of *consciousness*. However, it is complicated by the fact that in French (Chaadaev mostly wrote in French) the latter can be expressed by the word *la connaissance*, as well as *la conscience*. The basic meaning of *la connaissance* is knowledge and of *la conscience* is conscience. Thus there is a reasonable question of whether Chaadaev distinguished between "*consciousness—conscience*" and how he related them to each other, i.e., moral consciousness and "*consciousness—connaissance*," i.e., rational consciousness?

8. See Chaadaev, "Philosophical Letters," 86.

9. Ibid., 56.

10. See ibid., 64–65.

11. Ibid., 46.

12. Ibid., 56.

Quantitative analysis shows that in most cases *la connaissance* has a meaning of "knowledge" in the works by Chaadaev, and even where translation implies "consciousness," it deals primarily with the mental and cognitive human activity regardless of its content.[13]

In turn, *la conscience* usually gives a different semantic context: it is carried in the heart the intimate consciousness of God's will,[14] living conscience,[15] consciousness of one's weakness in the face of the divine force that is entailing us,[16] "the feeling of the universal will . . . the intimate sensation, the profound consciousness (*conscience*) of his real rapport with all creation,"[17] responsible to the supreme moral law consciousness of our own activities,[18] consciousness of our free will,[19] constituting the essence of our nature "germ of a superior consciousness,"[20] "an intimate awareness of the ways of God,"[21] "consciousness of the good,"[22] etc., in other words, it is consciousness implying quite a certain substantial moment and, of course, a higher consciousness of the rational or logical.

Finally, it is clear that even regardless of usage, Chaadaev distinguished between two types of consciousness: a lower as a mere consciousness of one's own existence ("ideological consciousness" of the modern philosophy, as he called it), or the shape of our being and a higher, "which lets us not only feel ourselves living but that we know even how we live," consciousness (*conscience*), that is a "given to us to act, in each moment of duration, upon the following moment, to make our life ourselves instead of letting it flow."[23]

So, according to Chaadaev, man is created in the image of God that reveals primarily in his freedom, an essential feature of which is the consciousness of conformity or non-conformity of our actions to God's will or the immutable moral law (the divine mind). This consciousness-conscience in man, in turn, is closely linked to his/her own mind, but not quite identical with it in the present (fallen) condition. Formally, the mind

13. See ibid., 55. Cf. Chaadaev, "Fragments," 144.
14. Chaadaev, "Philosophical Letters," 30.
15. Cf. ibid., 35.
16. Cf. ibid., 36.
17. Ibid., 46.
18. Cf. ibid., 48.
19. Cf. ibid., 53.
20. Ibid., 86.
21. Chaadaev, "Fragments," 131.
22. Cf. ibid., 112.
23. Ibid., 137.

cannot perceive, i.e., be conscious, and thus our current *Self* (*le moi actuel*) appears, but it is defective without initiation (return) to the divine mind. Christ gives us a perfect example of the moral and rational identity and hence the objective of a conscious movement toward a given identity, which is the main problem of the modern philosophy in its anthropological, rather than historical, dimension.

St. Innocent of Kherson

While the study of the philosophical heritage by Chaadaev has a long tradition, we cannot say the same about St. Innocent of Kherson. For all the uniqueness and originality of his theological works, they still have not found a thoughtful and careful researcher. Below I will address only those of their aspects that are most typical for the problem dealt with in this chapter.

The focus of St. Innocent's attention is, of course, Christ, and the saint gained all-Russian popularity due to the work *The Last Days of Jesus Christ's Earthly Life*, in which he tried to fill not only historical, but also psychological gaps in the Gospel narrative that, perhaps, obscured the dogmatic side of his teachings about Christ. The latter focuses mostly on the story of the Gethsemane praying of Christ. St. Innocent assumed that at this point through the special action of the divine will of Jesus was not only deprived of his divinity consciousness, but felt all of the weakness of the fallen human nature, the overcoming of which was, apparently, a matter of his personal hypostatic will. Otherwise, according to St. Innocent, we cannot imagine him as the model of the moral perfection for ourselves.

Such an approach may not require clarification of how the saint imagined the connection of the natural and the personal in Christ. On the one hand, using the traditional theological concepts of nature and a person, on the other hand, the saint combines them with the philosophical terminology of the modern times. Indeed, a person, according to his definition, is "a thinking creature, which has the arbitrariness and the unity of consciousness,"[24] having a "mental and moral autonomy,"[25] "his mind, his will, his power, his way of acting, as it is attributed to the subject—oneself."[26]

Thus, these definitions clearly show the outlines of the self-conscious Self of the new philosophy. The latter causes a number of problems, both in triadology and in christology: in the former, the problem of the correlation of the personal and natural will in the Persons of the Trinity (the personal

24. Innokentiy Khersonskiy, *Sochineniya*, 6:812.

25. Ibid., 712.

26. Ibid., 701.

and natural knowledge, the personal and natural actions); in the latter, the need for the presence of human *Self*, consequently, there should be *consciousness* inherent in the human nature.

In the first case, the saint stresses the difference between the consciousness of the divine persons and the human consciousness. The latter tends to be split in two, in a sense that a person is able to simultaneously see himself/herself as a source of several heterogeneous aspirations, which in turn comes from the fact that apart from the Self as the ultimate source of our aspirations, we feel the supreme law that is put into us, which requires its execution.[27] There is no such duality in God, "there the will is itself the law,"[28] that is why it is best to imagine God "as free in the highest extent" and to reduce to the concept of freedom all divine actions.[29] In this formulation of the issue there is apparently no problem of difference between the natural and hypostatic (gnomic) will by virtue of their actual identity.

The second, christological, problem is resolved by the saint as follows: although the "human nature cannot be unconscious, but [in Christ] it knows itself not alone, but in a way that its consciousness it filled with the divine consciousness, and thus makes the same thing with it."[30] Moreover, while the connection of the deity with humanity happens instantly and forever at the moment of Incarnation, the discovery of the divine consciousness in Christ takes place gradually, after his humanity has become conscious:[31] this makes it possible to explain as a manifestation of human ignorance (about the last day), as well as human weakness (in the Garden of Gethsemane), the overcoming of which is, in fact, the highest moral merit of Christ.[32] And to the question how the deity united with humanity in its entirety, and at the same time could remain unconscious, the saint answers directly, "it is a mystery."[33]

This response does not relieve us, however, from thinking about the consequences of St. Innocent's theological intentions, but now it is more important to focus on the fact that the doctrine of Christ is closely linked by St. Innocent with the doctrine of the church and of the person, and it is here that we encounter a number of surprising parallels to the ideas of Chaadaev.

27. Ibid., 678–79.

28. Ibid., 3:666.

29. Ibid.

30. Ibid., 6:812–13.

31. Ibid., 494.

32. Ibid.

33. Ibid.

The forties saw a dispute of St. Filaret with the then hieromonk Macarius (Bulgakov) about the place that the doctrine of the church should take in the dogmatic system. Macarius put it at the beginning, based on the ideas that the dogmatic sets forth first of all the teaching of the church. St. Filaret insisted that the best and based on the patristic tradition structure is given in the Creed, where the part about the church stands after the presentation of faith in the Holy Trinity. St. Innocent gives his own concept that is dramatically different from both points of view in his treatise, *Jesus Christ—the Redeemer of the Human Race*, putting the teaching of the church in the section where he considers the *royal* ministry of Christ: the church in this sense is the *kingdom* par excellence, however, a special kingdom, the kingdom of Christ. According to the saint, the lack of a relevant teaching in the Russian theological systems is a consequence of the Protestant influence. Protestants have neither church, no hierarchy, so the treatise on the church by the theologians who are following them was not related to the rest of the teaching, in the meantime, "the best place for the doctrine of the church is here, in the treatise of the kingdom of Jesus Christ, but here it still stands in none of our systems."[34]

Actually, Christ has power over the whole of humanity, but the church is his kingdom in a special sense that is highlighted by the well-known evangelical metaphors, "signifying the closest connection of one thing with the other."[35] The purpose of this kingdom is the restoration of the human race that is the victory over sin and death. Although Christ who dwells in eternity is the permanent and invisible head of this kingdom, we cannot say that it is not of this world. First, it is present in the world as the church on earth guided and taught by the hierarchy, which originates from Christ.[36] Second, the triumph of the future kingdom of Christ is prepared in the history: although mankind is not yet ready to live in direct theocracy,[37] but the triple alliance of the European monarchs concluded in the name of the Holy Trinity can be considered as one of the first steps in this direction.[38] Third, the kingdom is partly similar to the kingdoms of the world, including, for example, that there also exists its legislation, its rewards and its punishment, anathema to the church is "the same as political death in the state."[39] However, the laws of the kingdom are followed by its subjects not with their own

34. Ibid., 855–56.

35. Ibid., 857.

36. Ibid.

37. Ibid., 771.

38. Ibid., 862.

39. Ibid., 865.

forces, but by the power of grace, and with regards to the political societies the kingdom of Christ acts with moral rather than political means,[40] but those who are looking for the kingdom of God get the comforts as well, such as "long life, health, fame and respect."[41] Moreover, European civilization owes its successes to Christianity: even if it was not immediately found, but now "we can clearly see that the Christian nations have become dominant and control almost the whole world."[42]

At the same time, like Chaadaev, St. Innocent justifies the future unity of humanity in Christ from the anthropological point of view as well. When he says that Christ is the ideal and model for man, it means not only that he is our moral model (although this is very important), but also something more, "man was created in the image of Jesus Christ";[43] the image of God "has a face,"[44] in a sense, obviously, that is concentrated in the face of the Lord Jesus: "Jesus Christ has all perfections, which can touch a human heart with love. Our heart loves what is like itself. We can't see God; but Jesus Christ comes to us in a human form."[45]

And vice versa, if Christ is the image of God, given to us, we find the same image of God inside; that is why the knowledge of ourselves is so important to us, because all the best that we can say about God, can in turn be derived from this knowledge.[46] But this division into external and internal is a consequence of the Fall, man used to be one with God, and once again has to be united with him, as "there should be one mind, one will, one consciousness in the world."[47]

From this perspective, the concept of "consciousness" that has several levels is extremely important for St. Innocent. First, he links it with the concept of "self-personality," *Self*. The latter, being the point of connection of the soul forces: mind, feelings, will, "is mysterious in itself, lies in infinity"[48] and cannot be determined. Second, consciousness is conscience, the word that in every language expresses the same, a shared knowledge, a co-knowledge, and, as the saint writes, "in this case only co- is ours; but there is always someone else who knows us inside. This is God acting incessantly in our

40. Ibid., 644.
41. Ibid., 865.
42. Ibid., 781.
43. Ibid., 202.
44. Ibid.
45. Ibid., 290.
46. Ibid., 78.
47. Ibid., 290.
48. Ibid., 201.

hearts."[49] In other words, "conscience is consciousness, our participation in the knowledge of the divine,"[50] which takes place in three ways: the consciousness of the law, the consciousness of our thoughts and actions, and the verdict on them in terms of the law.

How does what is said relate to the freedom of man? On the one hand, the important evidence is the revelation of our own *Self*, which clearly shows us our freedom,[51] on the other, it does not deny the impact on us of God's grace, as to take action, does not mean to feel it, and God often does not want "through the perceptible opening of his actions to man to violate his identity . . . so that man could act with greater freedom, and so that's why his actions were morally higher and worthier God."[52]

In addition, since the concepts of *possibility* and *evil* cannot be applied to God, so far for him and only for him "freedom is the moral need as well,"[53] not connected with choice, which is an essential accessory of human freedom. Hence only God can be attributed an autonomous morality in the strict sense, "other creatures, as they are dependent themselves, then their morality comes partly from them, and partly from outside."[54] Hence another, even more important conclusion: since the concept of freedom is inseparably connected with the idea of an individual having the moral autonomy, the moral created beings "have a dual personality, private, or individual, and general."[55] This personal duality is again a consequence of the Fall: it disappears in Christ, in whom humanity is imbued with divinity until the loss of consciousness, and its overcoming is a matter of the future transformation of humanity, when the church covers the whole humanity, and all have "a general movement and feeling,"[56] when our consciousness is so imbued with the divine that it loses a sense of *Self*, and a man who now says: *I do*, will then say: *God does*.[57] This is the result.

49. Ibid., 180.

50. Ibid.

51. Ibid., 736.

52. Ibid., 902.

53. Ibid., 684.

54. Ibid., 851. Thus St. Innocent gives an answer to the Kantian doctrine of autonomous morality. In general, the criticism of Kant often takes place in his lectures.

55. Ibid., 851.

56. Ibid., 292.

57. Ibid., 293. Cf. ibid., 6:820.

Conclusion

It is not difficult to find it for the first paragraph of the teaching. As it has already been mentioned, the fact that the source of Chaadaev's concept of the church were the ideas of de Maistre has been firmly established and St. Innocent might also have been familiar with it. This is supported by one of his arguments, in which we can easily see the response to the well-known de Maistre's thesis about the "necrosis" of the Greek Church: "The Greek Church, in comparison with the other churches, reveals some lateness, or some semi-necrosis, which is an inevitable consequence of its external circumstances."[58] Moreover, the St. Innocent's texts often contain the statement that the position of the Orthodox Church must be the middle between the extremes of Catholicism and Protestantism, and his own concept of the church-kingdom, which has no analogues neither in the previous nor in the subsequent national tradition, is in fact a milder version of de Maistre's concept, fundamentally different from it only in one point, rejection of the need for a symbol of the church unity personalized in the pope. As for the extremes of Protestantism, then the prelate's definition of religion "from inside" as a moral divine kingdom, is reminiscent of the church-kingdom of Kant. Here, by the way, we could assume that Chaadaev, compared with de Maistre, who put more emphasis on the progressive development of the church, used the Kantian theory of moral progress.

It is more difficult to establish unequivocally the source for the second, anthropological, point of the teaching. In any case, the obvious closeness to both Chaadaev's anthropology and the anthropology of St. Innocent is found in the doctrine of the soul by Gotthilf Heinrich von Schubert, Schelling's well-known student, who saw in conscience a sense of unity between people, which on the spiritual level reveals itself as "a sense of God's will that is always good and the human will that is so often wrong."[59] No doubt that St. Innocent was familiar with Schubert;[60] it is probable that Chaadaev was also familiar with him.

As it has already been mentioned, St. Innocent's concept of the church did not have a direct continuation, while the one by Chaadaev with its pathos of the transfiguration of earthly society in the church, of course, proved to be in demand in the Russian religious and philosophical ideas in the late nineteenth and early twentieth century. In contrast,

58. Ibid., 3:663.

59. Schubert, *Die Geschichte der Seele*, 2:268–69, 276, 489.

60. It was at the insistence of St. Innocent, rector of the Kiev Theological Academy, that the teaching of psychology, which was read by Feofan Avsenev "by Schubert," as it was testified by the contemporaries, was introduced.

the anthropology of St. Innocent, who introduced the terminology and problems of the German philosophical idealism in the Russian theological tradition for the first time, eventually gave its rich fruits to Russian theological and philosophical personalism.

Finally, the parallelism of concepts discussed by the authors clearly shows an objective demand for the "examination" conducted by them independently of each other, "expertise" of the ideas that appeared at that time in the field of view of the Russian tradition, and that at first glance were external and alien to it; and it also shows that the intellectual fragmentation of the secular and ecclesiastical elite was not perhaps as big as it seems to us today.

Bibliography

Chaadaev, Peter. "Fragments and Various Thoughts." In *Philosophical Works of Peter Chaadaev*, edited by Raymond T. McNally and Richard Tempest, 112–255. Dordrecht: Springer, 1991.

———. "The Philosophical Letters Addressed to a Lady." In *Philosophical Works of Peter Chaadaev*, edited by Raymond T. McNally and Richard Tempest, 18–101. Dordrecht: Springer, 1991.

Chaadayev, Petr. "Pis'ma." In *Polnoe sobranie sochineniy i izbrannye pis'ma*, 1:6–409. Moscow: Nauka, 1991.

Innokentiy Khersonskiy i Tavricheskiy, arkhiepiskop. *Sochineniya*. 6 vols. Saint Petersburg: I. L. Tuzov, 1908.

Maistre, Joseph de. *Du pape*. Paris: Charpentier, 1843.

Schubert, Gotthilf Heinrich von. *Die Geschichte der Seele*. 2 vols. Stuttgart und Tübingen: J. G. Cotta'sher Verlag, 1850.

9

Chaadaev and Tyutchev

History, System, and Chaos[1]

Atsushi Sakaniwa

Peter Chaadaev and Fedor Tyutchev are outstanding representatives of nineteenth-century Russian thought. Of course, Tyutchev is currently appreciated primarily as a poet, but in his own lifetime he was regarded as the "lion of the season"[2] in social circles, on account of his European political and social views. He was also regarded as a brilliant analyst and admired for his intellect. Moreover, he was a famous dandy, no less popular in high society than Tyutchev was. Both figures possessed particular worldviews that did not coincide with either the Slavophiles or Westernizers models.

Different researchers have different views about when the friendship between the two began,[3] but there is some consensus that it was the mid-forties, after Tyutchev returned to his homeland. The two of them were regarded as mutually incompatible "antipodes" and—at the same time—true friends. Tyutchev wrote of Chaadaev: "[He is] the person with whom I agree less than anyone else and which, however, I love most of all."[4] On Chaadaev's attitude toward Tyutchev, Ivan Aksakov wrote that Tyutchev "could not help loving him, could not help recognizing that he

1. This paper is based on my article in Japanese: "Tyutchev and Chaadaev: History, System and Chaos," *Roshia Bunka Kenkyu* 11 (2004) 63–74.

2. Pigarev, *Zhizn' i tvorchestvo Tyutcheva*, 119. This expression belongs to Peter Vyazemsky, who was a friend of both Tyutchev and Chaadaev.

3. Boris Tarasov speculates that the two men attended a party celebrating the engagement of Tyutchev's cousin to Chaadaev's friend in 1822, or that they perhaps met in Carlsbad in the summer of 1825. See Tarasov, "Tyuchev i Chaadaev."

4. Zhikharev, "Dokladnaya zapiska," 108.

was European, more European than Tyutchev himself."[5] Their heated discussions sometimes bothered those around them.

Until now, many researchers have explored the theme of "Chaadaev and Tyutchev." For example, Yuriy Lotman, whose analysis of Tyutchev's views on the papacy and monarchy hinted at the polarity in the opinions held by the contemporaries.[6] Richard Tempest considered the thinkers responses and correspondence and introduced their friendship to us.[7] But, in my opinion, his comparative analysis of their views is not detailed enough. Boris Tarasov explored their thoughts in relation to Slavophilia and the philosophy of Friedrich Shelling, noting Tyutchev's "humility" and Chaadaev's "reasonable faith." He also pointed to the fact that neither of them could sincerely turn to religion. Further, Tarasov opposed their views about Christianity (Catholicism and the papacy).[8] I largely agree with Tarasov's findings but I think that the difference between their views, which Lotman describes as "mirrors facing one another"[9] merits a deeper and more dynamic analysis. Setting aside their understandings of Christianity, I would like to focus on the similarities and differences found in the thought of Chaadaev and Tyutchev.

Fragile "I" and "History"

First of all, I would like to introduce a poem written by Tyutchev. This untitled short poem was written at a time when Chaadaev was already in the public eye, following the publication of the "First Philosophical Letter." Tyutchev and Chaadaev were friends at that time.

Holy night ascended the horizon,
It would consoling day around itself,
The gallant day, so like a golden cloak,
A cloak flung mantling over the abyss.[10]

At first the poem was called "Identity." Here before the world of night, man stands alone, exposed—like a homeless orphan:

Each man, so like a homeless orphaned child,

5. Aksakov, *Biografiya Tyutcheva*, 70.
6. Lotman, "Tyutchev i Dante," 595–98.
7. Tempest, "Chaadaev and Tiutchev."
8. Tarasov, "Tyuchev i Chaadayev."
9. Lotman, "Tyutchev i Dante," 598.
10. Tyutchev, *Poems and Political Letters*, 74.

Now stands alone, feeble, frail, and naked.
Face to face with the somber bottomless pit.
Abandoned now entirely to himself,
His mind annulled, his reason meaningless,
And in his soul, as plunged in an abyss,
He finds no aid without, nor any bound.[11]

Such a fragile existence reminds us of the Russian people, whom Chaadaev portrayed in his *Philosophical Letters* as unrelated to humanity, belonging "to none of the great families of mankind . . . neither of the West nor of the East."[12] He went on to write that the Russians were "illegitimate children."[13] Therefore Chaadaev offered them entry into Europe.

Similarly, Tyutchev, a few years after Russia's defeat in the Crimean War, likened Russia to an unconscious person. Analogically, Chaadaev wrote that "nations must first learn to know and appraise themselves just as individuals do."[14] Thus, both bind personal identity and national identity. They judge and condemn the state and the people from the viewpoint of "history." Chaadaev wrote in his "First Letter": "We possess the traditions of neither [West nor East]"[15] and "we live only in the narrowest of presents, without past and without future, in the midst of a flat calm."[16]

In addition, Chaadaev insisted in the "Sixth Philosophical Letter" that "moral being is nothing other than being as created by the ages."[17] As if echoing Chaadaev, Tyutchev wrote the article "Russia and Germany" in 1844. There he observed that Russia did not hold a number of historical stages in common with Europe, such as feudalism, the papal hierarchy, religious wars and the Inquisition.

Both Chaadaev and Tyutchev could look at Russia from outside, from the position of the West and this was a crucial similarity between them. Still, as Tyutchev added in the poem "Russia and Germany," "the real apologist for Russia is 'history.'"[18] In a letter to his wife he wrote: "In humankind nothing is more human than the need to connect the past with the present." And again: "'to restore the chain of time'—that is the most urgent need of

11. Ibid.
12. Chaadaev, "Philosophical Letters," 34.
13. Ibid., 37.
14. Ibid., 115.
15. Ibid., 34.
16. Ibid., 36.
17. Ibid., 124.
18. Tyutchev, *Poems and Political Letters*, 160.

my being."[19] Thus, we can see, in both thinkers, a desire to embark on a movement from the point of view of "history" and a desire to understand the relationship between Russia and the individual.

Civilization = Europe = Christianity

I would like to examine further the two thinkers views on the problem of "Russia and Europe," especially the meaning of the equation "Civilization = Europe = Christianity." Tyutchev observed in *Russia and Germany* that only "Western Europe" is recognize as "Europe." But besides her, there is another Europe—"Eastern Europe," which includes Russia. At the same time, Tyutchev united the two Europes under the common concept of "Christianity." In 1848, in a letter to Peter Vyazemsky, he wrote, "The very great inconvenience of our situation is that we are compelled to call Europe, what until now we have called only 'Civilization.'"[20] Here, Tyutchev emphasizes the artificiality of separating Russia from other European countries. To understand the pattern at work here, just remember that, as a diplomat, Tyutchev advocated the preservation of the "Holy Alliance," then the European order, on the basis of Christianity.

Chaadaev in the "First Letter," considered Christianity the basis of all the peoples of Europe: "all Europe was called Christendom"[21] and "it is Christianity which has accomplished everything in Europe."[22] Moreover, he emphasized that it was Christianity that separated "us" from civilized Japanese and Christian Abyssinians, that "we" as Christians had been civilized in Europe.[23]

Yet Chaadaev insisted that Russia had to accept not Orthodox Christianity, but Catholicism and the papacy. Only through this other path could "we" get into Europe, in their divine earthly kingdom built by Providence, because "Our exotic civilization has so driven us toward Europe that, even though we do not have its ideas, we have no other language; we must, therefore, speak it."[24]

In "The Roman Question" (1850), Tyutchev also touched on the prospect of a united and universal church, but placed Orthodoxy at its center. As noted by Lotman, this view naturally concludes with a theory

19. Kozhinov, *Tyutchev*, 273–74.

20. Tyutchev to Peter Vyazemsky, March 1848, 444.

21. Chaadaev, "Philosophical Letters," 38.

22. Ibid., 46.

23. Ibid., 44.

24. Ibid., 152.

of Empire—a European Christian Empire, united under a Russian Tsar. The views of the two thinkers differ, then, in terms of who is placed at the center of the whole system—the pope or the tsar. Yet both imagined "the European world under one church." Both of them began with the equation "Civilization = Europe = Christianity."

Catholicism and the Papacy

We will now consider the opinions Tyutchev and Chaadaev held on Catholicism and the papacy. In "The Roman Question," Tyutchev recognized Rome as the root of the Western European world, that it was the Pope around whom the Christian system was created. At the same time, he wrote that Rome was setting up "a kingdom of Christ as a kingdom of this world"[25] and the Catholic Church "ceased to be a society of the faithful freely united in spirit and truth under the law of Christ in the midst of the great human society. It became an institution, a political power—a state within a state."[26]

Tyutchev recognized the value of the Catholic Church as a social system, but criticized it for straying from the original principle of Christianity. At the end of the article, he expressed his dream for the reunification of the two churches and, with deep emotion, wrote about the Tsar's 1846 visit to Rome. He dreamed about the unification of the social systems built by Catholicism and Orthodoxy, in a new unity, at the top of which would stand the Russian Tsar.

All of Chaadaev's *Philosophical Letters* praised the social system of Catholicism, but believed that the changes in the church and the papacy would occur, on the contrary, on the demand of "history." He said: "It is not the papacy which made western history, as our friend Tiutchev seems to believe, but it is completely on the contrary that history there which made the papacy."[27] In this sad statement, Chaadaev himself points to the yawning gap between himself and his friend-antipode.

Ivan Aksakov's evaluation of Tyutchev is based on the position of Chaadaev: "Chaadaev was deeply distressed, even annoyed, by Tyutchev's indecent and incomprehensible aberration, Russophilia, because he recognized Tyutchev's bright scientific knowledge, acquired directly from Europe."[28]

25. Tyutchev, *Poems and Political Letters*, 191.

26. Ibid., 192.

27. Chaadaev to Princess Ekaterina Dolgorukova, 22 January 1848, Chaadaev, "Fragments," 220.

28. Aksakov, *Biografiya Tyutcheva*, 70.

The two do differ in terms of results. But we must say that both look at the same events through the correlation of history and the papacy.

The Individual and Society

Removing the aforementioned essential difference, the thoughts of the two figures seem very similar, especially in terms of the balance between individual and society. Researchers have noted the anti-individualism in Tyutchev, who feared the overestimation of the "Ego" or personality. In the incomplete collection of his articles *Russia and the West*, Tyutchev wrote that revolution is the apotheosis of the "human self" in the most literal sense of the word.

Chaadaev, in the "Seventh Letter," following Pascal's "the whole succession of men is but one man who abides always," wrote: "Man has no other mission than the annihilation of his personal being and the substitution for it of a perfectly social or impersonal being."[29] In Chaadaev's philosophy, the principle of identity plays a very important role. Mikhail Gershenzon called this Chaadaev's "social mysticism."[30]

Their general preference for public order, personal freedom, a common commitment to organic and historic unity, their monarchism and providentialism make it possible to compare their position with Catholic conservatism, especially with the view of the Sardinian diplomat, Joseph de Maistre, who lived in Russia between 1803 and 1817. At this time, during the reign of Alexander I, Maistre had a certain influence over the Russian nobility. Among those he influenced was Chaadaev. Mariya Degtyareva wrote of Chaadaev's idea "Russia is not associated with Providence" that it seemed very original at first glance, but it is so similar to de Maistre's views that the lines appear to have been "written by the same hand."[31] Tyutchev's friend Ivan Gagarin, who became Catholic, called Tyutchev the "Orthodox de Maistre."[32] We can say that, in his own worldview, Tyutchev was like Maistre, except that Orthodoxy stood at the center of his thought. Of course, that is a sizable difference.

Still, it seems natural to assume that both Tyutchev and Chaadaev received the Catholic conservative idea of looking at Europe as an organic and historic unity. Both evaluated Europe with nearly the same system of ideas.

29. Chaadaev, "Philosophical Letters," 136.

30. Gershenzon, *Chaadayev*, 93.

31. Degtyareva, "Osobyy russkiy put'," 98.

32. Gagarin to Aleksandra Bakhmeteva, 16(28) October 1874, 45.

However, it is very important to note that, in their reflections formed within the framework of Catholic conservatism, an important role is played by "chaos" and the sense of fear toward said chaos.

Joseph de Maistre was Catholic, and of the Catholic universe. Chaadaev, although committed to that universe, stands outside it and Tyutchev, meanwhile, stands at the cusp. It seems to me that this sense of "chaos" brings Tyutchev and Chaadaev even closer to one another.

Systems, Chaos, and Visibility

Vadim Kozhinov formulated a common position for Tyutchev and Chaadaev "that strongly separates them from the Slavophiles" and "many Westerners": "Despite all the differences between them, the poet and the thinker were in the most profound and common beliefs. So, for them, like Pushkin, there was a paramount state, the governmental idea inextricably linked with Russia's role in the world."[33] Both thinkers held strict form and completeness of system in the highest regard, perhaps above content. By the way, I think that this position is largely due to the fact that neither could be truly religious people. In their thoughts on the theme "Russia and Europe," "system" plays a vital role.

Gershenzon writes about the "extraordinary system" he finds in the *Philosophical Letters*:

> It is the mind, unable to live outside the theoretical world, though very close to the scheme. By his nature, Chaadaev can't put up with vague, uncertain and disorderly things. He needs all to be in harmony and unity. Moreover, unity and continuity are the two main categories of his thinking, two tools, which discipline violently chaotic phenomena.[34]

Chaadaev's system exists to discipline the chaos. Thus it is his concept of unity and continuity that will enable us to understand his attitude toward Europe. The object, whatever falls out of system (which we could call Europe), will become chaos.

As shown in "Eighth Letter," for Chaadaev, "the earthly kingdom of Christianity" is the goal of humanity and Providence. In this context, thinking about the historical role of the Russian nation in a letter to Adolphe de Circourt, he wrote that the people "embraces the sublime beliefs of the Bible in their primitive expression such as they were conceived by the majority of

33. Kozhinov, *Tyutchev*, 303.

34. Gershenzon, *Chaadayev*, 94.

the faithful before the movement of Christian society had imprinted upon them the social character."[35] In his opinion, Russia is in a state of "chaos." Therefore, Russia has to be disciplined by Catholicism.

When comparing Chaadaev's "chaos" with Tyutchev's, one should pay close attention to the fact that Chaadaev mentions the clarity and rigor of perception several times. In his "Second Letter," speaking of the road to "celestial tradition," he wrote: "ever-shining [guiding] star that no cloud has ever veiled, visible to all eyes."[36] Within the radiance of the divine light, the human mind understands all. In other words, outside of this mind, there is only "chaos," from which Chaadaev wanted to escape. In the "Sixth Letter," assessing the papacy, he notices that it is a human institution, but "what is certain is that in its day it derived essentially from the true spirit of Christianity" and it is "a visible symbol of unity."[37] That's why he appreciates the Catholic faith and the papacy. On the contrary, he calls the Protestant church "*invisible*" and evaluates it as "*nothingness*."

In the poetic world of Tyutchev, his concept of "visibility" is different from Chaadaev's. For example, in his poem "Day and Night," the night world is represented by the image of the "abyss" with "its horror and gloom,"[38] and is thus identical to "chaos." But this "chaos" is hidden, covered with a "gold-brocaded cloak" of day.[39] At night, when cover of day is removed, the world of "chaos" becomes visible. That is also the theme of the poem "Why are you wailing so, night wind": "night soul's world" "thirsts to merge itself with infinitude."[40] Let us return briefly to the poem I referenced at the beginning of this paper. There is a man, touching "chaos." In the night world, a world of "chaos," a man understands his family heritage.

In the works of Tyutchev, while "chaos" is indeed terrible, it is, at the same time, as noted by Yuriy Lotman, "creative and fruitful beginning."[41] This is the fundamental difference between the concepts of "chaos" in Tyutchev and Chaadaev.

35. Chaadaev to Adolphe de Circourt, 15 June 1846, Chaadaev, "Fragments," 203.

36. Chaadaev, "Philosophical Letters," 65.

37. Ibid., 132.

38. Tyutchev, *Poems and Political Letters*, 66.

39. Ibid.

40. Ibid., 48.

41. Lotman, "Poeticheskiy mir Tyutcheva," 581.

Conclusion: the Fear of Chaos

When assessing the Russian history, Chaadaev and Tyutchev used the same system of relations: "Civilization = Europe = Christianity." This relationship ensures order. Yet, at the same time, they see the presence of unavoidable "chaos." The relationships the two thinkers had to this "chaos" differed. Chaadaev sees "chaos" and tries to understand how he might convert it into order. For him, there is only what is immediately given to us. Tyutchev, on the other hand, emphasizes that the "chaos" is in the system, or rather "under" the system and outside the visible world.

This "chaos," of course, is Russia. Thus Tyutchev's famous aphorism:

> Not by the mind is Russia understood.
> Nor is she measured by a common rule:
> She has a special stature of her own;
> In Russia one can only put his faith.[42]

Chaadaev thought more or less the same thing, but he didn't want to place unwavering faith in Russia.

The Soviet philosopher Georgiy Gachev called Tyutchev's Russia "the Cosmos of Chaos," and wrote that Chaadaev, in his philosophy of history, demonstrates the impossibility of "the Russian cosmos."[43] I agree with this but I can't with the following words, which also belong to Gachev: For Tyutchev "Chaadaev's theory is Nonsense."[44]

Chaadaev stands outside the cosmos, in the world of "chaos." He probably felt "chaos" on a deeper level than Tyutchev did, who only stood at the threshold; he never experienced the fear that Chaadaev did. But, perhaps, Tyutchev, a European-educated Russian, understood the meaning of Chaadaev's fear. Perhaps this was the source of the friendship of the two antipodes.

The ideas of two great thinkers—"mirrors facing one another"—complement each other, continue to live and be relevant in the modern civilized world.

42. Tyutchev, *Poems and Political Letters*, 144.

43. Gachev, "Tyutchev," 863.

44. Ibid., 864.

Bibliography

Aksakov, Ivan. *Biografiya Fedora Ivanovicha Tyutcheva*. Moscow: Kniga i biznes, 1997.

Chaadaev, Peter. "Fragments and Various Thoughts." In *Philosophical Works of Peter Chaadaev*, edited by Raymond T. McNally and Richard Tempest, 112–255. Dordrecht: Springer, 1991.

———. "The Philosophical Letters Addressed to a Lady." In *Philosophical Letters and Apology of a Madman*, 29–160. Translated by Mary-Barbara Zeldin. Knoxville: University of Tennessee Press, 1969.

Degtyareva, Mariya. "'Osobyy russkiy put' glazami 'zapadnikov': de Mestr i Chaadayev." *Voprosy filosofii* 8 (2003) 97–106.

Gachev, Georgiy. "Tyutchev." In *F. I. Tyutchev: pro et contra*, edited by Konstantin Isupov, 862–67. Saint Petersburg: Izdatel'stvo Russkogo Khristianskogo Gumanitarnogo Universiteta, 2005.

Gagarin, Ivan. Letter to Aleksandra Bakhmeteva. 16(28) October 1874. In *Literaturnoye nasledstvo*, edited by Sergey A. Makashin et al., 97:42–45. Moscow: Nauka, 1989.

Gershenzon, Mikhail. *Chaadaev: zhizn' i myshleniye*. The Hague: Mouton, 1968.

Kozhinov, Vadim. *Tyutchev*. Moscow: Soratnik, 1994.

Lotman, Yuriy. "Poeticheskiy mir Tyutcheva." In *O poetakh i poezii*, 553–94. Saint Petersburg: Iskusstvo, 1996.

———. "Tyutchev i Dante." In *O poetakh i poezii*, 595–98. Saint Petersburg: Iskusstvo, 1996.

Pigarev, Kirill. *Zhizn' i tvorchestvo Tyutcheva*. Moscow: AN SSSR, 1962.

Tarasov, Boris. "F. I. Tyuchev i P. Ya. Chaadaev. Zhiznennyye paralleli i ideynyye spory druzey-protivnikov." In *Tyutchev segodnya: Materialy IV Tyutchevskikh chteniy*, edited by Evgeniy Lebedev, 98–116. Moscow: Izdatel'stvo Literaturnogo Instituta, 1995.

Tempest, Richard. "Chaadaev and Tiutchev." *Studies in Soviet Thought* 32 (1986) 383–95.

Tyutchev, Fedor. Letter to Peter Vyazemsky, March 1848. In *Polnoye sobraniye sochineniy i pisem v 6 tomakh*, vol. 4, *Pis'ma 1820–1849*, 443–45. Moscow: Klassika, 2004.

———. *Poems and Political Letters of F. I. Tyutchev*. Translated by Jesse Zeldin. Knoxville: University of Tennessee Press, 1973.

Zhikharev, Mikhail I. "Dokladnaya zapiska potomstvu o Petre Yakovleviche Chaadaeve." In *Russkoye obshchestvo 30-kh godov XIX v.: Memuary sovremennikov*, edited by Ivan Fedosov, 48–119. Moscow: Izdatel'stvo Moskovskogo Gosudarstvennogo Universiteta, 1989.

10

On Some Features of Dissident Movement in Russia

The Sample of Peter Chaadaev

Andrew Schumann

Its own philosophy appeared perhaps too late in the Russian Empire, only emerging at the end of the nineteenth century. This fact can be explained by the fact that the university education in the Russian Empire started to be formed only in the eighteenth century under conditions which did not support the development of public discourse, namely: (1) the autocracy and rigid political censorship; (2) the low level of university education; (3) the accesses to university education only for a narrow part of noblemen; (4) the absence of editions of philosophical periodicals. Actually, on the one hand, there was no interest in philosophical texts because of the philosophical illiteracy of the Russian nobility as a whole, and, on the other hand, the political censorship made problematic any publication and distribution of free philosophical reflection.

Only at the beginning of the nineteenth century did an interest in European philosophy as an esoteric form of literature awaken within the framework of the common interest in European culture which grew in circles of the Russian nobility.

Peter Chaadaev, the Russian philosophical publicist, became one of the spokesmen of such an interest in philosophy as a mysterious and unclear literary genre in the literature of Europe. The interest in philosophy became a form of underground for Russian noblemen and Chaadaev was a famous representative of philosophy as an underground culture. In the pure meaning, Chaadaev cannot be considered even as philosopher. He was a publicist, who distributed short texts in the form of letters, written and sent out to different people. Chaadaev can be termed a "network thinker" or a "Facebook-thinker." Today Chaadaev would be a popular blogger and his philosophy would be reduced to popular writings on Facebook or Twitter. For him, philosophy was a genre of bright aphorisms. For example, on the Christian subject: "Christian immortality is life with the least amount of death, and not, as has been imagined, a life after death."[1] And also on political themes: "I prefer to wound my country, to afflict it, and to humiliate it rather than deceive it";[2] "The Russian liberal is a silly fly which flutters in a ray of sunshine; this sun is the western sun."[3] Chaadaev's popularity as a thinker among noble families increased rapidly due to his successful network communication. He conceived his activity as an aphoristic thinker as an original philosophy which was an alternative to the European one. He affirms that philosophy can be regarded as freethinking in France, as practice in England, as abstraction in Germany, and as a new form of network dialogue in Russia: "In France what does one do with thinking? One says it. What does one do with it in England? One practices it. What does one do with it in Germany? One digests it. What does one do with thinking in our country? Nothing at all, and do you know why?"[4] Most negatively, Chaadaev evaluates the German philosophy as unclear and esoteric:

> In Germany one sails along incessantly on the ocean of abstraction; the German is there more at home, more at ease than on earth; that is why there one carries intemperance of thought to the extreme. A very simple thing; why should pure thought without application, without body be restrained in its sailing? Where is the danger? When pure thought wishes to enter in life, when it becomes practical, when from the lofty region in which is soars, it comes to confront positive reality, then it must necessarily become moderated. But without that all the infinite space of nature would not be sufficient for it. Flaring up above all realities, it is always going to flare up: no reason for it to stop ever.[5]

It is evident that Chaadaev did not understand German philosophy at all.

The publicist activity of Chaadaev was very interesting for his contemporaries, but he was esoteric for them and unclear. As a result, in the context

1. Chaadaev, "Fragments," 141.
2. Ibid., 249.
3. Ibid.
4. Ibid., 138.
5. Ibid., 130.

of the Russian political censorship the contemporaries said about Chaadaev in extremely courteous and cautious terms: "I respect Chaadaev as philosopher, especially thanks to his thoughts on the Egyptian obelisks."[6]

Chaadaev considered himself as an outstanding Russian philosopher who is equal to the first-level European philosophers, and he expected to receive a high position in the sphere of national education from the Emperor. Meanwhile, he turned down a high position at the Finance Ministry.

After the publication of the *Philosophical Letters*, Chaadaev was announced as a madman. In response, Chaadaev changed the discourse format in the description of the Emperor and his decisions. So, in the *Apologia of a Madman* he designated the Emperor not in the standard way accepted among the contemporaries as Father and Monarch, but in a depersonalized form as "government": "After all, the government has only done its duty: it can even be said that the measures which it took in my case were completely liberal, since they did not exceed the expectation of the public. What could the most well-meaning government do other than conform to the general tone?"[7] In essence, in this designation there was something offensive for the Monarch. However, there were no direct negative estimations of the Sovereign.

The general meaning of Chaadaev's reply in the *Apologia of a Madman* is that philosophy must be accepted necessarily, although it is an alien cultural phenomenon, but, ultimately, it is useful for Russia. According to Chaadaev, all good had been borrowed in Russia from the outside:

> The most profound trait of our social physiognomy is spontaneity. Each fact in our history is an isolated fact, an imposed fact; each new idea, a detached idea, an imported idea. Therefore, we naturally lack the link between the event of the day and that of yesterday. But there is nothing in this point of view which could justly offend national sentiment. If it is true, it must be accepted, that is all.[8]

After the *Apologia of a Madman* Chaadaev definitively received the status of a dissident in the eyes of his contemporaries, although he was not a political opponent and furthermore a true political opposition. In particular, Chaadaev supported the bloody suppression of the November Uprising 1830–1831, mainly led by large segments of the society of modern-day Belarus:

6. Golubinskiy to Avdot'ya Elagina, 1 February 1833, 527.
7. Chaadaev, "Apologia of a Madman," 102.
8. Ibid., 105.

> After the suppression of the Polish revolt its main parties have been granted the refugee status in France. Using the small awareness of this country concerning the history and modern estate of Poland, they, without difficulty, could have represented their mad enterprise meriting not only pardons, but also praises.[9]

And further:

> Against the annexing of the present kingdom (of Poland) for the purpose of its transformation into a nucleus of new independent Poland, even with the assistance of several European states, a lot of educated Poles, in belief, would began to object that the well-being of people can be embodied only as a part of large political bodies and that, in particular, the Poles, the Slavonic people by nation, should share destinies of the fraternal people [Russians—A. S.] who are capable to enter so lots of force and prosperities to life of both people.[10]

In his opinion, the Poles were not worthy to have their own statehood, as well as both Belarusians and Ukrainians:

> The Poles constitute only one branch of the great Slavonic family. They, in olden time, constituted and now constitute population which is not numerous. The well-known Polish Republic during the time of its highest power was a state consisting of several nationalities, from them the Russians constituted the main body in the areas carrying the name: Belarus and Little Russia [today's Ukraine—A. S.]. This Russian population annexed to the Republic, united with the Poles only under the conditions to use all national laws and freedom, these rights were obeyed by the well-known *pacta conventa*. These rights and privileges have been roughly rejected with the course of time by Poland and constantly trampled among the most shocking religious prosecutions. As a consequence of these severe travails, the Russian areas were separated from the Republic and were incorporated to the family of the Slavonic people which accepted the name of the All-Russia Empire (in French: *L'Empire de toutes les Russes*). This separation, begun since 1651 and finished in the end of the eighteenth century, was an inevitable consequence of errors of the oppressing government, the intolerance of the Roman clergy and the quite natural draught of this part of Russian people to

9. Chaadaev, "Neskol'ko slov o pol'skom voprose," 512.

10. Ibid., 515.

dethrone the yoke of foreigners and to return to the bosom of own nationality.[11]

Hence, Chaadaev had a reputation as a dissident in Russian society, which focused interest on him even more and led to the distribution of Chaadaev's letters and aphorisms by the so-called *samizdat* (from the Russian expression "self-publishing"), copying by hands. Let us notice that the notion of dissident was introduced only in the sixties to designate representatives of the opposition movement of the USSR which did not try to struggle by violent means against the Soviet system and Marxist ideology, but appealed to the Soviet laws and officially proclaimed values. The dissidents in the USSR were not a political opposition in the narrow sense, but they were an intellectual underground—not obeying the dominating ideology and ignoring the stylistic and speech restrictions in the public discourse. Chaadaev has many features of the Soviet dissident and also he is not a political opponent in the pure sense.

A dissident movement is a phenomenon in Russia that represents an original subject for which there are no direct analogues to other discourses, including the West European discourse. The dissident movement is unique, first of all, as a special speech practice which is being embodied in a special way by a communicative community (*Kommunikationsgemeinschaft*) in the Karl-Otto Apel's meaning[12] where roles of speech behavioral agents are not typically distributed.

According to the late ideas of Ludwig Wittgenstein, any dialogue is performed within a language game (communicative community) and this game sets up a unique language. Therefore, any language is given within the contexts of the speech practice of concrete human groups involved in playing language games. Consequently, on the one hand, a universal language that would consolidate all people into a joint communication, i.e., into a joint game, is not possible, but, on the other hand, an individual language, i.e., a language of a single who was excluded from any possible communication is not possible, too. In this dimension, a universal ethics is also not possible. Ethics is always contextual to a given communicative community. Hence, following the Wittgenstein's late ideas, Apel developed a theory of the so-called applied ethics, i.e., the ethics which cannot be considered universal (because a universal language as such is inaccessible), and this ethics is limited by some discourses within concrete communicative communities.[13]

11. Ibid., 512–13.
12. See Apel, *Transformation der Philosophie*, 358–435.
13. See ibid.

In each communicative community there are membership rules, the so-called speech competence or "intersubjective arrangement (*Verstaendigung*) about language use."[14] The important element of speech competence consists in understanding and accepting basic roles of speech interaction agents. Examples of such roles[15] are as follows: (1) an epistemic role in the form of ability to train within the process of knowledge reception due to a self-critical cognitive-based relation to the objective reality; (2) a practical role in the form of ability to obey social norms; (3) a pathic role in the form of ability to self-critically consider an own subjective world.

Peter Chaadaev offered a special discourse in his *Philosophical Letters*. This discourse contained norms and rules which were frankly hostile to already existing norms and rules of public discourse for the nobility and officials in the Russian Empire at that time. This new discourse updated epistemic, practical, and pathic roles of speech behavior agents in a special way.

Chaadaev's public position, on the one hand, was regarded as a defiance for the society and an unjustified claim to the existing tradition of public dialogue, and, on the other hand, caused a strong interest of his contemporaries to him and, even more, it led to a movement of admirers of Chaadaev the person.[16] Actually, we can see the creation of an artificial, new communicative community which had some new rules and norms of public discourse and was parallel to already existing communicative communities of the Russian intelligence. In his response to the public negative reaction, the *Apologia of a Madman*, Chaadaev definitively set up a special dissident discourse. In this discourse the most important information is transmitted beyond official channels, in particular through the *samizdat* that the Soviet intelligence knew well. Thereby, Chaadaev became the first example of the Russian philosopher-dissident. Later, the given position was realized by different thinkers many times with, for instance, Alexander Zinoviev, the logician and publicist, became one of such thinkers.

In Chaadaev's dissident discourse, the Russian intellectual underground was formed for the first time. As well as for the Soviet dissidents, for Chaadaev it was so important to be recognized by Europe. And through the brothers Turgenev he sent a letter to Friedrich Wilhelm Joseph Schelling with the earnest entreaty to write a reply:

> I don't know whether you remember a young man of Russian nationality whom you saw at Karlsbad in 1825. He had the

14. Ibid., 381.

15. See Habermas, *Theory of Communicative Action*.

16. See Gershenzon, *Griboedovskaya Moskva*; Sverbeev, "Vospominaniya o Chaadaeve"; Khomyakov, "Neskol'ko slov o 'Filosoficheskom pis'me.'"

> opportunity of often conversing with you about philosophical subject and you did him the honor of saying to him that you got some satisfaction in communicating your thoughts to him. You told him, among other things, that you had modified your ideas on many points, and you advised him to await for the appearance of a new work, which you were writing then, in order to find our about your philosophy. This work has not appeared, and this young man was myself. In the meantime, sir, I have read all your writings. To say that following in your footsteps, I was elevated to those heights to which your genius has carried you by such a beautiful flight this would be, perhaps, presumptuous on my part . . . I would be very indiscreet, a man unknown in the European world, to pretend to surpass one of such great literary reknown; but you will permit me, I believe, to say to you, that the study of your works has opened a new world to me; by the light of your spirit I have been able to see imperfectly into the domain of spacial thought which had been entirely hidden from me, this study has been a source of fertile and delicious meditations for me . . . Today I just learned through a friend who lately has passed some days in your presence that you are teaching a philosophy of revelation.[17]

After one year later, Chaadaev received the following response from Schelling:

> During that time when we are finishing the work, already begun by us a long time ago in calm, which results are in establishing the new intellectual world that was till now inaccessible to philosophy, we are pleased to learn that other persons are on the same road as we, that they understand us in advance, and that not a poor and miserable spirit of individual, but a general spirit of time has excited us and has wished to emerge in us and through us.[18]

Schelling's reply meant for the Russian public circles that indisputably recognized the philosophical status of Chaadaev. Their correspondence was widely announced through Chaadaev's friends to be a true proof of that Chaadaev is a recent Russian philosopher at the European level, indeed. For this purpose Chaadaev needed this reply from Schelling.

Schelling was probably the most talented German philosopher in the whole history of German philosophy. He started to study at the Tübinge University in 1790, i.e., at fifteen years old, with the characteristic *ingenium*

17. Chaadaev to Schelling, 1832, Chaadaev, "Fragments," 153.

18. Chaadaev to Schelling, 1833, Chaadayev, "Pis'ma," 450.

praecox (early talent). In 1792 he graduated with his master's thesis, titled *Antiquissimi de prima malorum humanorum origine philosophematis Genes III. explicandi tentamen criticum et philosophicum*, and in 1795 he finished his doctoral thesis, entitled *De Marcione Paulinarum epistolarum emendatore* (*On Marcion as emendator of the Pauline letters*). In 1798, at the age of only twenty-three, Schelling became an extraordinary (i.e., unpaid) professor of philosophy at the University of Jena.

Schelling was one of the best friends of Georg Wilhelm Friedrich Hegel, who was five years older. However, Hegel did not show a special talent and Schelling was the leader in their friendship always. The relationships of the friends were sharply changed only in 1807, when Hegel published his first serious book, at age thirty-seven, the *Phänomenologie des Geistes* (*Phenomenology of Spirit*). From this moment on, the new star of Hegel promptly rose in the sky of philosophy, and Schelling's fell at age thirty-three, effectively becoming a philosophical pensioner. It was no wonder that it was so painful for him to see Hegel's rise and he began to hate Hegel and completely broke off their relationship.

For a long time, Schelling prepared his triumphal return to philosophy with a victory over Hegel. In this manner he represented before the public his lectures 1841–1842 in Berlin, under the general title *Philosophy of Revelation*. These lectures were heard by the best representatives of German society at that time—politicians, officers, militaries, university professors. Among the hearers there were Søren Kierkegaard, Mikhail Bakunin, Jacob Burckhardt, Alexander von Humboldt, Friedrich Engels, and many other brilliant thinkers.

Chaadaev also looked forward to Schelling's triumph over Hegel and wrote to Schelling the following letter:

> Since you did me the honor of writing to me, many things have taken place in the philosophical world, the one thing which interested me most was your appearance in the new theater to which a prince, a friend of genius, called you. As soon as I had learned of your arrival in Berlin, I wanted to address my good wishes to you for the success of your teachings in the center of German science; diverse circumstances, independent of my will hindered me from doing this; today I have only to felicitate you on your triumph. I don't presume to believe that my compliments could touch you infinitely, and if I had nothing else to say to you, perhaps I would have abstained from writing to you, but I couldn't resist the desire of informing you about our powerful interest in your present teaching, as well as profound feelings

> with which the small group of our philosophic minds greeted your entry into this new period of your glorious career.[19]

The expected triumph broke down. Schelling did not cause a public resonance for his ideas as he had hoped. He appeared to be underestimated by his contemporaries and yet, nevertheless, in the ideas of his lectures Schelling anticipated Heidegger's *Dasein*-analysis and existentialism.

Hegel's basic opening is in the historicity of concepts. The absolute spirit can comprehend himself in nature only due to the "science about phenomenological knowledge." The latter attends to a movement exclusively in the aspect of its organization comprehended in concept, in other words, it attends to history as a purely spiritual process, as such a formation that completely makes himself indirect. In other words, here "the goal, absolute knowledge, that is, spirit knowing itself as spirit, has the recollection of spirits as they are in themselves and as they achieve the organization of their realm."[20]

Schelling states that a true revelation of absolute spirit proceeds not in history, but in prehistory. There are two kinds of time: historic and prehistoric and establishing prehistory gives a starting point for the historic time:

> Thus, the historic and prehistoric times are not only relative differences of one and the same time, but they are two essentially different and disconnected, mutually exclusive times, and, therefore, they are limiting times. Since this is the main difference between both times that in prehistory the consciousness of mankind is subjected to an interior necessity, to a process which brings the mankind away from the external real world, while every people, which becomes by its internal decision to be a people, is established by the same crisis also from the same process as such and the people is free from that now to carry out own actions due to a more external, worldly and profane character making them historic.[21]

Obviously, all of the details of the philosophical dispute of Schelling and Hegel were absolutely obscure for Chaadaev since he did not have any special philosophical background. Chaadaev's choice to bear Schelling as an example for imitation was determined by the following circumstances:

1. His status of unrecognized genius in philosophy who only in the long-term future becomes a shining star.

19. Chaadaev to Schelling, 1842, Chaadaev, "Fragments," 182.
20. Hegel, *Phenomenology of Spirit*, 735.
21. Schelling, *Schriften zur Religionsphilosophie*, 588.

2. The status of religious thinker with a high Christian reflection.

Such a choice formed special features of the dissident-intellectual, the representative of the Russian intellectual underground:

1. The status of unrecognized genius.
2. The status of a prophet, who scattered symbolical aphorisms around himself.
3. The replacement of producing an intellectual product (books, researches) by a network dialogue.

The status of unrecognized genius and prophet is received easily, through posturing and shocking within the limits of network dialogues. A similar example was Alexander Zinoviev. He belonged to the Moscow Logical Circle—an informal association of students, post-graduate students, and graduates of Philosophical Faculty of the Moscow State University in 1952–1958, they were going to set up new foundations of dialectical (content-genetic) logic. However, he was not an outstanding logician and became popular in another way. In 1975 he wrote and distributed in the West his novel the *Yawning Heights* which was published in 1976 in Switzerland. This text was a satirical treatment of Soviet power. So, Zinoviev became the prominent Soviet dissident who coined the term *homo sovieticus.*

Thus, Chaadaev was a network thinker who has been excited by Schelling's public pose. He decided to transfer this pose to conditions of the Russian discourse, and to embody it. This pose is one of the dissident-intelligent who has a reputation as a prophet and unrecognized genius, but, at the same time, in the pure sense he does not make an intellectual product.

Bibliography

Apel, Karl-Otto, editor. *Sprachpragmatik und Philosophie*. Frankfurt am Main: Suhrkamp, 1976.

———. *Transformation der Philosophie*. Vol. 2. Frankfurt am Main: Suhrkamp, 1973.

Chaadaev, Peter. "Apologia of a Madman." In *Philosophical Works of Peter Chaadaev*, edited by Raymond T. McNally and Richard Tempest, 102–11. Dordrecht: Springer, 1991.

———. "Fragments and Various Thoughts." In *Philosophical Works of Peter Chaadaev*, edited by Raymond T. McNally and Richard Tempest, 112–255. Dordrecht: Springer, 1991.

———. "The Philosophical Letters Addressed to a Lady." In *Philosophical Works of Peter Chaadaev*, edited by Raymond T. McNally and Richard Tempest, 18–101. Dordrecht: Springer, 1991.

Chaadayev, Petr. "Neskol'ko slov o pol'skom voprose." In *Polnoe sobranie sochineniy i izbrannye pis'ma*, 1:512–15. Moscow: Nauka, 1991.

Gershenzon, Mikhail O. *Griboedovskaya Moskva. Chaadayev. Ocherki proshlogo.* Moscow: Izdatel'stvo Moskovskogo Gosudarstvennogo Uuniveriteta, 1989.

Golubinskiy, Fedor. Letter to Avdot'ya Elagina. 1 February 1833. In Petr Chaadayev, *Polnoe sobranie sochineniy i izbrannye pis'ma*, 2:526–27. Moscow: Nauka, 1991.

Habermas, Jürgen. *The Theory of Communicative Action.* Vol. 1. Translated by Thomas McCarthy. Boston: Beacon, 1994.

Hegel, Georg Wilhelm Friedrich. *Phenomenology of Spirit.* Translated by Terry Pinkard. Originally published 1807 as *Phänomenologie Des Geistes.* https://archive.org/details/GWFHegel1807PhanomenologieDesGeistesPhenomenologyOfSpirit.

Khomyakov Aleksey S. "Neskol'ko slov o 'Filosoficheskom pis'me,' napechatannom v 15 knizhke *Teleskopa* (Pis'mo k g-zhe N.)." In *Sochineniya v dvukh tomakh*, vol. 1, *Raboty po istoriosofii*, 449–55. Moscow: Moskovskiy filosofskiy fond, Izdatel'stvo Medium, 1994.

Schelling, Frierdich Wilhelm Joseph von. *Schriften zur Religionsphilosophie: 1841–1854.* In *Schellings Werke. Sechster Hauptband, Schriften zur Religions-philosophie, 1841–1854.* Munich: Beck, 1965.

Sverbeev, Dmitriy. "Vospominaniya o Petre Yakovleviche Chaadaeve." *Russkiy arkhiv* 6 (1868) 976–1002.

PART III

Influences

11

Peter Chaadaev

The Founding Myth of Russian Philosophy[1]

Janusz Dobieszewski

The founding myth is a concept relating in particular to the remote beginnings of human culture. It deals with the genesis and origins of the events of the history of culture, civilization, and social life which remain vital—due to their constant currency and perpetual presence in memory, or, at the very least, the unceasing attention granted them by historians. Yet, this concept is also applied to contemporary situations, occurrences taking place before our very eyes, when this idea is used to endow to such current events a special importance, profundity, deep rootedness. With the aid and through the use of the founding myth we attempt to penetrate the very birth of some important event which interests us and to describe its orientation coordinates in a way that would be symbolic and particularly significant. We are certain that somewhere at the origin of this phenomenon some defining quality was revealed, a quality demarcating its weak and vital points; that in this origin the given phenomenon was revealed in all its purity, authenticity, spontaneity, in all its perfectly expressed energy and vital power. We are aware that later on this phenomenon would be liable to complications and distortions through inner changes and outer influences and such alterations would in many aspects warp its truth, thus compelling the scholars to return in thought and interpretation precisely to the beginning.

1. The essay was written as part of the research project "Epistemology of the Religious Experience in Russian and Jewish Thought" supported by the grant of the National Science Center, Poland, no. 2014/13/B/HS1/00761.

Founding myths, it goes without saying, characterize religions—and religions themselves cultivate their founding myths with exceptional care and attention, as their central, continually actual and vibrant principles. Moreover, they are also associated with country states, social and political movements and even scientific disciplines. Thus, for instance, the founding myth of Christianity is the doctrine of Jesus as the son of God; of Buddhism—the awakening and enlightenment of Siddhartha Gautama; of Islam—the prophetic life of Muhammad; the founding myth of Russia—the call to the Varangians; of the French Republic—the taking of the Bastille; of the Soviet Union—the "Aurora's" shot; of the Polish People's Republic—the Manifesto of July 22; and of contemporary Poland—the Round Table; the founding myth of physics is Newton's apple or, perhaps, Archimedes's bathtub; and of the medical craft—the Hippocratic oath.

Founding myths refer to the legendary or fabulous settings, which are unverifiable, and yet highly suggestive, engaging the imagination and interpretative drive of the audience; they may also refer to real facts and actual events, though most frequently these are still characterized by ambiguity, remaining in the sphere of conjecture, lively disputes, controversies; the figures and events invoked are still subject to questions and doubts, and may not be safely filed away *ad acta* under any decisive heading. This initiates or even creates a demand for a certain atmosphere of mystery around the founding myth, lending an aura of particular uniqueness, exceptionality and charisma to the central figures of such myths. The founding myths constitute the turning points, critical episodes, a recapitulation which draws final conclusions of the state of the world as it was up until a given moment, but above all, this is the intrusion of a new, different world which initiates "the true beginning" in some field. Such intrusion may be direct (horizontal) or more distant (vertical), but always transcendent in relation to the previous state of the affairs, while the heroes of the myth appear marked by the divine, supernatural quality, a certain mission which turns their lives into a sacrificial service and an inspired labor. Elaborations and embellishments of various kinds spring up easily, situations are dramatized and exaggerated. Moreover, the ambiguity of the founding myth invites heterodoxy, heresy, at times even reformulating turns which testify to the lively and engaging nature of myth. The upholders and defenders of the myth are not merely guardians of memory; the founding myth demands continuous, consistent work, attention, vigilance; it functions under the constant threat of reinterpretation or even demolition. The Round Table mentioned above as the founding myth of the contemporary Poland may serve as a vivid example in which since a while the content or meaning of the myth is the subject of impassioned disputes and heated debates in Poland, as well as quarrels and mythological reversals.

The reflections above were intended as the background for the clear, concise, and yet free from any reducing oversimplification, presentation of the well-acknowledged role of Peter Chaadaev in the history of Russian philosophy. The use of this term to describe his work and life serves well to capture the particular qualities of Chaadaev's phenomenon, such as its spectacular fecundity combined with the air of ambiguity, enigma or even uncanny strangeness usually associated with it.

It may be noted that some sources date the birth of Russian philosophy to the late medieval period and Old Slavic thought; Gregory Skovoroda, the eighteenth-century mystic and moralist, is sometimes named as its originator; it is hardly possible to overlook the great intellectual ferment of the Enlightenment—extensive though derivative—of the epoch of Catherine the Great; the quality and quantity of the works of Vladimir Soloviev can hardly be overestimated, causing some scholars to view him as the founding father of the Russian philosophy. And yet, it is Chaadaev who had played this role most effectively and convincingly, as the formula of the founding myth makes abundantly clear. This formula may not be associated with the Old Slavic thought, with Skovoroda or eighteenth-century Enlightenment, it may not be traced—even in reverse—to Soloviev. It was precisely Chaadaev who encapsulated "the awakening of independent original Russian thought" (Nikolai Bierdyaev[2]); the greatest Russian thinkers continuously "recurred to Chaadaev's themes" (Vasilii Zenkovsky[3]); "Chaadaev turned out to be the pioneer of the new paths in Russian thought" (Razumnik Ivanov-Razumnik[4]); "no one in Russia had spoken in such a universal voice before him" (Dmitry Merezhkovsky[5]); "his ideas had the defining influence on the state and development of Russian philosophy" (Igor Evlampiev[6]); let us not omit Alexander Herzen's famous reflection on Chaadaev's "First Philosophical Letter": "It was a shot that rang out in the dark night; whether it was something foundering that proclaimed its own wreck, whether it was a signal, a cry for help, whether it was news of the dawn or news that there would not be one—it was all the same: one had to wake up."[7]

2. Bierdyaev, *Russian Idea*, 34.

3. Zenkovsky, *History of Russian Philosophy*, 170.

4. Ivanov-Razumnik, "Zapadniki i slavyanofily," 399.

5. Merezhkovskiy, "Chaadaev," 415.

6. Evlampiev, *Istoriya russkoy metafiziki*, 1:50.

7. Herzen, *My Past and Thoughts*, 2:261.

The most significant and momentous event in Chaadaev's own life (and in the life of Russia in relation to Chaadaev) was the publication in 1836 of the first in the series of *Philosophical Letters*.[8] The reaction of the authorities was inordinately spectacular: Chaadaev was pronounced insane, subjected to medical and police supervision which was only lifted after a year on condition that "he would not dare to write anything."[9] And though Chaadaev did not publish anything further, he did leave a few manuscripts, and he also conducted fascinating correspondence with a few individuals, and it is precisely through the context of the social life led by him until his death in 1856, conflated by his unpublished works (quite well known to many of his contemporaries), that the events around the "First Letter" became magnified and enriched, lifted to the rank of the founding myth.

The spectacular decision of the authorities in 1836 had a significant effect on the entire development of the Russian thought and Russian reality: it instilled in the subsequent rulers an attitude of suspicion toward any theories rooted in or associated with Chaadaev's ideas. And since such qualities are characteristic for almost all Russian philosophical and social theories starting from the Slavophiles and ending with Marxists, the philosophical and social thought itself became suspect; Chaadaev became something of an "original sin" of the Russian thought, which was the first step, as yet insufficient, on the path to the status of the founding myth.

Moreover, such politicization of the thought by the authorities produces a mirror effect, a reflected politicization on the part of the creators, a process which in a sense predetermines thinkers to become political, even if their original intentions were quite far from it. If Chaadaev's abstract, devoid of any direct political accents theory is viewed as a politically threatening expression of madness, such situation must have made obvious the question of the nature of reality in which such assessment is possible on the one hand, and on the other—a question of the content of thought which would cause such reaction. No matter how these questions might have been answered, such situation caused, first, a remarkably high political potential of Russian philosophy, with the exceptionally well-pronounced element of the issues of social life in it; second, it generated the high level of self-consciousness and self-criticism of the Russian thought and its constant self-acceleration, produced by means of the above mentioned unceasing self-questioning, ongoing enquiry about its place in social life and its chance for freedom.

8. There were eight epistles in total, though the publishers sometimes included one more, ninth letter; the publication of the remaining letters took place after Chaadaev's death.

9. See Gershenzon, *Chaadayev*, 140.

But to return to Chaadaev's "First Philosophical Letter": it was a radical and outspoken state-of-the-nation reckoning of Russia's current predicament and its position in history. Russia, in essence, lacks such historical situation; it belongs in geography rather than history. We are dealing here with an absence of development or progress, with a lack of any mechanisms for accumulation of knowledge and experience. Intellectual life here always returns to the point of entry, since it is unable to externalize and perpetuate any new ideas. "We live only in the most narrow kind of present without a past and without a future in the midst of a shallow calm . . . we have absorbed nothing, not even traditional ideas of mankind."[10]

From such position, Russia could not possibly have created anything that could be included into the treasury of human accomplishments that would even in a smallest degree benefit the development of the humankind, moreover—it had done nothing for itself. As a result, the life of Russia "renders us equally indifferent to good and evil, to truth and falsehood."[11]

Such were the opinions that ignited the decisively adverse reaction of the authorities (and of the general public opinion), and at the same time produced an image of Chaadaev as a Westernizer and a radical critic of the Russian sociopolitical establishment—an image we see reflected in the passage from Herzen cited above. This was the convention used later to write about Chaadaev not only by Plekhanov, but also by Mikhail Gershenson who was connected with the Russian religious philosophy circles and who called the decision of the authorities after the publication of the "First Letter" "the most cynical, contemptuous victory of the rude physical force over thought, word and human dignity, without precedent until today even in Russia."[12] Such an image of Chaadaev is focused almost entirely on the "First Letter" and seems to advance his myth and legend, and yet it is a rather one-sided perspective, and while it certainly perpetuates the legend of the disgracefully persecuted philosopher, it hardly suffices—precisely because of its limited nature and obvious blatancy—to formulate the pattern of the founding myth. The comments of a Polish scholar may appear both inspiring and persuasive in this context: in Chaadaev's case,

> the instructions of the Imperial secret services were not extensive, and the medical and police observation to which the thinker from Basmannaya street had been submitted was brief, just as brief was the exile of Nadezhdin [the publisher of *Teleskop* journal who printed the "First Letter"—J. D.], who was allowed to

10. Chaadaev, "Philosophical Letters," 21.

11. Ibid., 24.

12. Gershenzon, *Chaadayev*, 137.

> conduct scholarly activity, and both exiles did not culminate in the acts of martyrdom. Moreover, Chaadaev himself did much to romanticize the entire "*Teleskop* Affair" by concluding many of his letters with a "Madman" signature and by describing in great detail the state of his mind.[13]

Dmitry Merezhkovsky, discussing Chaadaev's rather average personal courage, remarked that he was "a wise man, and not a martyr."[14]

Yet the most essential for the entire affair is the actual content of Chaadaev texts. The image of Chaadaev as a Westernizer and sociopolitical radical may be justified—and even then only in some measure—only if the "First Letter" is set aside from Chaadaev's complete, though not extensive intellectual oeuvre. Indeed, as was already suggested earlier, some interpretations suggest that Chaadaev appears to fulfill a double purpose: "He plays the role of the author of the 'First Letter (interpreted as the unconditional and inescapable 'verdict' on Russia) and also the role of an individual, of a man in his full integrity."[15] However, these scholars seem to select only the first role, and persist in seeing only the "First Letter" as Chaadaev's entire contribution to the intellectual history of Russia. Such perception is narrow, superficial and crippling, reducing the philosopher's entire work to a single fragment, and stopping short at a legend, which may be attractive, but which cheats us of the far more profound and comprehensive vision of Chaadaev's oeuvre as the founding myth of Russian philosophy. The focus on the famous legend of the "First Letter" also inevitably leads to an embarrassing psychologization of almost all Chaadaev's remaining works, and in particular his "pro-Russian" and nearly "pre-Slavophile" writings, as well as written in 1837 *Apologia of a Madman* which from this point of view appears merely a testimony of the philosopher's cowardice and of his retreat from the positions demarcated in the "First Philosophical Letter."

Meanwhile, neither is the "First Letter" (or, furthermore, the entire body of the "Letters") anti-Russian, nor is *Apologia* Slavophile in the degree suggested by the rash stereotype delineated above. In the first of his *Philosophical Letters* Chaadaev, having first praised the historical development of Europe, goes on to say:

> I am certainly not claiming that there are only vices among us and only virtues among Europeans, God forbid! But I do say that, in order to judge nations, the pervading spirit which constitutes their existence must be studied, for it is this spirit alone

13. Jedliński, *Rosyjskie poszukiwania*, 190.

14. Merezhkovskiy, "Chaadaev," 409.

15. Kozhinov, "Pushkin i Chaadaev," 707.

> which can lead them towards a more perfect moral state and towards continuous development . . . assuredly all is not reason, virtue and religion in Europe, far from it.[16]

The "First Letter" is concluded by the opinion exemplary in its tone of rationality and compromise: "Despite all that is incomplete, vicious, evil in European society as it stands today, yet it is nonetheless true that God's reign has been realized there in some way, because it contains the principle of indefinite progress and possesses basically and essentially all that is needed for God's reign to become established definitely upon earth one day."[17] The subsequent *Philosophical Letters* complicate the issue even further, and the "Seventh Letter" ends with a statement which appears to be almost a transition to *Apologia*: "Today the forces of the sovereign society have grown so much, its work upon the rest of humanity has increased so greatly, that soon we shall be swept along body and soul in the universal whirlwind, that is certain: we surely could not remain in our desert any longer."[18] The criticism of Europe in *Apologia* is, moreover, not based on the reversal of the previous assessment, but on the adjustment of the emphasis, on "animation" of the comparatively static descriptions from the *Philosophical Letters*. Therefore, when Chaadaev seems to admit in *The Apologia* that he "had perhaps praised too much" the European countries in his *Philosophical Letters*, he still immediately qualifies this statement: "[They] are nonetheless the most complete models of all kinds of civilization," even though this civilization "is oppressed by its tradition . . . and obstinate memory of the days gone by" and requires a regeneration which should come from those who are "able to march forward" (i.e., the Russian people) and who "are permitted to aspire to types of prosperity which are vaster," though not nearly as far-reaching as the visions of the Slavophiles.[19]

We would seek to suggest that Chaadaev's position should be regarded as an inherently consistent and unified vision when it comes to the issue of Russia vs. Europe. The enraged reactions to *Apologia of a Madman* of those who read it as an apparent break with the noble and heroic honesty of the "First Letter" might be seen as the result of the drastically superficial reading. Contrary to such superficial opinions, the idea of Russia's historic mission is already present in the subsequent *Philosophical Letters*, and thus long before the *Apologia*; as a Polish scholar rightly notes, "we must therefore reject the view that the ideas of the *Apologia of a Madman* were caused

16. Chaadaev, "Philosophical Letters," 24, 29.

17. Ibid., 29.

18. Ibid., 96.

19. Chaadaev, "Apologia of a Madman," 109.

by the thinker's tactical concessions to the demands of the political powers and enraged public opinion."[20]

Such an approach to the relation between the *Philosophical Letters* and the *Apologia of the Madman* allows us to postulate yet another, perhaps even more important thesis: Chaadaev is a thinker who transcends the opposition between Slavophiles and Westernizers, and his philosophy precedes this opposition, lays down its groundwork. And it is precisely this that lends the status of the founding myth to the life and work of Chaadaev. As a Westernizer, or—a contention which sometimes may be encountered, however infrequently—as a Slavophile, Chaadaev would be seen as the master, the creator, the founding father of these movements (especially of the Westernizers), which would therefore allow us to pinpoint his exact location on the map of the intellectual nineteenth-century Russia between the thirties and of the fifties. And thus, as the thinker who precedes the dispute between the Slavophiles and the Westernizers, as the initiator of his dispute, Chaadaev becomes the founding myth of Russian philosophy in its entirety, of its universal field of interest which would first become differentiated into Slavophiles *vs.* Westernizers, and later would continue its transformations. Meanwhile, Chaadaev himself remains detached from any such movements, always appearing as a precursor, forerunner—as the founding myth whose meaning and nature differs from the usual position and significance of an originator, founding father, figure of authority or canonical forefather standing at the origin of any particular movement in Russian philosophy.

It becomes evident that the concept of the founding myth is understood here as a certain synthesizing quality, a totalizing feature, a quality that establishes and problematizes certain potential, suggests solutions which become fixed positions constituted by the founding myth's sphere of meaning; such a problematization is frequently expressed as an opposition of sorts, as a more or less articulated dispute between diverse points of view or projects (in our case, as we well know, it is the antagonism between the Slavophiles and the Westernizers). Such disputes frequently encompass almost the entire sphere of intellectual culture; they also are subject to reformulations and evolve into successive forms of oppositions, not necessarily and not always binary. Such a view of Chaadaev as the forerunner of the opposition between the Slavophiles *vs.* the Westernizers, who yet transcends this argument, is easily found in the literature of the subject and thus it appears adequate and apt both in the aspect of the internal content of Chaadaev's views, and in the context of the role played by him in the history of Russian philosophy.

20. Przebinda, *Od Czaadajewa do Bierdiajewa*, 104.

Such a synthetic, all-embracing quality of the myth introduced here—in particular, in the context of the later formulation on its basis of the opposing arguments or binary structures in the form of attitudes or intellectual approaches in Russian thought—such qualities lend to the myth a measure of ambiguity, already noted above, a certain inner tension, a mysterious, enigmatic character. This testifies to its comprehensiveness and impacts the profundity and range of the philosophical thinking presented here. At the same time, this challenges the unreflective consciousness and common-sense which would prefer rather to reduce Chaadaev's thought to one of the sides of the opposition it lays the foundations of, to shift it into the region of psychology, or to accuse it of logical inconsistencies and contradictions detected all too easily.

This fascinating property of Chaadaev's thought—its synthesizing capacity accompanied by a measure of ambiguity, or even uncanny oddity (i.e., its integral contradiction from the rational point of view) is perfectly expressed by Andrzej Walicki:

> He was the first to formulate—in drastic terms—a number of basic problems that were later taken up by the thinkers representing very different worldviews: by the Slavophiles and the Westernizers, by Herzen and Dostoevsky, by Chernyshevsky and Soloviev. He was an admirer of the West who was repulsed by the liberal and bourgeois Europe; an opponent of revolution who furnished intellectual stimulus for revolutionaries; a religious thinker who was accepted by the antireligious or the non-religious progressive intelligentsia that emulated Herzen in regarding him as a symbol of protest against the stifling atmosphere of autocratic Russia.[21]

Let us now further develop and particularize this comprehensive, synthetic, meaning of Chaadaev's thought characteristic for the founding myth, based for the large part on the coexistence of opposites which as yet remain in perfect equilibrium, in a certain inclusive harmony or concord, from which only later they will begin to separate in various forms of Russian philosophical and social thought.

Chaadaev has found for his comprehensive, unifying and universalist vision of the world a most perfect form in the Christian idea and worldview. Christianity was a keystone of the Europe's accomplishments and values, a source of power and energy for the human action, and at the same time it was a "common denominator" of such action, a guarantee of its inclusion in the common history of humankind. It is thanks to Christian idea that

21. Walicki, *History of Russian Thought*, 158.

the life of societies has been transformed into a progression of facts and ideas, into a continuous, unimpeded advancement. As Chaadaev wrote, "See what a diversity of characters, what a multiplicity of powers, it sets in motion; what a variety of different qualities serve but one purpose; what a diversity of hearts beat for but one idea!"[22] And yet, the full and complete understanding of the unifying power of Christianity consists in perceiving and understanding its two aspects—the mythical and the sociohistorical: "People understand nothing about Christianity, if they do not realize that in it there is a purely historical aspect which forms so essential a part of the dogma that in a certain way it includes all of Christian philosophy, since it reveals what Christianity had done for men and what it can do for them in the future"; Christianity is the power of "visible action," which brings along a "social idea."[23] Both of these aspects of Christianity possess a certain tendency to become independent, to particularize: thus, Catholicism is characterized by prevalence of sociohistorical aspect and Orthodoxy is dominated by the dogmatic mystical aspect. This tendency toward a one-sided realization of Christianity proves that to sustain the integrity befitting its nature it would require special care, attention, active endeavors, personal concern; this integrity is not a given, should not be taken for granted as something that "falls out of the sky."

These two contrasting tendencies, although rooted in the same origin, are conveyed in the sphere of Russian philosophy in the two, perhaps, most general (even in relation to the Slavophile-Westernizer argument) directions: in the circles of liberators and social thinkers on the one hand, and among the religious philosophy adherents on the other, since for both of these factions Chaadaev's thought represents a common foundation and since both do aspire to trace their origins to Chaadaev. In social philosophy such reference to Chaadaev may be seen most clearly in Herzen; in religious philosophy it appears in numerous laudatory comments by many of its representatives, most systematically in Mikhail Gershenson's monograph, *Chaadaev: His Life and Thought*. Let us note, however, that the unifying energy of Chaadaev's thought was preserved to some extent even in its theoretically one-sided or partial extensions. Thus, in Russian social philosophy there was always a certain presence of the religious immanenticism, emphasized by Zenkovsky and Berdyaev; the Russian religious philosophy in its turn always contained the remarkably strong historiosophical and sociopolitical aspect. We may find similarly comprehensive and synthetic motifs in the Slavophiles or the Westernizers as well. In our opinion, this

22. Chaadaev, "Philosophical Letters," 30.

23. Ibid., 26, 28.

signifies that the founding myth of Chaadaev was not only a founding myth of Russian philosophy in a historical or formal sense, but that it still remains its constantly present tendency, a peculiar predisposition, a "mood," which may also be easily found in the consequent one-sided particularizations growing out of this founding myth.

The origins of Chaadaev's thought—splitting into many distinct developments in the later stages—are yet another manifestation of its synthetic, unifying nature. French Catholic traditionalists are usually identified as such origins (Louis de Bonald, Josepf de Maistre, Hugues de Lamennais), as well as classical German philosophy, Hegel and Schelling in particular. In our case, the second origin appears of special significance, due to its comprehensive twining unity, important in the context of the future development of Russian philosophy. It is commonly represented as an opposition or a dispute of the two tendencies, originating either from mysticism, aestheticism, *Naturphilosophie* or Schelling's positive philosophy, or from historicism, immanenticism, rationalism and Hegelian philosophy of negation. Chaadaev is frequently associated with Schelling's philosophy, (which, *nota bene*, is frequently associated also with the Slavophiles), yet, Chaadaev himself had written to Schelling: "In following you along your sublime routes, it often occurred to me to stop at places other than those you came to."[24] On the other hand, the sociohistorical understanding of being, and the idea of the cunning of reason seem to strongly suggest Chaadaev's belonging to the Hegelian circle (which, by the way, is associated with the Western thought). It thus appears that we are dealing with a coexistence of Hegelian and Schellingian inspirations in Chaadaev's thought, and only in later Russian philosophical landscape we may distinguish more clearly a separate following of either Hegel or Schelling.

Making yet another effort to grasp the unity, comprehensive integrity or syntheticity of Chaadaev's thought, so difficult to accurately conceptualize, a thought which only later gains expressive clarity in the concepts which follow and grow out of it, while simultaneously gaining particularity and embeddedness in contrasting duality, we may note an inclination to embrace and combine the ideal and the real, a mutual infiltration of transcendence and immanence (as well as the frequently encountered in Russian thought pantheistic threat, so decidedly rejected in the declarative mode), and a connection between the given and the required.[25]

An additional and indirect argument in favor of the unity and integral totality of Chaadaev's thought—the qualities which have been identified

24. Chaadaev, "Fragments," 153.

25. See Evlampiev, *Istoriya russkoy metafiziki*, 1:55, 58.

as prerequisite for the status of founding myth—is the perception of the philosopher by his followers and the scholars of Russian thought as of the founding father who had inspired almost all the key currents in Russian philosophy, including those which appear to contradict each other. As already noted, Chaadaev is seen as the creator, or as the origin at the very least, both by the Westernizers (Alexander Herzen, Georgi Plekhanov), and by the Slavophiles (Nikolay Chernyshevsky); he is also seen as the precursor of Soloviev and Russian religious philosophy (Mikhail Gershenzon[26]), of the attempts to combine Christianity with liberalism (Vasily Zenkovsky[27]), of Dostoevsky's idea of the Russian general humanitarian instinct (Gershenzon[28]), of Narodniks (Chernyshevsky, Gershenson,[29] who emphasizes Herzen as an intermediary), of subjectivism (in the conviction of the possibility of Russia's conscious choice of its future—Plekhanov[30]), finally of the project of the new religious consciousness (Dmitry Merezhkovsky[31]) and God-Building (Plekhanov[32]), or even of nihilism and rational egoism.[33] No wonder then that in this aspect as well we are given perhaps the most convincing proof of Chaadaev's nonpartisanship,[34] and it comes as no surprise that while Chaadaev's seal seems to mark every Russian philosopher, yet he "established no school of his own,"[35] and any attempts to assign such role to him are one-sided and in essence understate his significance in the history of Russian philosophy.

Next to the integral totality and syntheticity that the founding myth possesses, unlike its consequent developments, we should identify as the essential features of the founding myth its aura of mystery, enigmatic quality, its air of extraordinary rareness, suggesting an intervention from another dimension. And in that aspect as well the figure of Chaadaev appears as remarkable, original and striking due to his personal qualities and his destiny. Chaadaev possessed exceptional, immediately noticeable talents and evident predispositions to great acts and accomplishments, and yet also a melancholy, withdrawn, cold and distant air, a certain coolness and detachment

26. See Gershenzon, *Chaadayev*, 168–69.
27. See Zenkovsky, *History of Russian Philosophy*, 151.
28. See Gershenzon, *Chaadayev*, 168–69.
29. Ibid., 280.
30. Plekhanov, "Chaadayev," 302.
31. Merezhkovsky, "Chaadayev," 314.
32. Plekhanov, "Chaadayev," 299.
33. Ermichev and Zlatopol'skaya, "Chaadayev v russkoy mysli," 34.
34. Filippov, "Legenda russkoy literatury," 339.
35. Ermichev and Zlatopol'skaya, "Chaadayev v russkoy mysli," 15.

from the world, and a peculiar opacity in relation to those around him. Religion was an important element and aspect of his philosophical views, and at the same time a personal quality, a personality trait. The intensity and rank of his religious feeling placed Chaadaev essentially in opposition to freedom seeking movements, which are usually strongly anti-religious. And yet, this religiosity was strikingly alien to the traditionalistic Russian society—Chaadaev's religion was above confessional belonging, he was even somewhat charmed by Catholicism, though his confessional detachment was never uncritical or amorphous; for instance, he viewed Protestantism with decided revulsion. Romantic melancholy was close to his heart, and yet these sulks would be interrupted by sudden bursts of violent and decisive action, leading one of Chaadaev's correspondents to form the following suggestive appraisal of his personality: "discouragement and impatience—these are the two of your weaknesses,"[36] flaws, we may note, which are in direct contradiction to each other. Religious and pantheistic anti-individualism of Chaadaev's views merged with extreme, almost morbid focus on the autonomy of the "I," which granted the self a superiority over any decisions or assessments, even those that would limit the "I." This made Chaadaev appear an attractive ally to the liberation projects, inspiring enhancement of the individualistic element in the Russian religious philosophical concepts.

Until today the exact circumstances of the commotion around the publication of the "First Philosophical Letter" remain unclear, and the circumstances of Chaadaev's decision to withdraw from military service are no less mysterious, as are his liaisons with Catholicism, his "management" of his private affairs. Coolness and detachment on the one hand, and on the other—a need to live publicly and remain in the public eye; this combination of qualities leads scholars and researches to read his figure as that of a holy fool, a *yurodivy*, and such assessments, despite their obvious rashness and cheap appeal to popular taste, are not entirely without reason.[37]

This text defined the life and work of Peter Chaadaev as the founding myth of Russian philosophy. It is not likely that such definition may be applied to any other Russian thinker. But the nature and power of Chaadaev's founding myth, its propensity to produce specific and particular, one-sided developments, as well as to cause continuous attempts to retain the unifying and totalizing power of this myth causes a periodic appearance on the scene of Russian philosophy of certain repetitions, replicas of the founding myth, which renew and reanimate the paths of development

36. Levashova to Chaadaev, 1834–1835, 454. Cf. Jedliński, *Rosyjskie poszukiwania*, 123, 153.

37. Kuznetsov, "Metafizicheskiy Nartsiss," 739.

for Russian philosophy. Vladimir Soloviev's work may be certainly seen as such a recurring influx of energy of the founding myth, and later, perhaps, the publication of the *Vekhi* collection. And even though both of these events in the history of Russian philosophy possess a far greater wealth of substantive content, they still remain a repetition, a copy of the original, that is, of Chaadaev's founding myth. In this aspect even Soloviev appears as merely an epigone of Chaadaev.[38]

Bibliography

Bierdyaev, Nicolai. *The Russian Idea*. Translated by Reginald Michael French. New York: Macmillan, 1947.

Chaadaev, Peter. "Apologia of a Madman." In *Philosophical Works of Peter Chaadaev*, edited by Raymond T. McNally and Richard Tempest, 102–11. Dordrecht: Springer, 1991.

———. "Fragments and Various Thoughts." In *Philosophical Works of Peter Chaadaev*, edited by Raymond T. McNally and Richard Tempest, 112–255. Dordrecht: Springer, 1991.

———. "The Philosophical Letters Addressed to a Lady." In *Philosophical Works of Peter Chaadaev*, edited by Raymond T. McNally and Richard Tempest, 18–101. Dordrecht: Springer, 1991.

Ermichev, Aleksandr, and Alla Zlatopol'skaya. "P. Ya. Chaadayev v russkoy mysli. Opyt istoriografii." In *Petr Chaadayev. Pro et contra: Lichnost' i tvorchestvo Petra Chaadayeva v otsenke russkikh mysliteley i issledovateley. Antologiya*, edited by Aleksandr Ermichev and Anna Zlatopol'skaya, 7–40. Saint Petersburg: Izdatel'stvo Russkogo Khristianskogo Gumanitarnogo Universiteta, 1996.

Evlampiev, Igor. *Istoriya russkoy metafiziki v XIX–XX vekakh. Russkaya filosofiya v poiskakh absolyuta*. 2 vols. St. Peterburg: Aleteyya, 2000.

Filippov, Iosif. "Legenda russkoy literatury." In *Petr Chaadayev. Pro et contra: Lichnost' i tvorchestvo Petra Chaadayeva v otsenke russkikh mysliteley i issledovateley. Antologiya*, edited by Aleksandr Ermichev and Anna Zlatopol'skaya, 331–53. Saint Petersburg: Izdatel'stvo Russkogo Khristianskogo Gumanitarnogo Universiteta, 1996.

Gershenzon, Mikhail. *P. Ya. Chaadaev. Zhizn i myshlenie*. Saint Petersburg: Tipografiya M. M. Stasyulevicha, 1908.

Govorukha-Otrok, Yuriy. "Vl. Solov'yev i Chaadayev." In *Petr Chaadayev. Pro et contra: Lichnost' i tvorchestvo Petra Chaadayeva v otsenke russkikh mysliteley i issledovateley. Antologiya*, edited by Aleksandr Ermichev and Anna Zlatopol'skaya, 207–15. Saint Petersburg: Izdatel'stvo Russkogo Khristianskogo Gumanitarnogo Universiteta, 1996.

Herzen, Alexander. *My Past and Thoughts*. Translated by Constance Garnett. Vol. 2. London: Chatto and Windus, 1927.

Ivanov-Razumnik, Razumnik. "Zapadniki i slavyanofily. Chaadayev." In *Petr Chaadayev. Pro et contra: Lichnost' i tvorchestvo Petra Chaadayeva v otsenke russkikh mysliteley i*

38. Govorukha-Otrok, "Solov'yev i Chaadaev," 207.

issledovateley. Antologiya, edited by Aleksandr Ermichev and Anna Zlatopol'skaya, 285–400. Saint Petersburg: Izdatel'stvo Russkogo Khristianskogo Gumanitarnogo Universiteta, 1996.

Jedliński, Marek. *Rosyjskie poszukiwania sensu i celu*. Bydgoszcz, Poland: Epigram, 2015.

Kozhinov, Vadim. "Pushkin i Chaadayev." In *Petr Chaadayev. Pro et contra: Lichnost' i tvorchestvo Petra Chaadayeva v otsenke russkikh mysliteley i issledovateley. Antologiya*, edited by Aleksandr Ermichev and Anna Zlatopol'skaya, 696–725. Saint Petersburg: Izdatel'stvo Russkogo Khristianskogo Gumanitarnogo Universiteta, 1996.

Kuznetsov, Pavel V. "Metafizicheskiy Nartsiss i russkoe molchanie: P. Ya Czaadayev i sud'ba filosofii v Rossii." In *Petr Chaadayev. Pro et contra: Lichnost' i tvorchestvo Petra Chaadayeva v otsenke russkikh mysliteley i issledovateley. Antologiya*, edited by Aleksandr Ermichev and Anna Zlatopol'skaya, 729–52. Saint Petersburg: Izdatel'stvo Russkogo Khristianskogo Gumanitarnogo Universiteta, 1996.

Levashova, Ekaterina. Letter to Petr Chaadaev. 1834–1835. In Petr Chaadayev. *Polnoe sobranie sochineniy i izbrannye pis'ma*, 2:454–55. Moscow: Nauka, 1991.

Merezhkovskiy, Dmitriy. "Chaadayev." In *Petr Chaadayev. Pro et contra: Lichnost' i tvorchestvo Petra Chaadayeva v otsenke russkikh mysliteley i issledovateley. Antologiya*, edited by Aleksandr Ermichev and Anna Zlatopol'skaya, 309–18. Saint Petersburg: Izdatel'stvo Russkogo Khristianskogo Gumanitarnogo Universiteta, 1996.

Plekhanov, Georgiy. "P. Ya. Chaadayev." In *Petr Chaadayev. Pro et contra: Lichnost' i tvorchestvo Petra Chaadayeva v otsenke russkikh mysliteley i issledovateley. Antologiya*, edited by Aleksandr Ermichev and Anna Zlatopol'skaya, 287–308. Saint Petersburg: Izdatel'stvo Russkogo Khristianskogo Gumanitarnogo Universiteta, 1996.

Przebinda, Grzegorz. *Od Czaadajewa do Bierdiajewa. Spór o Boga i człowieka w myśli rosyjskiej (1832–1922)*. Krakow: Polska Akademia Umiejętności, 1998.

Walicki, Andrzej. *A History of Russian Thought from the Enlightenment to Marxism*. Translated by Hilda Andrews-Rusiecka. Stanford: Stanford University Press, 1980.

Zenkovsky, Vasilii V. *A History of Russian Philosophy*. Vol. 1. Translated by George L. Kline. London: Routledge, 2006.

12

Peter Chaadaev on the Religious Basis of the Russian History Vector

Yuriy Ivonin
Olga Ivonina

Peter Chaadaev went down in the history of Russian social thought as one of the authors of the so-called "Russian idea"—a complex reflection on the historical fate of Russia and its place in space and time in world history. Tomas Masaryk considered Chaadaev as "the first Russian who tried to follow the German thinkers to understand more clearly and articulate the essence of the philosophy of history and history in general, that was necessary exactly for Russians in order to orient in developing Europeanization."[1] James Billington, a historian of Russian culture, found it significant that Chaadaev's reflection on the meaning of world history, though the Russian historical method was influenced by European tradition of romanticism, was written in Russian, by the truly Russian thinker and was turned to Russia.[2]

Thus, Chaadaev's works can be regarded both as the source of the Russian philosophy of history and as that style of thinking which is keeping with the modern way of reflection in setting and resolving theoretical and methodological problems of the humanities.

It is necessary to remark upon the unique nature of Chaadaev's discourse, which formed a special style of Russian philosophy of history where profound philosophical generalizations were closely associated with the answers to practically significant problems of Russia improvement. The

1. Masarik, *Rossiya i Evropa*, 230.
2. Bilington, *Icon and the Axe*, 316.

Russian thinker's understanding of history as both science and art, as a moral judgment on the past and prophecy of the future of the country and the world in many respects anticipated the subsequent discussion on the subject and method of historical knowledge, its social function. Chaadaev can be considered as a pioneer of the so-called multi-disciplinary approach in Russian humanities: in his works, eternal questions about the fate of Russia and Europe took the form of artistic images and metaphors; the history of philosophy rooted from the magazine controversy, letters and essays but not from special studies. It was the first time that Chaadaev proposed the holistic paradigm of knowledge of human nature, combining the elements of philosophy, religion, science, and art, which all Christian thinkers—from Alexei Khomyakov to Nikolai Berdyaev—later consciously opposed to formal standards of scientism and strict disciplinary limitations.

Russian and foreign researchers recognize the fact of significant changes in the historical concept of Chaadaev: thesis of his *Philosophical Letters* (1829), written with deep criticism to the Russian historical process, are significantly different from the ideas of *Apologia of a Madman* (1836), where he advocated the universal messianic calling of Russia. In other words, the pro-Western sentiment of the author eventually evolved toward Slavophile intuitions. First manifesting itself in Chaadaev's works, the symbiosis of Westernizers and Slavophiles concepts was inherent to the majority of Russian thinkers—the so-called Russian Europeans. Chaadaev's attempt is extremely interesting because his historical concept reveals the deep ideological unity of Westernism and Slavophilism, rooted in the author's Christian views.

Chaadaev was one of the first Russian religious thinkers of the nineteenth century who raised the question of the necessity of philosophy of history as a combination of religious metaphysics and historical narrative. Like most of his contemporaries, Chaadaev acknowledged that history has a special place in the development of social and national identification. However, he was skeptical about contemporary historical science, believing that historical knowledge should not be reduced to pure narrative. In his opinion, a historian should subordinate historiography to philosophy of history, seek understanding of the historical process from the viewpoint of metatheory, which was regarded as religious metaphysics in Chaadaev's works.

According to Chaadaev, a new philosophy of history would be significantly different from the former one in its objectives, methods and value for system of modern knowledge. It would make the greatest revision of the previous ways of understanding the past, dispel false myths, expose any undeserved fame and reputation to scrutiny, and judge the past, taking it as the basis for predicting the future.[3]

Chaadaev believed that the important task of the philosophy of history is to form national identification by understanding the meaning of the historical path of each nation and its mission in world history. Only having understood their true purposes and the place in the family of nations, having learned the lessons of the past and repented of their sins would nations be able to unite for a common goal and develop a common understanding the general interest of humanity on the basis of the moral law. Thus, as Chaadaev thought, a new philosophy of history could perform the task of forming national identity as well as every nation's awareness of involvement in search for ways to achieve universal ideal.

Chaadaev thought that the majestic destiny of historical knowledge should be the revealing of the divine purpose which gives the human world harmony and completeness. In his opinion, it is the philosophy of history that is capable to find a manifestation of a single plan for the development of mankind, and thus to grow to the standards for scientific knowledge—comprehension of the universal laws of life. As one of them, Chaadaev regarded the progressive development of humanity on the path of "the great apocalyptic synthesis"—all peoples and nations as one unit.[4]

In his understanding of the world history vector, Chaadaev was close to Christian Modernism. Like Schelling and Hegel, he considered Christianity as a *historical* religion that acknowledges the value of both: the mortal and eternal, earthly and heavenly planes of human existence. Chaadaev thought that universal Christian doctrine of the world and human was supplemented with social function of Christianity, which encouraged social changes in the real world. To Chaadaev's mind, the true spirit of Christianity was embodied in the idea of God's kingdom as the result of humanity's combined effort to reach the ideal of truth, unity and harmony.[5]

This idea opposed the traditional definition of Christianity as a religion of the individual salvation of each believer who has withdrawn himself from sinful world. Chaadaev believed that Christianity's true nature was to *change this world socially.* Chaadaev thought that unity of social and religious evolution of Christian humanity, which embodied the unified divine design of the world and humanity, could explain duality of the world history. Similar views on Christianity could be traced later in Vladimir Soloviev's and Nikolai Berdyaev's works.

3. Chaadaev, "Philosophical Letters," 73.
4. Ibid., 101.
5. Ibid., 19.

Being in the center of contemporary ideological discussions, Chaadaev demonstrated his affinity to different social ideas. His works combined traditions of German idealism and romanticism, critic of rationalism and individualism with faith in social progress and triumph of social justice, close to the ideology of the Utopian Socialists.

Originating from such a synthesis, Chaadaev's concept of the world history was consistently Europe-centrist and progressive. Chaadaev thought that the change of historical process geographical orientation from East to West unearthed different sides of human nature in the world history such as contemplation and passive obedience to necessary order, which are inherent to eastern nations, and human activity, desire to turn divine commandments into social transformation, which are inherent to European nations.

Chaadaev considered Christian Europe to be an ideal historical community. He regarded Europe, united in spirit and worldview, as determining all aspects of social life. Chaadaev believed Christian faith to be responsible for the religious and political unity of the West, accelerating social progress on the basis of common values of justice, right and order, uniting different people in a giant "great family of Christian people, European society."[6] During its history, European society preserved its Christian basis for development, showing sustainability and continuous progress.

Chaadaev saw United Europe as a union in spirit and worldview which determines all sides of social life. That internal unity, which was formed in the Middle Ages, shown itself in the New Time. Europe's political unity was continuation of spiritual unity of Christian world, which was so unmovable that no social shocks during Reformation and Renaissance could change the *progressive* vector of European history. Chaadaev didn't give too much importance to the rise of nationalism, although he considered ideology of national state as a return to pagan ways. However, he thought that the spiritual unity of European nations would embody itself socially and overpower political particularism of the New Time.[7]

The publication of the "First Philosophical Letter" (written in 1829) in *Teleskop* magazine in the fall of 1836, as it was later acknowledged by contemporaries and further researchers, shocked Russian society by the harshness and mercilessness with which it judged the present and the past of Russia. As Alexander Pypin remarked, the letter "has congregated so many bitter emotions, so irresistible understanding of shortcomings of Russian life as there was no one else from the leaders of our mental

6. Ibid., 76.

7. Ibid., 75.

life—and how much authority, accustomed to panegyric, probably not even thought possible."[8]

The reaction of the ruling powers to the publication (banning the *Teleskop*, the exiling of its editor to Siberia, and placing the author in a mental institution) and opposition (Alexander Herzen considered the letter to be a signal for the awakening of Russian independent mind) had given Chaadaev's ideas a special, symbolical meaning. Chaadaev's nihilism toward the Russian historical and cultural tradition became an object of hot discussions, in which all political and intellectual parties participated. Mikhail Gershenson—one of Chaadaev's biographers—explained the extremely high level of emotions of the public to Chaadaev's thoughts about the destiny of Russia as the critics inability to fully understand the theoretical basis of Chaadaev' historical concept. Gershenson rightfully thought that Chaadaev's judgment of Russia was the result of his religio-philosophical concept and almost none of his contemporaries understood that.[9]

However, rejecting accusations of anti-patriotism, Chaadaev said many times that his criticism of Russia was to be explained by his religious understanding of world history as evolution of the united community of Christian nations. Christianity's universalism and cosmopolitanism as the one and the only Truth determines, to Chaadaev's mind, the only objective judgment of world history which cannot be warped by national bias, or rigidness of methods and objectives of a philosopher. Chaadaev believed that as a philosopher he found himself in the situation when newly-found truth opposed to public opinion:

> Love of the fatherland is certainly a very beautiful thing, but there is one thing better than that; it is the love of truth. Love of fatherland makes heroes, love of truth makes wise men, the benefactors of humanity; it is love of fatherland which divides peoples, which feeds national hatreds, which sometimes covers the earth with mourning; it is love of truth which spreads light, which creates the joys of the spirit, which brings men close to the divinity. It is not by way of the fatherland, it is by way of the truth that one mounts to heaven.[10]

His judgment of Russia as a historically pitiful nation without history and ideas was the result of the author's methodological position as well. Like Schelling and Hegel, Chaadaev saw history as continuity of developing

8. Pypin, *Kharakteristika literaturnyh mneniy*, 186.

9. Gershenzon, *Chaadayev*, 146.

10. Chaadaev, "Apologia of a Madman," 102.

ideas, not as sequence of real events. In his opinion, Russia didn't have this intellectual history.[11]

Lacking ideological content, Russian history could not be considered as part of worldwide historical progress. As Chaadaev stated, "For us historical experience does not exist; ages and generations have flowed by fruitlessly for us. It would seem that in our case the general law of humanity has been revoked."[12]

The categories of the East and the West, used by Chaadaev for characterizing historic-cultural identity of Russia, are fairly relative, as they correlate with axiological poles of Byzantium as the East of the Christian world, and United Europe as the West.

The author considered the despotic manner of management, servile character of collective conscious and religio-cultural particularism to be the embodiments of Byzantium in the sociopolitical routine and mentality of Russian people. To Chaadaev's mind, the acceptance of Christianity from the Byzantine Empire clove Russia from the brotherhood of European nations. The Orthodox faith turned out to be the main factor in the cultural isolation of Russia, assisting to conservation and self-preservation of social organism, but obstructing further progressive development.

Furthermore the political servility of Byzantine Orthodoxy which had been accepted by Russia, hindered the development of civil liability, independent public opinion, and contributed to low social standards and anti-intellectualism of Russian society. Chaadaev wrote: "A church herself submitted to material power and tending to elevate it into a kind of Christian Caliphate. There you have the heritage which we received from Byzantium with the dogmatic integrity and the primitive purity."[13]

Taken from Byzantium, Christianity was accustomed to being a spiritually underdeveloped society, so the Russians interpreted it unilaterally ascetically—as the practice of individual salvation and cast aside the basic foundations of Christianity, which condition the development and progress, to the edge of the collective conscious and artistic creativity. To the monastic severity and servile obedience formed by Orthodox faith, Chaadaev opposed the social activity and liberating potential of European Christianity. Chaadaev believed that servility was the main factor in Russian history, the source of total obedience and the paralysis of the will. In Chaadaev's words:

11. Ibid., 104.

12. Chaadaev, "Philosophical Letters," 25.

13. Chaadaev to Adolphe de Circourt, 15 June 1846, Chaadaev, "Fragments," 202.

"Everything in Russia bears the stamp of servitude, customs, tendencies, instruction and even liberty itself."[14]

In his further speculations on the destiny of Christianity in Russia, Chaadaev invariably returned to the conclusion, made in the "First Philosophical Letter"—not being a truly Christian society, Russia could not keep developing together with world civilization. As Chaadaev stated, "Alone in the world, we have given nothing to the world, taken nothing from the world, bestowed not even a single idea upon the fund of human ideas, contributed nothing to the progress of the human spirit, and we have distorted all progressivity which has come to us."[15]

In order to assess Russia's level of development in comparison with other historical communities, Chaadaev used the notion of "young social organism." Chaadaev seems to be familiar with Herder's idea of different historical destinies of "young" and "old" nations, and, perhaps, with Sergei Solovyov concept of the two "historical ages" of a nation.[16] However, in his *Philosophical Letters*, Chaadaev underlines not only the prolonged period of Russia's "youthfulness," but its special character which makes it different from all other nations. The immature self-identification of Russian people doesn't hold such ideas as duty, justice, right and order which formed social history of the West. The Russian mentality lacks orderliness, logical continuity, and discipline of conciseness. Chaadaev believed that such specificity of Russian self-identification originated not only from spirituality, but also from the special path of historical evolution—with its non-continuous rhythm, multitude of stops and disjoints in the process of communication with other civilizations.

In his historical concept, Chaadaev stressed constant *potential, underdevelopment of natio-cultural self-identification and unpredictability of Russia's historical path*. To Chaadaev's mind, the indefiniteness of "Russian Idea" is very diverse. It is shown in instability and frailty of cultural standards, unsteadiness of social institutions and reversibility of great achievements. The country was in a constant state of choice between alternative ways of development. Chaadaev remarked:

> Look around you. Don't you think we are all very restless? We all resemble travellers. There is no definite sphere of existence for anyone, no good habits, no rule for anything at all; not even a home; nothing which attracts or awakens our sympathy or affection, nothing lasting, nothing enduring; everything departs,

14. Chaadaev, "Fragments," 119.

15. Chaadaev, "Philosophical Letters," 25.

16. Ivonina and Ivonin, *Ex Occidente Lux*, 13.

> everything flows away, leaving no traces either without or within ourselves.[17]

Chaadaev thought that the constant alternatives in Russia's historical choice could be explained by the lack of cultural traditions, which assured continuity of social standards and instinctive automatism of behavioral patterns in other nations. That is why he considered the Russian people to be the bastard child of world civilization.[18]

The philosopher thought that Russia's potential led to its cultural anonymity, weak historical memory, historical infancy. All of this makes historic-cultural identification of Russia and its place in the world history *objectively impossible.* In Chaadaev's words:

> That follows from the fact that we have never advanced along with other people; we are not related to any of the great human families; we belong neither to the West nor to the East, and we possess the traditions of neither. Placed, as it were, outside of the times, we have not been affected by the universal education of mankind. This admirable interconnection of human ideas throughout the passing centuries, this history of the human spirit which led men to the position which they occupy in the rest of the world today, had no effect upon us.[19]

Such an understanding of Russia's place in the world history could be called as *atopy and achrony* of Russian evolution.

Chaadaev took the historical evolution of the Western Europe as a paragon, which was the most important criterion of the author's opinion about the Russian Idea. That's why Chaadaev considered Europe's historical experience to be the only way for Russia—the country which never had any historical initiative, never participated in humanity's creativity—in order to join universal progress. Chaadaev believed that there was no alternative for Russia other than to return to the family of civilized nations. If the country continues to exist out of space and time of world history, and even more, stays culturally isolated deliberately, it makes the country's survival problematic. In Chaadaev's opinion, "We must try to prove to Russia herself, if possible, that she marches to her own doom every time that she directly opposes to the old civilized races, who are more powerful a thousand times than she, due to the long and laborious work of their intellects and due

17. Chaadaev, "Philosophical Letters," 20.

18. Ibid., 22.

19. Ibid., 20.

to the continuous, persevering exercise of their faculties rather than their material forces."[20]

Thus, the author of *Philosophical Letters* saw the *essentials* of Russian historical process as overcoming national and religious particularism and Russia's backwardness, compared to European nations, by assimilating the cultural legacy of the Western civilization.

Chaadaev emphasized that it is not only modernization that is objectively necessary in order to normalize the Russian historical process, but he also highlighted Russia's predisposition to adopt the achievements of other nations. Chaadaev considered communicability and intellectual plasticity as well as a readiness to lose current identity to be inseparable traits of national character which can ease Russia's modernization process. He stated:

> This taste for abdication, firstly the fruit of a certain complexion of mind particular to the Slavic race, exalted subsequently by the ascetic character of our beliefs is a necessary fact, or, as people say today in our country, an organic fact. One must accept it with good grace, just as the country accepted the different foreign or national yokes which weighed upon it one after the other.[21]

Chaadaev believed that Peter the Great's reforms were the first attempt by Russians to enter the reaches of world progress and Russia's self-identification as a European power. In Chaadaev's words: "the inspiration that Peter the Great gave to the people's spirit, and the course of actions of all further monarchs, introduced European civilization to us."[22]

Also, Chaadaev mentioned cultural uncertainty and legitimization of radical transformation of monarch's image by the servile, "Byzantine" mind of people. Interestingly, he didn't consider such cultural mutations as something abnormal. The problems of social and cultural schism, which were evoked by Peter the Great's social reforms, and which were so painful to the Slavophiles as well as Westernizers, were not meaningful to Chaadaev. He wrote:

> In his land Peter the Great found only a blank sheet of paper, and he wrote on it: Europe and West; since then we belonged to Europe and to the West. One must not be mistaken about it: whatever the genius of this man was, his work was possible only within a nation whose precedents were not imperiously governing the development which it had to pursue, whose traditions

20. Chaadaev, "Fragments," 238.

21. Chaadaev to Alexander Turgenev, before 1843, Chaadaev, "Fragments," 189.

22. Chaadaev, "Zapiska grafu Benkendorfu," 226.

> did not have the faculty of creating a future for it, whose memories could be erased with impunity by an audacious legislator. If we were so docile to the voice of the prince who dragged us into a new life, the reason is that we had nothing in our past existence which could legitimize resistance.[23]

Thanks to Chaadaev, the evaluation of Peter the Great's reforms became the main theme of historiographic discussions between Slavophiles and Westernizers. Chaadaev's motto—"I love my motherland as Peter the Great taught me to"—was, in fact, the motto of Russian Europeanism. His expectation for the radical transformation of Russian monarchs, who could with "one great gust of the wind," destroy the previous order, "create an abyss between the past and the future" of the country was an idea of "revolution from top" as an optimal way to change Russian history vector in conditions of eternal submission of people to the will of sovereign.

Contrary to some Slavophiles, he didn't consider Peter the Great's reforms as an abuse of Russian history and the self-identification of Russian people, but quite the opposite—he saw the mission of the Great Emperor as to be predestined by God for the country which didn't have fruitful history and great individuality. Moreover, the deeds of Peter the First reflected the deep nature of national spirit—ability for self-renunciation. By his own renunciation of old Russia, with its prejudices, ignorance, all institutions, way of life and manners, Peter I "liberated us from all these precedents which encumber historical societies and impede their development; he opened our intelligence to all of the great and beautiful ideas existing among men; he handed us over totally to the West, such as the centuries have made it, and he gave us all its history for a history, all its future for a future."[24]

Despite Russia's self-identification as a part of the West, its progress in after-Peter's the Great time showed that Europeanization wasn't still irreversible. To Chaadaev's mind, such a contradiction was the result not only of the significant asynchrony of Russia's reforms with transformations of the West but also because of wrong choice of the object of reforms. Russia's tendency to adopt Europe's achievements began at the same time when Europe's creative impulse *objectively* began to fade. As a result, Russia didn't acquire the legacy which made Europe reach the peak of its progress. On Russian soil, Western standards of progressive development deformed significantly and, even, became the factors of social instability. Chaadaev considered the Decembrists, with their narrow political interpretation of

23. Chaadaev, "Apologia of a Madman," 104–5.

24. Ibid., 104.

European progress, as the example of the false familiarization of Russian intellectuals with Western values.

Denial of the "criminal path" of revolution, which originated from the enlightening concept of progress, consolidated the Russian philosopher with the representatives of European romanticism and traditionalism (Louis de Bonald, Joseph de Maistre, Hugues de Lamennais). Chaadaev's comprehension of European revolutions between the thirties and of the fifties of the nineteenth century made him doubt that Western historical process could be regarded as a paragon. In a letter to Alexander Pushkin he expressed his shock at July's Revolution in France as "universal disaster old Europe so unexpectedly suffered." Suddenness of the revolution made Chaadaev question his previous ideas regarding Europe's historical evolution as gradual, continuous, organic process of development. Furthermore, he acknowledged that he couldn't see the future way of Western civilization.

The ill-fated transformations of the old Europe forced Chaadaev to reconsider his previous thoughts about Russia's historical way. Like the Slavophiles, he believed that Providence smiled on Russia by choosing it for a special religious mission and keeping it away from the community of Christian nations. The philosopher justified Russia's world mission with the help of theology as the mission to the country which lacks the sense of national exclusivity and smug egoism. Chaadaev stated: "Providence has made us too great to be egoists; that it placed us beyond nationalistic interests, and has charged us with the interests of humanity."[25]

Regarding Russia's calling, all the drawbacks of the previous path of progress (historical youthfulness, unformed self-identification, national and religious particularism) turned into virtues and acquired special, religious, meaning. Isolation from the West, which Chaadaev earlier considered as the main factor of Russia's slow progress, then was viewed as wise move to distance Russia from upheavals, which thrown back revolutionary Europe into "mud of woeful mediocrity" and "self-satisfied well-being." Not having entered the new age of the world history—the age of middle class triumph with its cult of material prosperity and self-confidence—Russia was truly free in choosing historical path, worthy for the Christian country.

Russia's lack of historical experience and relatively youthfulness made it free from fatal pressure and intellectual traditions of the past, and gave strength to its transforming universal mission. In the context of messianic vision of Russia's history, even domestic anti-intellectualism, which Chaadaev earlier damned as the main factor of ruptures and dead-ends of Russian history, became positive. Due to the fact that Russians, unlike the people of

25. Chaadaev to Alexander Turgenev, 1835, Chaadaev, "Fragments," 160.

the West, regarded ideas as the product of mind games and did not see any connections with the interests of nation and individuals, Russia was able to adopt European ideas unselfishly and unbiased, according to their internal value. Naturally, in his letter to Alexander Turgenev, Chaadaev likened the Russian people to the public that "to judge the play," that is being performed on the stage of the world history.[26]

Chaadaev's enthusiasm about these ideas is especially seen in the thirties, when he formulated his peculiar "dialectic of retardation" which was actively used by Russia's radical-socialist public (however, not in the context of the philosopher's religious philosophy of history) in the nineteenth and twentieth centuries. It was Chaadaev who put forward the thesis that Russia's lagging behind is its advantage over the Western countries and it would allow it to progress on the path of historical progress farther than European nations managed to. Chaadaev hoped that Providence returning to Russia would manifest itself in *positive* religious calling and *positive objective* for Russia's historical progress. Russia would *finish Europe's evolution*. He also hoped that in the future the image of strong power would be replaced by perception of Russia as the leader of Europe's intellectual and cultural progress.[27]

To Chaadaev's mind, Russia's progress and the implementation of European values shouldn't be "modernization to catch up with." He supposed that Russia would be able to avoid all continuous stages of Western evolution and go straight to the final, progressive state of society. Assimilating the experience of Western nations should optimize Russia's evolution, make it expedient and not as wasteful as Europe's one, which advanced by trial and error. He denied that it was Russia's fate to repeat European's dangerous delusions and disasters.[28]

Amazingly, Chaadaev, dreaming of Russia in the thirties as the final stage of Europe's progress, didn't care for individual freedom which provided basis for Europe's ability for positive changes. From his point of view, genius can overcome any obstacle and doesn't need any institutional guaranties of its expressions. What Europe obtained in freedom, Russia would get with better results by public mobilization, thanks to the efforts of supreme power. It was potential of the country, lack of own social and intellectual traditions that would allow the state to fulfill progressive ideas in their fullest, without sordid resistance of population with its ever-changing ideals.

26. Chaadaev to Turgenev, 1 May 1835, Chaadaev, "Fragments," 159.

27. Chaadaev to Turgenev, 1835, 162.

28. Chaadaev, "Apologia of a Madman," 109.

That was the way Russia could overcome its retardation and became vanguard of European progress by only an act of state transformation. Provided supreme power was guided by ideas of progress and enlightenment, Russia would perform not the "catching-up" but accelerated modernization. He called for the state to perform "powerful *elan* which should carry us along in one single effort, where the other peoples could only have arrived by unheard of efforts and by frightening calamities."[29]

It is worth saying that expectations for "powerful charge" didn't sum up Chaadaev's philosophy of history. In 1837, Chaadaev was already disappointed with his ideas of Russia's messianic purpose and his understanding of Providence's mission yet again became undetermined. Chaadaev's pessimism toward Russia's historic fate only strengthened during the Crimea War. He explained Nicolas I's expansion policy as a reaction to European revolution of 1848 and perverted interpretation of Russia's calling as a savior of the West. Identifying the ideology of official populism with the Slavophile "retrospective utopias" and reproaching them for betraying the spirit of Europe and freedom, Chaadaev opposed them with his own vision of patriotism. In the "Letter of an Unknown to an Unknown" (1854), he wrote:

> This is not the way that we loved our country in our youth. We wished her well-being . . . to wish her a little liberty if that were possible. We thought of her as great and powerful, full of future . . . We were far from imagining . . . that Russia had a special mission to absorb in herself all Slavic people and thereby to bring about the regeneration of the human species . . . We especially did not think that Europe was on the point of receeding [*sic*] into barbarism and that we had been charged with saving civilization . . . We treated Europe with civility, even sometimes with respect; for we know that Europe had taught us many things, among others, our own history.[30]

So, at the end of his life, Chaadaev returned to the same disappointing conclusion about Russia's place in the world history that was in his "First Philosophical Letter." He saw Russia as concentration of servility and threat to other country's freedom. Chaadaev stated:

> In speaking about Russia people always believe that they are speaking about a political power like others. But that is not so at all. Russia is an entire world obeying the will, the caprice, the fantasy of only one man, whether he is called Peter or Ivan, no matter, it's always an incarnation of arbitrariness. Russia is

29. Chaadaev to Turgenev, 1 May 1835, 158.

30. Chaadaev, "Fragments," 243–44.

> a country which, contrary to all the laws of human societies, advances only towards its own enslavement and those of the people who are neighbors. Hence it is as much in its own interest and that of other nations that it would be useful for Russia to pursue a new path.[31]

Andrzej Walicki called this tragic evolution from *Philosophical Letters* to *Apologia of the Madman* the tragic paradox of Chaadaev. The philosopher, glorifying history, denied historical experience of his own country; being a pupil of the European traditionalists and reactionary romantics, he inspired the most radical movements of Russian revolution by the *tabula rasa* theory. Represented by Chaadaev, a Russian patriot suffered crushing defeat in discussions on the fate of his Motherland and still is not able to determine national and religious identity and historical calling of Russia.[32]

Bibliography

Bilington, James H. *The Icon and the Axe: An Interpretive History of Russian Culture*. New York: Knopf, 1966.

Chaadaev, Peter. "Apologia of a Madman." In *Philosophical Works of Peter Chaadaev*, edited by Raymond T. McNally and Richard Tempest, 102–11. Dordrecht: Springer, 1991.

———. "Fragments and Various Thoughts." In *Philosophical Works of Peter Chaadaev*, edited by Raymond T. McNally and Richard Tempest, 112–255. Dordrecht: Springer, 1991.

———. "The Philosophical Letters Addressed to a Lady." In *Philosophical Works of Peter Chaadaev*, edited by Raymond T. McNally and Richard Tempest, 18–101. Dordrecht: Springer, 1991.

———. "Zapiska grafu Benkendorfu." In *Sochineniya*, 225–32. Moscow: Pravda, 1989.

Gershenzon, Mikhail. *Chaadaev*. Moscow: NIMP, 2000.

Ivonina, Olga, and Yuriy Ivonin. *Ex Occidente Lux: russkaya ideya semyi Solovyevykh*. Novosibirsk: NGUEU, 2011.

Masarik, Tomas G. *Rossiya i Evropa*. Saint Petersburg: Izdatel'stvo Russkogo Khristianskogo Gumanitarnogo Universiteta, 2000.

Pypin, Alexander. *Kharakteristika literaturnyh mneniy ot dvatsatykh do pyatidesyatykh godov*. Saint Petersburg: Kolos, 1909.

Walicki, Andrzej. *A History of Russian Thought from the Enlightenment to Marxism*. Translated by Hilda Andrews-Rusiecka. Stanford: Stanford University Press, 1979.

31. Chaadaev to Turgenev, 1 May 1835, 240.

32. Walicki, *History of Russian Thought*, 90–91.

13

The Problem of Personality in the Philosophy of Peter Chaadaev and Russian Theological Personalism[1]

Konstantin Antonov

By theological personalism I mean that current in Orthodox twentieth-century thought which is connected with such names as Georges Florovsky and Vladimir Lossky. This stream has a number of essential features, among which it has to be mentioned first of all a special attention to the uniqueness and nonrationalisability of subjectivity, an understanding of the relation between God and man as sort of dialog and focusing on the faith as a particular kind of personal act exceeding normal human cognitive capacities. In this respect, its source may be traced back to the polemic response of Friedrich Heinrich Jacoby to the philosophy of Spinoza and German classicism. For many of the members of this stream it was normal to establish a more or less strong correspondence between the early Christian notion of *hypostasis* and the modern one of "personality."[2]

Since Vladimir Lossky, the following trend became dominant in Orthodox personalism. It consists in claiming that the personalism is rooted in the tradition of the Orthodox Holy Fathers and meanwhile is maximally distant from the tradition of prerevolutionary academic theology, the religious and philosophical renaissance of the beginning of the twentieth

1. The article was written with support of the grant of the Fund of the Development of St. Tikhon's Orthodox University *Genealogy of Ideas of Theological Personalism (on the Material of Russian Religious Thought of the Nineteenth through the Beginning of the Twentieth Century)*, no. 04–1215.

2. See Lossky, "Theological Notion of the Person."

century and Russian religious philosophy in general.[3] It looks like this genealogy needs some correction since it tends to reject an evident fact that personalistic thought was invented in Modernity.[4] Meanwhile, careful and unprejudiced investigation can not only clarify our view of Orthodox thought in the nineteenth and twentieth centuries but also discover the causes of efficiency and popularity of personalistic theology which were unseen by this movement itself.

From this point of view, addressing the roots and especially the works of one of the first representatives of the Russian religious philosophy, Peter Chaadaev, may be of considerable significance. Thus the task of this chapter is a reconstruction of Chaadaev's doctrine of personality and comparing it with the conceptions of Russian personalism of more recent times.

Chaadaev certainly was not a personalist in the modern sense of the term. This distinguishes him from his junior colleague Ivan Kireevsky, in whose later "Fragments" we find the following: "For only reasoning and free personality is what is essential in the world. It alone has a distinctive significance. Everything else has only relative significance."[5] At the same time he understands faith as a central relation constituting human life, as "consciousness of a relationship of the living divine personality and the human personality."[6] Nevertheless, the topic of personality occupies a visible yet barely definable place in the philosophical legacy of Chaadaev.

This should not surprise. Historians of Russian thought beginning from Vladimir Ern talk a lot about its personalism. Notice that "personal significance of its creators" correlates with the thematisation of "personality" in their works.[7] The personalistic language is used here not only relative to human reality but also relative to God. Chaadaev, as it was already said, is one of the founders of the Russian religious-philosophical tradition and already for this reason it doesn't look a coincidence that he was interested in the problem of personality. However, the question about the motives of this interest seems worth asking: what makes Chaadaev think about the specificity and foundations of the individual human being, what constitutes his attitude to this individual being?

3. See Maler, "Ponyatiye lichnosti"; Chursanov, *Licom k licu*; Williams, *Theology of Lossky*.

4. Shichalin, "O ponyatii 'lichnosti.'"

5. Kireevsky, "Fragments," 284.

6. Ibid., 285.

7. Ern, "Nechto o Logose," 89.

"Personality" in Chaadaev's Works: Terminological Problems

Answering the questions considered above, let us begin by addressing the specific number of essential complications which the substantial analysis of this topic necessarily encounters.

First of all, Chaadaev does not always use the word "personality" and its derivatives as a philosophical category, often using it in an ordinary way.[8] But the frequency which he uses these words with calls for explanation and, in this precategorical use, "personality" means simply a single person. He talks about: "(great) historical personalities," "Biblical personalities," "personal feeling," and so on.[9]

Sometimes he uses "personality" to stand for "specificity." Thus in his description of English nation he uses *lichnost'* in authorized Russian translation of the "First Letter" instead of *physionomie* in French ("features" in English version[10]). Here he links its disposition to personal diversity with the specificity of modern time. Knowing general "traditionalist" Chaadaev's attitude one could expect negative connotations here but instead of them we find the indication of the religious character of basic tendencies of English history.

Another difficulty is that even the categorical use of the word "personality" by Chaadaev is not clear enough. Not only do we never find any definition of personality but we will also hardly manage to give such a definition ourselves after considering all of the contexts of Chaadaev's categorical use of this word.

The comparison of nations with particular persons which is often met in Chaadaev's writing[11] rather characterizes his philosophy of history and society than his anthropology. We find out from here only that if a nation has self-consciousness and is a "moral being" "just like personality" then the personality also possess self-consciousness and morality which seems to be obvious.

Add to this the following "antidemocratic" passage: "It is evident that individuality (*de personnalité*) and freedom exist only insofar as there is diversity of intelligence, moral powers, and knowledge."[12] This implies the existence of an elite within a single nation and so between nations and from

8. One can note that Russian translations often use *lichnost'* instead of the French *l'individu* and sometimes vice versa, *sebialubie* instead of *personnalité*.

9. Chaadaev, "Philosophical Letters," 71, 88, 77.

10. Ibid., 29.

11. See ibid., 72–73.

12. Ibid., 68.

this he infers the necessity of an existence of a single nation "who had preserved the tradition of God's initial communications in a purer and more definite manner than others"[13]—the people of Israel.

With some more sense this word appears in the context of historiosophic speculations about the meaning of the Reformation, which "set the world back again into the disunity of paganism; it reestablished great national entities, isolated men's souls and minds, plunged man again into the solitude of passion (*personne*)."[14] Here we see clearly negative connotations. Individualization and atomization lead to loneliness, and are represented here as a result of betray of Christian way, the returning of the world to the dissociation of paganism.

Chaadaev's very talk about personality is ambiguous: the personal reality is claimed to be both a vicious illusion and a necessary basis of consciousness. Stemming from original sin, it makes human existence individualized and radically egocentric: "this individual, isolated idea, which permeates him at this moment, instead of this personality which isolates him from all around him and clouds up everything before his eyes and which is not at all the necessary condition of his particular nature."[15] Personhood is identified with egoism.[16] Such individualization meanwhile is not the only way of personal existence "but solely the consequence of his violent alienation from universal nature.[17] This alienation may be overcome and then new perspectives will be opened for humanity: it will "recover the idea and also the comprehensive personality, as well as the whole power of pure intelligence in its original link with the rest of things."[18] From illusions of egocentric self-consciousness we come by way of self-denying to "push our own submission to the point of complete forfeiture of his own freedom,"[19] to some other genuine but also personal existence.

How is this possible?

13. Ibid., 67.
14. Ibid., 82.
15. Ibid., 46.
16. See ibid., 132.
17. See ibid., 46.
18. See ibid.
19. Ibid.

The Idea of Personality in the Context of Mystical Experience and Theory of Consciousness

In order to solve this problem one may address Chaadaev's testimony about his own mystical experience and to his understanding of consciousness, knowledge, and history, where the central role belongs to the concept of tradition.

Forms of Transcending

Concerning the first, there are a number of testimonies in Chaadaev's texts which may be interpreted as descriptions as sort of ecstatic or in more contemporary words "transpersonal experiences" or "altered states of mind." Most of them are located in the "Third Philosophical Letter." They report two types of transcending: the overcoming of (1) space-time limitedness of the subject and (2) the separateness of subjects in an act of something like moral empathy.

So, the personal individualization shows itself first of all in space-time localization of a human being. Chaadaev is close to Augustine in his understanding of time, although he modifies it substantially. Time exists first of all in human consciousness: "We create all time by ourselves, that is certain; God did not create time; he allowed man to make it."[20] And the past and the future are primarily efforts of recollection and imagination and Chaadaev considers them as "acts of will." These efforts form human individuality but at the same time they constrain him/her and Chaadaev perceives this constraint as something suppressing: "this fatal thought of time, which obsesses and oppresses me on all sides . . . which so cruelly dominates and crushes me."[21] It looks as if Chaadaev sees time-consciousness as one of the consequences of the original sin which settled the power of illusions other humanity. Paradoxically Chaadaev believes that this illusion may be defeated by an act of will, "throwing away the ghost of past" and future, leave the present moment for eternity:

> No more limits to my existence, no more obstacles to the vision of infinity; my glance plunges into eternity; the earthly horizon has disappeared; the heavenly vault is no longer fixed to the earth at the end of the immense plain which stretches before my eyes; I see myself in this unlimited continuity, not divided into days or hours or fleeting moments, but one continuity forever,

20. Ibid., 47.

21. Ibid.

> without movement and without change, in which all separate beings are lost in each other and, finally, in which everything eternal subsists.[22]

The boundaries of an individualized person are torn apart along with time. The pathos with which Chaadaev speaks here with about "this superior life" shows that he is talking about the "altered states of mind" which he really experienced. Something like this grows on also with the space. Both happened to be *a priori* forms of fallen human consciousness determining his egocentric worldview according to Chaadaev. Unlike Kant, Chaadaev believes that this *a priori* may be overcome.

Analogous overcoming of personal limitations and egocentrism are possible in everyday relations between people: "Is it not within our power to identify ourselves on any level with beings similar to ourselves? Are we not capable of applying their needs, their interests to ourselves and transferring their feelings to ourselves, so that we finally begin to live only for them and feel only through them?"[23]

One can develop this capability in oneself up to the extreme limits: "we can mingle with the moral world so well that, provided we know about it, we may experience everything that happens in nature as if it were happening to us . . . to make each of our thoughts, each of our actions harmonize with the thoughts and actions of all men in one harmonious whole."[24] One can see behind these descriptions the personal experience of moving from one mode of being to a principally different one.

One may suppose that experiences of these states became a foundation for distinguishing between two types of personal existence one of which is assigned positive connotations while another negative.

His purely philosophical analysis of the problem of freedom and human cognitive activity leads to the same result.

Freedom and Consciousness

The feeling of freedom is directly given to humans. This very experience is responsible for our personal self-consciousness. Freedom links people with God. "This image of God, this likeness with him—this is our liberty."[25] In this establishment of the link between freedom, personality and godlikehood

22. Ibid.
23. Ibid., 48.
24. Ibid.
25. Ibid., 56.

Chaadaev comes closer than ever to the ideas of theological personalism. The problems of the "tragedy of freedom" (Sergey Levitskiy) constituting a link between freedom and evil, also belong here. In this passage Chaadaev anticipates the dialectics of freedom developed in the twentieth century by Nikolai Berdyaev: "An idea comes to be associated with that of my liberty, an awesome idea, its terrible, merciless consequence the misuse of my liberty and *evil* which results from it."[26]

The main illusions of human self-consciousness are also connected with this place of a man in the world: the idea of personal individualized existence, its space-time definiteness, false understanding of the freedom itself.

The dialectics of freedom by Chaadaev is as follows: completing freedom as arbitrariness, stepping away from the law a man unavoidably becomes dependent on his environment and this way "destroys himself": "When we abandon ourselves to these outside influences, when we go beyond the law, we annihilate ourselves."[27] But at the same time the illusion of freedom persists. On the contrary, by recognizing his dependence and purporting to obey, man reaches liberation and self-realization.

In general Chaadaev formulates it in the following way: "If we accept liberty as a given reality, such reasoning does not hinder us from recognizing dependency as the fundamental reality of the moral order."[28] This thought he makes more specific when he describes the life of consciousness as an interaction between two forces: "the one force which we are aware of, our *free choice*, our will, the other, which dominates us without our knowing it, the action of an *exterior force* upon our being, and then see what the consequences will be."[29]

Personal self-consciousness is immediately linked with the freedom experienced by human beings. The latter as we saw is an illusion which occurs against the background of profound dependence on external forces. This dependence is made clear by Chaadaev in reflection concerning the obedience of a man to the moral law, forms of communal being, to the course of history, divine predestination as signs of universality. For example, Chaadaev writes: "The feeling of duty, and hence submission is necessarily at the basis of each moral activity, no matter how spontaneous or how isolated it appears."[30] In the same way our mind obeys to mathematics and

26. Ibid.
27. Ibid.
28. Ibid., 44.
29. Ibid., 53.
30. Ibid., 46.

logical analyses.[31] And the higher the level of conformity the more effective its work is: "Consequently, the real principle of our intellectual power is in reality nothing more than a kind of *logical abnegation*, identical with moral abnegation and originating from the very same law."[32]

From the same false perspective the main modern theories of knowledge arise. The polemics between empiricism and apriorism is based on false individualistic understanding of man which doesn't take into account the problems related to the fall and original sin: "In both cases we always deal with the reason which we find in ourselves today, but not with the reason which was given as a present to us in the beginning; therefore, we could never investigate the genuine spiritual principle at all, but this distorted, disfigured principle, perverted by man's arbitrariness."[33]

Interfering this polemics Chaadaev proposes his own solution to the problem of knowledge. It is based on the recognition of the social and historical nature of a priori forms of cognition which organize our sensory experience:

> *Archetypes* of Plato, *innate ideas* of Descartes, *a priori* of Kant, all these diverse elements of thought, which were necessarily recognized by all profound thinkers as in advance of any kind of operation by the soul, as preceding all experimental knowledge and all the appropriate activity of the mind, all these preexisting seeds of reason . . . are summed up in the ideas which come to us from the intellectuals who preceded us in life and those who have been charged with the task of introducing us to our personal existence.[34]

The ideas which organize consciousness and knowledge are definitely not innate, they are conveyed from generation to generation sometimes becoming either opaque or clear at different times. These ideas do not always convey deliberate teaching. Chaadaev is one of the first who thematizes the significance of different forms of non-verbal communication:

> The main vehicle for the formation of spirits is, of course, the word: without it is impossible to imagine either the source of intelligence in an individual or his development within humanity. However, the word alone is not enough to produce the great phenomenon of universal intelligence; it is far from being the sole means of communication among men; consequently, it

31. See ibid., 44–45.

32. Ibid., 45.

33. Ibid., 65.

34. Ibid., 66.

> would have to include all the intellectual activity being done in the world. A thousand invisible ties unite the thoughts of one reasonable being with those of another; our most intimate thoughts discover every means possible for reproducing themselves outside; when they are disseminated, when they cross one another, they fuse together, they unite, they pass from one spirit to another, they sow, they fertilize, and finally, they engender universal reason.[35]

This very process of the transmission of ideas constitutes history according to the Russian thinker. Therefore he understands history as tradition and at the same time as an "education of mankind" (Gotthold Ephraim Lessing).[36] This account makes Chaadaev address the problem of the beginning of the history. He describes it as the unity of two events. The first is the primordial revelation which is thought as a prior communicative act connecting God with man. And the second is the original sin breaking this prior communication:

> On the day when man was created God spoke with him, and man heard and understood him: this is the true genesis of human reason; psychology will never find a more profound explanation. Later, he partially lost the ability to hear the voice of God; this was a natural consequence of the gift of unlimited liberty which he had obtained. But he did not lose his recollections of God's first words which resounded in his ear.[37]

The rejection to take into account this fundamental relation which is revealed to people by Christian doctrine is the main disadvantage of new European philosophy. As a result, illusions of consciousness are seen in it as its immediate data, the present human self recognizing its own autonomy and uniqueness becomes in the center of its consideration as a basic reality. Here is the source of the opposition of faith and reason characterizing the Enlightenment. Chaadaev believes that a new era must substitute it. This era will recognize the specificity of Christian rationality and will complete a new synthesis: "the grand operation of the fusion of souls and of the world's different moral forces into one soul, into a single force."[38]

35. Ibid., 61.

36. "Education of mankind" or "education of humanity" is one of Chaadaev's favorite expressions which he uses many times (ibid., 20, 22, 28, 40, 77, 296) and which shows his rootedness not only in French traditionalism, but in German humanistic thought as well.

37. Ibid., 63.

38. Ibid., 101.

Chaadaev, Christianity, and Personalism in the Context of Modernity

Chaadaev's thought therefore appears anti-personalistic at first glance. The idea of uniqueness and autonomy of human personality is recognized by him as the unconditional illusion of consciousness, the consequence of original sin which the practice of systematic obedience of the will must be opposed to. This practice must lead to the modernization of man and his thinking. This in its turn leads to the acquisition of a new genuine personality recognizing its inclusion in the unity of world consciousness, accomplishing an intensive inner work for the sake of becoming part of the tradition. One has to note, however, that in spite of the described suspicion, personalistic problems are at the heart of Chaadaev's theory. The thinker eventually considers it as the most common trait of the thought and culture of modernity and tries to include it into the structures of Christian thought. He manages to preserve some distance relative to it due to the use of the basic assumptions of Christian anthropology. In it the ideas of man's creation as God's image, his freedom and fall are combined and united together.

Therefore, in spite of the fact that problems of personality are not considered by Chaadaev systematically and not favored by him, he must certainly be thought of as one of the precursors of the theological personalism of the twentieth century.

There is a correspondence between Chaadaev's distinction between false and true personality and personalistic distinction between person and individual and his idea of tradition anticipates the problem of church.[39] The situation is made yet harder because, as modern culturological investigation shows, such complex models of individuality may themselves be considered as outcomes of the modern understanding of personality.[40]

What was said allows us to see the sources of theological personalism and the connections between philosophical and theological ideas of modernity in a new light.

Bibliography

Chaadaev, Peter. "The Philosophical Letters Addressed to a Lady." In *Philosophical Works of Peter Chaadaev*, edited by Raymond T. McNally and Richard Tempest, 18–101. Dordrecht: Springer, 1991.

39. See Zenkovsky, *History of Russian Philosophy*, 155.
40. See Kemper, *Ineffabile*.

Chursanov, Sergei. *Licom k licu: ponyatie lichnosti v pravoslavnom bogoslovii XX veka.* Moscow: Izdatel'stvo Pravoslavnogo Svyato-Tikhonovskogo Gumanitarnogo Universiteta, 2014.

Ern, Vladimir. "Nechto o Logose, russkoy filosofii i nauchnosti." In Vladimir Ern. *Sochineniya*, 71–108. Moscow: Pravda, 1991.

Kemper, Dirk. *Ineffabile. Goethe und die Individualitätsproblematik der Moderne.* München: Wilhelm Fink Verlag, 2004.

Kireevsky, Ivan. "Fragments." In *On Spiritual Unity: A Slavophile Reader*, translated and edited by Boris Yakim and Robert Bird, 275–92. New York: Lindisfarne, 1998.

Lossky, Vladimir. "The Theological Notion of the Human Person." In *The Image and Likeness of God*, 111–23. New York: St. Vladimir's Seminary Press, 1974.

Maler, Arkadiy. "Ponyatiye lichnosti v sofiologii i neopatristike." In *Sofiologiya i neopatristicheskiy sintez. Bogoslovskiye itogi filosofskogo razvitiya*, edited by Konstantin Antonov and NataliyaVaganova, 225–50. Moscow: Izdatel'stvo Pravoslavnogo Svyato-Tikhonovskogo Gumanitarnogo Universiteta, 2013.

Shichalin, Yuriy. "O ponyatii 'lichnosti' primenitel'no k triedinomu Bogu i bogocheloveku Iisusu Khristu v pravoslavnom dogmaticheskom bogoslovii." *Vestnik Pravoslavnogo Svyato-Tikhonovskogo gumanitarnogo universiteta. Seriya I: Bogoslovie. Filosofiya. Religiovedenie* 1 (2009) 47–72.

Williams, Rowan. *The Theology of Vladimir Nikolaievich Lossky: An Exposition and Critique.* DPhil, University of Oxford, 1975.

Zenkovsky, Vasilii V. *A History of Russian Philosophy*. Vol. 1. Translated by George L. Kline. London: Routledge, 2006.

14

Peter Chaadaev as the Founder of the Geographic Deterministic School of Russian Historiosophy

Grigory Olekh

First, we would like to give some explanations about the theory of geographic determinism which will be discussed in more detail. As is well known, the basic postulate of this theory states that the physical environment is the predominant factor in the development of human society, which determines the manners and customs of the people, their daily way of life, occupations, laws, governmental and public order. The roots of the idea about the priority of nature in the development of man and mankind go back to antiquity. Outstanding ancient thinkers such as Hippocrates, Aristotle, Herodotus, Polybius, Strabo, and others in their reasoning insisted that the fate of individuals and peoples are bound up in the place in which they live.

Early geographic and deterministic views of antiquity were resurrected and taken up in modernity. The creators of the classic European theory of geographic determinism became a French politician, philosopher, economist, and lawyer of the sixteenth century, Jean Bodin; a French writer, lawyer, and philosopher of the end of the seventeenth and first half of the eighteenth century, Charles Montesquieu; a German poet, novelist, theologian, and historian of culture of the middle of the eighteenth century and early nineteenth century, Johann Herder; and others. Bodin's views on the character of the relationship between nature and human society are detailed in his work *The Method of Easy Comprehension of History* (1566). The author establishes a direct causal link between climate, landscape, soil, on the one hand, and the physical appearance and mental structure of people, or "nature of people," on the other hand.[1]

The idea of Bodin catches and develops his compatriot Montesquieu in his famous treatise *The Spirit of the Laws* (1748). In the context of our story, this work deserves a special mention. The fact is that the work of Montesquieu, published in 1827, in Paris, was part of Peter Chaadaev's personal library and, thus, clearly has been the subject of his special interest. The fourteenth book of Montesquieu's treatise, entitled "On the Laws in Their Relation to the Properties of the Climate," contains a chapter appropriately titled "How People Vary in Different Climates." Here the author discusses the differences of the physiology of the peoples of the Northern and Southern countries and the diversity of their national characters. "It is the variety of wants in different climates that first occasioned a difference in the manner of living, and this gave rise to a variety of laws,"[2] Montesquieu summarizes his observations. In passing we note that some of his conclusions today sound pretty straightforward and even far-fetched. So, slavery, the author of the treatise describes as a consequence of the hot climate, which depletes the body and weakens the spirit and freedom as a result of cold climate, giving the mind and body a "known force." Aristocratic governance is derived from the presence of fertile soil, and the governance of folk from its scarcity. However, Montesquieu's main idea of the dominant role of geographical environment in the formation of public and state order of peoples, of course, perfectly legitimate.

Herder's book *Outlines of a Philosophy of the History of Mankind* (1784–1791), published in Leipzig in 1812, was also acquired by Chaadaev for his personal library and also joined the circle of his mandatory reading. Of course, the Herder's reasoning about the influence of nature on the people looks a little thinner than those of Montesquieu, but he does not negate this influence. On the contrary, all of the work of Herder is imbued with a deep conviction in the defining value of the natural elements in the evolution of mankind. "The structure of our Earth, in its natural variety and diversity, rendered all these distinguishing periods and states of man unavoidable."[3] In two voluminous parts of the book is described in detail the millennial natural history of the planet, the differences in the organic structure of the peoples inhabiting it, explained how the climate effects on the psychological state and physical constitution of man.

1. See Bodin, *Method of Easy Comprehension of History.*
2. See Montesquieu, *Spirit of the Laws*, 253.
3. Herder, *Outlines of a Philosophy of the History*, 19.

The first distributors of the ideas of the European classical theory of geographic determinism in Russia were, ironically, two historian-antagonists, that led between a fierce polemic—Ivan Boltin and prince Mikhail Shcherbatov, who, incidentally, was the grandfather of Chaadaev on the maternal side. So in the understanding of Boltin, who felt the influence of the French Enlightenment, the main cause of known sequence of phenomena and events is the impact of the physical conditions on human beings. Making objections to historical essay on Russia by Nicolas-Gabriel Le Clerc, Russian historian noted:

> I'll follow those which . . . although guess the climate as a dominant reason in the dispensation and the formation of men, but does not deny other promoting causes . . . climate has a major effect in our bodies and manners; other causes, like education, form of governance, examples, etc., are the secondary or incidental: they only facilitate or rather impede its actions.[4]

Similar views were held by Mikhail Shcherbatov. On the interaction between natural conditions and civilizations he wrote in his novel-utopia *Journey to the Land of Ofir* (1783).

Thus, it would be appropriate to say that the theoretical constructions, built later by Chaadaev, were erected not on empty ground, but on a firm foundation created by several generations of outstanding thinkers of the past, both European and Russian. However, we note that Chaadaev does not stop at the achieved level of comprehension of historical reality, and makes his own, very courageous, at times extremely paradoxical judgments, later received confirmation and more intense development in the Russian historiosophy and historiography.

It would suffice to add that the geographic and deterministic views of Chaadaev, unfortunately, had never been spelled out by him in a systematic, complete form. His brief, scattered, but very accurate and precise thoughts have to be collected literally bit by bit in a number of his works—*Philosophical Letters, Apologia of a Madman, Fragments and Various Thoughts 1828–1850*, etc. This circumstance imposes on researcher of theoretical heritage of the Russian philosopher a special responsibility and requires a special care and good faith in interpreting the texts.

First of all, it is necessary to reliably verify a valid commitment of Chaadaev to geographic deterministic paradigm per se. "Each people—says the philosopher—carries in its breast a particular element which imprints its seal upon its social being, which determines its pilgrimage across the centuries and marks its place in humanity. This constituted element

4. Boltin, *Primechaniya na istoriyu.*

in our case is the geographical element, there—that is what people don't want to understand"[5]—he exclaims with unconcealed vexation and bewilderment in the same phrase after the comma, as though addressing it to his possible opponents.

Clearly marking out his general theoretical position Chaadaev then smoothly moves to its application in the analysis of the historical development of Russia.

> There is, he says, one fact which imperiously dominates our historical movement, which runs like red thread through all our history, which contains in itself, so to speak, all its philosophy, which is evident in all eras of our public life and determines its character, which is at one and the same time an essential element of our political greatness, and the true cause of our intellectual impotence: it is a fact of geography.[6]

> Our entire history, he adds, is produced by the nature of the immense topography which has fallen as our . . . In a word, we are nothing but a geological product of the vast latitudes in which some unknown centrifugal force launched us. We are but a curious page in the physical geography of the earth.[7]

Specifying his geographic and deterministic approaches, Chaadaev expresses several fundamental considerations about the peculiarities of the historical dynamics of Russia.

(1) Determining the place of Russia among mankind, its role and significance in world history, the philosopher argues that we should talk about the country's loss of global flow of development, the estrangement of Russian civilization from the East and from the West, about its "planetary orphan hood" primarily because of its geographical location. So, talking about the alienation of Russia from the Eastern traditions, Chaadaev observes: We are not the East.

> We are simply just a northern country, and on the basis of our ideas as much as that of our climates, far removed from the perfumed valley of Kashmir and the sacred shores of the Ganges. True, some of our provinces border on the eastern empires, but our centers are not there, our life is not there and will never be

5. Chaadaev, "Fragments," 124.

6. Chaadayev, "Apologia sumasshedshego," 538. This passage is missing in English translation.

7. Chaadaev, "Fragments," 124.

> there, unless the earth's axis be displaced or unless a new cataclysm again transforms the southern formations into polar ices.[8]

The real trouble of the Russian people, writes the philosopher, is precisely that he "consisted in having been relegated to the extremities of the civilized world, far from the centers in which all the lights naturally had to accumulate, far from the sources from which they shined forth for centuries"; as a result, Russian people "came into the world upon a sterile soil upon which empires did not flourish, which generations did not venerate, where nothing spoke to us about ages gone by, upon which there was no vestige of previous civilizations, no reminder, no monument of the world which has disappeared."[9] Due to geographical remoteness from the civilizations of the East and the West, the Russians were, according to Chaadaev, buried alive in a vast tomb, where they lived only the life of a fossil.[10]

(2) In an effort to comprehend deeper "the natives of a juvenile civilization,"[11] by which Chaadaev means Russia, to understand the origins of the paradoxical combination of its political greatness and mental impotence, material strength and moral nullity, the writer refers to the theme of social immobility of Russian society. "The epoch of our social life which corresponds to this moment was filled by a dull and somber existence without vigor and without energy, in which the only thing that animated us was crime, the only thing that pacified us was slavery."[12] "Look from the beginning to the end our annals—in another passage exclaims Chaadaev—you will find its on every page the profound impact of power, continuous effect of soil, and almost never meet the expressions of public will."[13]

The thinker offers his certainly an original response to the question he posed himself about the reasons of impotence of society and omnipotence of the state in Russia. Nature, he indicates,

> It is the nature of the immense topography which causes us to diverge in countless directions and scatters us in space from the very first days of our existence; it also imposes on us a blind submission to the force of things, to every power which proclaimed itself our master. Thus in a milieu made in such a way there is no regular, daily contact of intellects. In this complete isolation

8. Chaadaev, "Apologia of a Madman," 107.

9. Ibid., 110.

10. Cf. ibid., 108.

11. Chaadaev, "Fragments," 117.

12. Chaadaev, "Philosophical Letters," 21.

13. Chaadayev, "Apologia sumasshedshego," 537–38. This passage is missing in English translation.

> of individual reason there is no logical development of reason, no spontaneous elan of the mind towards a possible amelioration, none of these general common feelings among souls which might reunite them in unison, in enormous blocs before which all the material powers must necessarily bow.[14]

In the above snippet, there is a great idea, later taken to adopt by geographic deterministic school of Russian historical science about the influence of territory size and population density on the relationship of society and the state. Russian historical phenomenon according to Chaadaev is precisely that the extremely low population density leads to a weak or almost complete lack of horizontal communications in society, and this, in turn, entails reduced social activity of society and total dominance of the state over society.

(3) Special attention should be given to judgment of Chaadaev about the need "to take into account the principle which pushes this immense empire beyond its limits and causes it to exert a formidable pressure on the rest of the world."[15] As believed the philosopher, not the last role in the centuries-old Russian expansion, transforming the country in the biggest power on the planet, plays the geographical factor. The truth the thinker himself does not give an exhaustive explanation for this striking phenomenon in the history of Russia, but only in passing pointedly notes: "We look like nomads, even more than the nomads who let their herds graze on our steppes, for they are more attached to their deserts than we to our cities."[16] In a letter to Alexander Turgenev before autumn 1843 Chaadaev, discoursing on the oddities of historical destinies of his fatherland, again returns to theme of territorial vastness of the country and makes a few additional comments to his thoughts about this subject. Population, he says, "was caused either by the very effect of the geographical nature of Russia, or else by the empty spaces which foreign invasions created, or else finally by this taste for migration so natural to the Russian people, a taste to which we owe in great part the enormous extension of our empire."[17]

(4) It is worth mentioning another important thesis voiced by the philosopher. The commitment of the Russian people to relocations, he believes, as his penchant for self-denial were the main reasons for the emergence in Russia such an unique historical phenomenon, which was a serfdom. In the same letter to Turgenev Chaadaev explains: the state "had to put an end to

14. Chaadaev, "Fragments," 124.

15. Ibid., 238.

16. Chaadaev, "Philosophical Letters," 20.

17. Chaadaev to Turgenev, before 1843, Chaadaev, "Fragments," 191–92.

the vagabond existence of the peasant," therefore, it took the enslavement of the Russian countryside. "Such was the motive behind the first administrative measure which tended to prepare the peasant for a more stable social state," to installation of immobility "of a not very numerous population between 64 and 45 degrees of latitude."[18]

Revealing the inner content of the propensity of the Russian people to humility and self-denial, the philosopher indicates his low self-esteem, that peasants, representing an absolute majority of the people, with the establishment of serfdom had lost personal freedom, but never felt any insulted, humiliated, disgraced this change in his fate.[19] What is the fundamental reason for such extraordinary victimization of the Russian man?—asks Chaadaev. And he is trying to find nontrivial answer to this delicate question. Perhaps, he says, it's all about the turn of mind peculiar for the Slavic race. But why is it that this property of self-denial reaches its greatest power in Russian man? And then the philosopher for a better comprehension of the elusive historical reality once again calls on the assistance the geographic deterministic approach. In his "Second Philosophical Letter" Chaadaev intuitively groping the way towards explanation the indigenous features of national character by influence of natural environment. So, perhaps, he was the first Russian thinker who drew attention to the extremely adverse properties of the habitat of the Russian people. "We, he says, imprudently settled down in this cruel climate," "we scarcely even think of sheltering ourselves from the extremes in the seasons—and this in a climate of which one may seriously question whether it was intended for the life of thinking creatures at all." The adverse climatic conditions have a depressing effect on people, encouraging them to be satisfied with little. On this basis, summarizes Chaadaev, there creates mass asceticism and self-denial, as "neglect of all the comforts and joys of life," preventing any progress.[20]

The uniqueness of the theoretical contribution of Chaadaev to the arsenal of Russian historiosophical and historiographical thoughts is that brief and sketchy ideas of the philosopher, his brilliant insights and paradoxical guesses, thickly scattered on all his works, became the starting point for the emergence of many original scientific schools, trends and directions. So, the Chaadaev's thesis about Russia as the eternal outcast in the global human community in the future, as it is known, has spawned a whole set of theories about Russia as a "median," "intermediate," "peripheral," "polymorphic," "hybrid" civilization, which is destined to be whether the chasm separating

18. Ibid., 192.

19. See ibid.

20. See Chaadaev, "Philosophical Letters," 32–33.

the East and the West, or bridge, connecting them, or both. The opinion of Chaadaev about the Russian people as an ethnos, inclined to renunciation and selfless devotion, has formed a powerful stratum of philosophical and ethical constructions about Russian people as the God bearing people, messianic people, embodying the idea of world human brotherhood.

We, however, are interested, above all, in the further interpretation of the actually geographic deterministic views of Chaadaev. Therefore, we now turn to the views of prominent Russian scientists, mainly historians, starting from the second half of the nineteenth century and until the beginning of the twenty-first century, that is, over the last 150 years, those on whose works lies a clear trail of Chaadaev's presence.

The historical and philosophical ideas of Chaadaev were a prerequisite for the emergence of geographic school in national historical science. It should be considered the founding father of this school is Sergey Solovyov, who in fundamental twenty-nine-volume work *History of Russia from the Earliest Times* (1851–1879) identifies three main factors in the historical process: nature of the country, nature of the tribe and the course of external events, however, the first of these three gives the greatest importance. The course of events, he said, constantly obeys the natural conditions. The dwelling place of the Russian people is extensive monotonous plain and the monotony of natural forms leads to monotony of occupations, the monotony of occupations—to monotony of customs, and all this together—to a vast unified state. The state becomes the main organizing principle of folk life, because the small number and dispersion of the population, the weakness of the division of labor and a lack of large cities deprived society the ability to self-organization. Thus, notes Solovyov, the state we have is surgical bandage on a sore organ, suffering from loss of internal communication, internal cohesion. The nature has a serious impact on the national character: the soft nature soothes manners, the harsh—hardens its. In our case, we are talking about the second of two possible options. Finally, the environment determines the direction and intensity of historical movement. Since the ancestors of the Russian people had to settle there, where the "nature is stepmother to the man" as his development was significantly slow. Adverse climatic conditions have caused, among other things, the immediate prerequisite for the emergence of peculiar social organization of the Russian society—the system of serfdom. Solovyov on this matter notes: "Attaching of the peasants was the result of ancient Russian history: in it by the most tactile, the most terrible way expressed bankruptcy of a poor country incapable by its own means to meet the needs of its state provision."[21]

21. See Solov'yev, *Sochineniya*, 1:56–73; 7:7–9, 25–26, 102.

Vasily Klyuchevsky, a talented pupil and Solovyov's successor, clarifies, complements and improves the geographical approach to the analysis of past of Russia. In his main work *The Course of the Russian History* (1904–1910) he calls, as well as Solovyov, three driving forces in the historical process, but defines its somewhat differently. They are nature, society and personality, as a result of the interaction of which is built and operates a public organism, creates a known set of material and moral qualities of the society. And still the importance of the natural environment, said Klyuchevsky, prevails over the influence of the other two factors, because nature is ultimately "affect everyday life and spiritual order of people." Drawing further interaction of nature and man, the historian underlines the significant place of nature in this process, but also notes the active transforming role of the man who modifies the nature according to his needs.[22]

In *The Course* by Klyuchevsky, in addition to the general theoretical reasoning, there is a specific description of the influence of climate, landscape, soil, vegetation and rivers on the economic, political, social, moral and psychological life of the Russian people. Here a comprehensive picture of the adverse impact of geographic environment on the labor activity of the peasant population of the country is given. Among the peculiarities of Russian agriculture are: the dispersion of the population, the dominance of small hamlets and villages, the insignificance of peasant plowing, pettiness of homestead arable plots, the mobile nature of agriculture, dominance of shifting cultivation and the development of small rural handicrafts, reinforced the development of forest, river and other lands. About mobility of domestic agriculture Klyuchevsky makes remarkable explanation of this kind:

> We are dealing with vagrant and finely dispersed rural population, which, without the means or intentions widely and assiduously to develop lying in front of him vast forest spaces, was content with scarce arable plots and having grabbed a few harvests, throw its on indefinite vacation to on another virgin land to repeat the previous operations.[23]

Thanks to this agricultural technology, peasant villages "its primitiveness, a lack of the simplest everyday facilities produce . . . the impression of a temporary, casual encampments of nomads, not today, then tomorrow intending to throw their barely hatched places to move to new."[24] In this context, the assertion of the historian that history of Russia is the history of

22. See Klyuchevsky, *Sochineniya*, 1:40, 79.

23. Ibid., 1:50, 87, 311.

24. Ibid., 312.

the country, which is colonized, and that the main element of the centuries-old expansion is rural colonization, sounds like a transparent allusion to intervene in this process by the mighty forces of nature.[25]

Describing a folding in the course of such continuous colonization of Muscovy, Klyuchevsky drew attention to a number of its remarkable properties. First, he says, it is the deeply militarized state, constantly fighting for its existence. Second, it is the state, which transformed all of the estates, from top to bottom, in its animated tool, staff, differing only by a set of duties, but completely devoid of civil rights. The historical pattern is that the expansion of the state territory is increasingly oppressed the people's freedom; a growing number of annexed lands, increases the magnitude of power, but reduces the "lifting force of people's spirit."[26]

A great place in work by Klyuchevsky paid to features of Russian national character which is matured in unfriendly geographical environment. The willfulness of climate and soil, the vagaries of nature encourage Russian man (and he is, par excellence, a peasant) to rely not on himself, not to his skill and ingenuity, but on the happy occasion. Instability of the weather creates improvidence, impracticality and its unpredictability weans from long-term planning and habituates to the discussion already traversed path; short summer pushes to hard hasty, hurried and sloppy work, but weans from the habits to work a regular, constant and thorough.[27]

So, the representatives of the Russian historical-geographical school during the second half of nineteenth to the early twentieth century put forward and have tried to substantiate several key methodological points:

1. Geographical factor acts among other factors (ethnic, religious, foreign policy, etc.), but plays a pivotal role in the historical fate of Russia, like other countries and peoples.
2. The consequence of the actions of the geographical factor turns out to be a permanent process of folk (mostly peasant) colonization, supported and encouraged by the state, and the transformation of Russia in the largest state of the planet.
3. A huge spaces with low population density are depriving Russian society self-organization capabilities, turning it into an obedient tool in the hands of supreme power.
4. System of Russian serfdom is a special way of overcoming of resource poverty of the country and meeting the immediate needs of the state.

25. See ibid., 2:273.
26. Ibid., 2:372; 3:3, 8.
27. Ibid., 1:315–17.

5. Geographical factor not only generates a specific socioeconomic and political system, but also the moral-psychological type of people.

Upon closer examination of these positions it is easy to detect the confirmation, clarification, and even revision of individual Chaadaev's geographic deterministic ideas. So, a new interpretation is given to the causes of the problem of Russian permanent territorial expansion. Its main driving force is now called the fallow system of peasants land management. It is given a different, in comparison with Chaadaev's, interpretation of the causes of the end of serfdom in Russia: the reason is declared not so much desire of the states to bind to land a forever wandering peasantry, but its desire to collect from fatal poor population at least minimum surplus product on state needs. However, still the main theses of Chaadaev about the defining influence of environment on the fate of Russian civilization and properties of Russian national character, about the scarcity of the population on the large territories as a prerequisite for the despotic state and the servile society—preserved its actual sounding and got a further justification.

A little apart in relation to the mentioned participators of the national historical and geographical school are two notable domestic thinkers—geographer, ethnographer, and sociologist of the nineteenth century Lev Mechnikov and biophysicist and historian of the first half to the middle of the twentieth century Alexander Chizhevsky. They both stand firmly on the positions of geographical determinism, but the object of their study is not so much Russian as how many world historical process.

It remains to mention three newest twentieth-century modifications of Russian geographic deterministic school, the foundation of which was laid by Chaadaev in the first half of the nineteenth century. They are: (1) ethnogenetic direction, formed by the talented ethnologist, historian, archeologist, and geographer Lev Gumilyov from the fifties to the eighties; (2) school of socio-natural history, founded in the early nineties by the historian-orientalist, philosopher Eduard Kul'pin-Gubaydullin, and (3) neoclassical historical-geographical school, founded by the historian Leonid Milov from the second half of the eighties to the end of nineties.[28] Thus, a powerful impetus to the search for scientific truth, given by the outstanding Russian philosopher Peter Chaadaev, contributed to the emergence of a number of wonderful geographic deterministic theoretical constructs, reliably explaining the unique nature of the Russian historical process.

28. For more detail, see Olekh, "Geografo-deterministskiy podkhod."

Bibliography

Bodin, Jean. *The Method of Easy Comprehension of History*. Translated by Beatrice Reynolds. New York: Columbia University Press, 1969.

Boltin, Ivan N. *Primechaniya na istoriyu drevniya i nyneshniya Rossii g. Leklerka*. Saint Petersburg, 1788. http://takya.ru/nuda/iz-primechanij-na-istoriyu-drevniya-i-nineshniya-rossii-g-lekl/main.html.

Chaadaev, Peter. "Apologia of a Madman." In *Philosophical Works of Peter Chaadaev*, edited by Raymond T. McNally and Richard Tempest, 102–11. Dordrecht: Springer, 1991.

———. "Fragments and Various Thoughts." In *Philosophical Works of Peter Chaadaev*, edited by Raymond T. McNally and Richard Tempest, 112–255. Dordrecht: Springer, 1991.

———. "The Philosophical Letters Addressed to a Lady." In *Philosophical Works of Peter Chaadaev*, edited by Raymond T. McNally and Richard Tempest, 18–101. Dordrecht: Springer, 1991.

Chaadayev, Peter. "Apologia sumasshedshego." In *Polnoe sobranie sochineniy i izbrannye pis'ma*, 1:523–38. Moscow: Nauka, 1991.

Herder, Johann Gottfried. *Outlines of a Philosophy of the History of Mankind*. Translated by Thomas Churchill. New York: Bergman, 1966.

Klyuchevsky, Vasiliy O. *Sochineniya*. 9 vols. Moscow: Mysl', 1987.

Montesquieu, Charles de Secondat. *The Spirit of the Laws*. Translated by Thomas Nugent. Kitchener, Ontario: Batoche, 2001.

Olekh, Grigoriy L. "Geografo-deterministskiy podkhod k izucheniyu istorii Rossii: Kratkiy istoriograficheskiy ocherk." *Sibirskiy nauchyi vestnik* 18 (2014) 198–205.

Solov'yev, Sergey M. *Sochineniya*. 18 vols. Moscow: Mysl', 1988–1991.

www.ingramcontent.com/pod-product-compliance
Lightning Source LLC
LaVergne TN
LVHW010936100826
845153LV00001B/65

* 9 7 8 1 5 3 2 6 4 3 6 0 6 *